Awakening Power II

The key to changing the world — from a global perspective to a hyper-universal perspective

SAT DHARMA

BALBOA.PRESS
A DIVISION OF HAY HOUSE

Balboa Press books may be ordered through booksellers or by contacting:

Balboa Press
A Division of Hay House
1663 Liberty Drive
Bloomington, IN 47403
www.balboapress.com
1 (877) 407-4847

Scripture taken from The Holy Bible, World English Bible (WEB), Public Domain

Print information available on the last page.

ISBN: 978-1-9822-4734-8 (sc)
ISBN: 978-1-9822-4733-1 (hc)
ISBN: 978-1-9822-4732-4 (e)

Library of Congress Control Number: 2020908364

Balboa Press rev. date: 07/10/2020

Contents

PART I: EXPLORATION

Chapter 5 Are you still waiting for the savior from each field to save you? 1

5–1 Are you waiting for the salvation? Show your own power! 2
The wrong soul fallacy (The fallacy, persistence, projection and self-deception of cultivation and soul); "Never abandon the secular duties", said the mentors from different generations

5–2 The heroic journey of transcending the self and transformation 14

5–3 The Heroic Mission 113

Chapter 6 "Seeing" is the Great Awakening 117

6–1 The True Meaning of "Seeing" and Discernment 118
Do you Really Want Life to Be Different?; How to Truly See New Opportunities; The Power of Stillness – Utilize the "Unseen" Power to "See" Again

6–2 The Compassion, Wisdom, Strength, and Beauty of Divinity; the Divine Wonder of Prayer 178

PART II: CULTIVATION

Chapter 7 Searching for the Universal Value of the True Self...........193

    7–1 The Power of Identifying with the True Self
and 16 Types of Universal Values 200

    7–2 The Path to Transforming the Individual and
Society..212

Chapter 8 A Global Initiative for the Spiritual Industry....................218

    8–1 From a Global View to a Super Cosmic View..........219

    8–2 A Clean Life – A Practical Blueprint for the 6Cs.... 230
Clean Heart

    8–3 The 6Cs of a Clean Life.. 235
Clean Medicine; Clean Education; Clean Community;
Clean Economy; Clean Energy; Clean Life

    8–4 A New Heart and a New World – Ushering In
a Golden Paradise across the Globe 260

About The Clean Life Foundation... 267
Notes 269

PART III

EXPLORATION

Chapter Five: Are you still waiting for the savior from each field to save you? Be brave and embark on your own heroic journey!

Chapter Six: to "see" is a great awakening—the secret of the omniscient eye Are you still waiting for the savior from each field to save you?

Chapter 5

Are you still waiting for the savior from each field to save you?

Be brave and embark on your own heroic journey!
"Don't look for it outside. Go back to the inside of yourself, because the Truth lies inside each one of us!" ——S.Aureli Augustini (AD 354-430)

Are you waiting for the salvation? Show your own power!

"The real holy of holies resides in each one of us." ——Jesus Christ.

"All beings are originally Buddhas." ——*The Sutra of Perfect Enlightenment*

From time immemorial, mentors have been expounding on the one, same truth——the real "holy of holies" resides in us.

The wrong soul fallacy (The fallacy, persistence, projection and self-deception of cultivation and soul)

When it comes to spiritual cultivation, many people have become more suspicious of it and attached negative tags to it because of the news a while back about how some people lost their lives in an institute of spiritual cultivation called "the Sun and the Moon." Spiritual cultivation refers to the cultivation of a person's soul, namely the enhancement of his spirituality and the practice in advancement (the evolution) of his life. When hearing the term "spiritual cultivation," many people would immediately associate it with some common stereotypes such as "religions" or traditional religious practices. Although the term "spiritual cultivation" is used in many different religions, the fact is that in the 21st century, it carries a wider and more comprehensive connotation.

Spiritual cultivation——to cultivate your soul is a journey to self-realization, a return to one's Svabhava, a display of one's inherent strength, and the reflection of a perfect life. A real spiritual practice transcends religious divisions. It takes shelter in selfless love. It is a pilgrimage you make in your heart. Do you foster spiritual cultivation because you want to be a happier person, have a better relationship, or have a more integrated soul? Or is spiritual cultivation an excuse for you to justify all of your different behaviors? If your answer is the latter, spiritual cultivation will only make you divorced from reality, because you will suppress yourself, unwilling to face the truth, and unable to face your true self, and you will end up suffering even more. Many people tend to paint an idealized picture of spiritual practices: "For some, this may manifest in a kind of idealistic, mystical hysteria where everything is wonderfully positive, magical and beautiful but has little relationship to the normal world and fails totally to include the dark, painful side of life. For others, it can lead to a fanaticism that drives them into strict and intense practice in order to attain spiritual realizations, desperately seeking spiritual salvation will often cover deep-seated problems that are not resolved". *152

Some people look on spiritual practices with rose-colored glasses. They believe as long as they do something related to religion every day, many of their problems will be solved. Or maybe they have a poor relationship with their family, so they indulge themselves in religious surroundings and cling to some organizations of spiritual cultivations. However, once they return home, they are still unable to deal with the strained relationships with their family.

Rob Preece coined the term "spiritual flight" to describe this kind of mindset: "Spiritual flight may seem like a form of emergence but unfortunately is not. It is quite possible to embark on a spiritual path that is largely dominated by avoidance or is a kind of false emergence. Flight into idealism and intellectual spiritual knowledge, combined with a yearning for purity and perfection free from worldly contamination are, regrettably, signs of a continued psychological malaise. The disposition…may seem like renunciation. It is, however, most often a reflection of flight". *153 What seems to be a spiritual path to awakening turns out to be an escape to one's comfort zone and a form of self-deception that allows one to dodge one's problems. Therefore, on the surface, this person might be fully dedicated to spiritual practices, but as a matter of fact, he only sees what he wants to see, and when it comes to the duties he has to carry out day in and day out, such as dealing with issues concerning his financial state, his job, or his material well-being, he tries every possible way to avoid them.

Other people rely on some external power to make decisions for them, so whenever they encounter difficulties, they seek divination from fortune tellers as their solutions, because they are reluctant to believe they can sort out these problems. When a person adopts this kind of mindset and attitude to do spiritual practices, he is still keeping all his issues unsettled and simply ignoring them.

When we visit Jerusalem or other holy sites, we often find that "the holy of holies" is located in the innermost part of a religious building (such as a cathedral), and you need the permission from a member of the clergy, such as a high priest or a chief Catholic father, to be led into "the holy of holies".

Jesus Christ told us: "The real holy of holies resides in each one of us".

The Buddha also remarked: "All beings are originally Buddhas".

From time immemorial, mentors have been expounding on the one same truth——the real "holy of holies" resides in us. If you regard spiritual cultivation as an escape, you will never return to the real holy of holies inside you. To go back to your inner holy of holies means to be your true self——to go back to "the center of the sacred" within you, because that is where the source of your strength and wisdom is.

Some monks or nuns think that since they have put on their organizations' "uniforms" or have vowed to "observe the precepts," they should only say something nice, and do something virtuous, but they are afraid of saying what's on their minds, and afraid of getting into conflicts with people. They appear to be peaceful and composed, but deep down, they are simply stifling many of their emotions. However, our emotions are one of the gates to self-understanding, and to ignore them is to cut off our connections with our hearts. Some people have wrong views about people who follow the religious orders. They believe those who have chosen to pursue religious practices should be full of love. They should not turn down others' requests, because this shows their lack of compassion. As a result, they cannot draw a boundary between themselves and other people, and their lives slide into absolute chaos.

Still there are others who exaggerate the meaning of "enduring humiliations". They believe everything is preordained, and there is nothing human beings can do to change their fate. Being a passive predestinarian makes one indifferent to this world, and causes one to disregard one's real feelings.

The Sixth Patriarch, Huineng, once said: "Buddhism is in the world. It is not realized apart from the world. Seeking enlightenment apart from the world is like looking for horns on a hare" (*Buddha Nature and Animality*, edited by David Jones, page 78). Living in the real world is the most assiduous cultivation of spirituality one can foster. Nevertheless, some people have a deep contempt for this evil world of the five kinds of turbidity, and see spiritual practices as a way to "enhance" their souls. They consider themselves superior to others and tend to criticize other people or other organizations.

Many people believe those who pursue spiritual cultivation should always have a positive attitude and always remedy their wrongdoings. Therefore, they are very harsh towards themselves. They don't tolerate their mistakes or imperfections. They demand a lot from themselves and from others. They only see other people's flaws and faults. They are very eager to do spiritual practices, because they want to improve themselves and others as soon as possible, but they don't know how to calm down and concentrate on the present. They are reluctant to face their opposite selves and the dark sides in their hearts, so they are unable to discover the real causes of conflicts. Nor are they able to accept the different sides of themselves. Thus, they cannot organize different parts of themselves into an integrated whole, and they cannot be completely at one with themselves.

Being "composed", "just and open", or "peaceful", these are but different masks one wears. However, there are "shadows" lying under these masks——all kinds of emotions or grudges that are about to explode, such as being angry, jealous, greedy, domineering, or other more severe traumas. Some people pursue the "perfection" of their spirituality, but what they do only makes them further removed from the state of completeness. To avoid problems or deny their existence will not solve these problems. Nor will this kind of attitude make one a more mature person.

Some spiritual practitioners put too much emphasis on outward appearance and religious dogmas. They even use these dogmas to constrain their conscious minds. Some organizations of spiritual cultivation try to manipulate their followers by exploiting ideas such as "earning one's merits" (encouraging their adherents to donate money, because the more money they give, the more merits they will accrue), and "atoning for one's sins" (persuading their adherents that they are all grave sinners, so they have to make the utmost effort to redeem their sins), or simply by "issuing threats" (they warn the adherents that if they don't take any action to attest to the truth of the preaching delivered to them, they will suffer severe consequences. Or they intimidate the adherents by saying that the cost they will have to pay for betraying their spiritual mentors will be a trip down to the bottom of Hell, etc.). All these maneuvers prevent us from being at ease with ourselves, from settling comfortably and peacefully in our immense, illimitable, and imperishable Svabhava.

The end of the 20ᵗʰ century saw the emergence of many new movements, which, while they helped awaken many people, also gave rise to many "strange" phenomena. Some religions, in an attempt to isolate their followers from the influence of the new ideas in a new era, have carried out many actions to defend their creeds. They even went so far as to ban their followers from reading books of the new era or obtaining any relevant information. However, we cannot entirely blame these religions for these unusual occurrences, because many "believers" also make the rejection of other religions their rallying point, and instead advocate their own idiosyncratic dogmas. There are also people who live in this new era of the awakening of our conscious mind and are daunted by some outlandishly progressive ideas or behaviors they don't have detailed knowledge of.

The differences a new era presents to us, as well as the advancement of technology and the development of consciousness, all tell us that people who pursue spiritual cultivation have to adopt very different and diverse methods, in order to comply with the Buddha's advice that "rules should adapt to different eras". Each time we usher in a new era, because of the changes in environments and collective consciousness, some phenomena will occur to change us and get us integrated into a new stage in history. The times we live in now are no exception. Around the 1950s and 1960s, when the mind of the whole galaxy was about to leave the Age of Pisces and enter the Age of Aquarius, there were drastic changes in the Earth's energy field, and as a consequence, many people also underwent the "peak experience" (a temporary state of enlightenment). Nonetheless, after going through the peak experience, many people also started to suffer from severe depression and melancholy. At that time, many religions could not find the cause for what happened to these people, so they treated them as if they were "possessed by demons", which unfortunately inflicted excruciating pains on many who were in the process of a major spiritual transformation. Some of them were even sent to psychiatric hospitals because they were believed to be mentally ill. Under the care of medical staff, they lived the rest of their lives unhappy and dejected. Others were lucky and were discharged from the hospital, but they never dared to mention anything about the peak experience, lest they be seen as clinically insane again.

In the 1970s, some psychics started to appear, such as Seth, Jane Roberts, and Edgar Cayce, etc. With extraordinary psychic abilities, they helped many people who were undergoing tremendous spiritual transformations to get over the traumas of having their souls live in darkness. In addition, they passed onto people many spiritual messages that enabled us to have a better understanding of the wisdom hidden in "the unknown". The introduction of some Eastern traditions of spiritual cultivation, such as the teachings of Tibetan Buddhism or the trainings of Yoga, etc., also led many people to the path of spiritual practices. As an increasing number of spiritual messages became available, and different skills in cultivating one's spirituality have also been developed. Moreover, the fact that platforms were offered to some spiritual leaders living at the end of the 20th century, people such as Krishnamurti, Sai Baba, Babaji, Yogananda, Swami Rama, Osho, and the Supreme Master Qing Hai, for their views to be heard, helped broaden the scope of spiritual cultivation in our world.

As a matter of fact, if we want to trace the world history of spiritual cultivation, it could go back to tens of thousands of years ago. Therefore, there is no need for us to feel intimidated by spiritual cultivation. On the contrary, we should be open to it; trying to understand its charm, which so many people have succumbed to; trying to see its value, and why it could have changed so many people's lives.

A real spiritual cultivation is a way to unearth the infinite treasures hidden in our hearts. Being flexible and not being a stickler for rules when we experience spiritual awakening directly will allow us to have a deeper sense of what "enlightenment" is, of what Jesus Christ means to human beings, and of what it means to attain Nirvana in this life. Moreover, we can apply our newly acquired knowledge to how we live our daily lives so that it will not become empty words, a means of escape, a way to delude ourselves, and an experience that is merely a reflex with no real substance. In this way, we can feel raptures of joy that come with the exploration of our spirituality, rather than wallow in the superficial emotions of self-complacency.

Rather than just become a prudish and reserved practitioner, we can actually experience the indiscriminating great love. We can become a union with the state of original enlightenment. We can stop distinguishing one thing from another and start to become aware that we are simply clinging to "the dogmas of our own religions".

In *Reform of the New Era, Coming Home Now,* it is also pointed out that the "flow of light" means "the light of the wisdom of original enlightenment will flow everywhere to edify tens of thousands of people." Regardless of whether you are a lay practitioner, or an ordained monk or nun, as long as you have firm intentions to become enlightened and attain Nirvana, as long as you commit your heart and soul to the pursuit of ultimate liberation, we will be ready to share with you the mantras of great profundity, as well as the blessings from every Buddha ever existed, and from Jesus Christ.

Guru Rinpoche once said: "People who chose to practice Tantric techniques are as numerous as stars in the night sky, but those who really achieved enlightenment are as few as stars in the morning sky". In the 21st century, it is of paramount importance to choose a truly effective, multidimensional and verifiable method, or an organization that teaches this method, to do spiritual practices; because, whether you want to become enlightened or unearth the treasures hidden in the very depths of your heart, it is the way through which you can be peaceful, be at ease with yourself, and be joyful. Only with determination and perseverance, only by following your heart and practice diligently, can you uncover your innate wisdom and enter your inner Dharmadhatu (Sphere of Absolute Reality) by means of introspection. As the saying goes: "Real wisdom comes from emptiness, and your essential nature is the entrance into the wisdom of emptiness". This is the tradition and the methods of practice that, from time immemorial, have been passed down from generation to generation.

To commit yourself to spiritual cultivation, you have to start by putting your "heart" into it, so that in your daily existence, in the job you do, in your domestic life, in all kinds of relationships you have, and in your emotions, you will be able to see your true self, accept who you are, and accomplish self-realization. On this literal "life's journey", day by day, you will gradually become more aware, and become more awake.

Do you want to wait until miracles happen or do you want to be brave and perform your own miracles?

Transcend dualism, transcend your own consciousness, and stop discriminating between light and darkness, because love doesn't discriminate. You have to be brave enough to jump into a "shithole". "Shithole" means darkness, fear, collective consciousness, and your adventure into the real world. This is why we were born on this planet——to know ourselves. Be brave and step into darkness and into your fear. Every holy site has its bright and dark sides, and what we need to do is to turn both brightness and darkness into neutral light of wisdom. There is longstanding antagonism of light and darkness. Do you still want to choose "light" and reject "darkness"? **When you praise what is "meritorious," you also praise what is "evil" at the same time. If you criticize what is "evil," you are just allowing "evil" a larger space for existence.** Do you want to see the true value of darkness, or do you choose to criticize it, distinguish it from light, and avoid it? "Rather than curse darkness, you can light a candle". You should approach darkness and embrace it, and you will see how light and darkness become "oneness," the "oneness" that you have never imagined, that you can't ever imagine. The truly beautiful process is the process through which you can transcend the original polarity between light and darkness. We are not here to make light glow brighter. **We are here to bring the two opposite sides together. This is our precious ethos, and the precious essence of our dharma.**

"Never abandon the secular duties", said the mentors from different generations

Life itself is a Bodhimanda (Position of Awakening). Everything you own is a Bodhimanda. For the general public, to perform spiritual practices means to go to a monastery and accept the eight precepts, to go on religious retreats, to practice meditation, to chant Buddhist sutras, or to go to church. They think those places are the real "Bodhimanda", and those activities are the real "spiritual practices". Here at SatDharma, we have a completely different view. Your workplace is a Bodhimanda.

Your home is a Bodhimanda. **Your whole life is a Bodhimanda.** You have to face yourself under any circumstances, because you have no place to escape to. You used to be able to live the life you wanted in your "comfort zone", but once you are awakened, how can you still have a "comfort zone"? You know you cannot deceive your heart anymore, because if anything you do is not from the bottom of your heart, from your innate Buddha nature, what is intrinsic to you will immediately respond. Denunciation, misery, fatigue, stress, arrogance, etc., these are the voices that will pop up in your head, ripping up the sense of composure and tranquility you enjoy.

To all of you, the "Buddhas". Please don't underestimate yourself. You always learn more from the challenges you face in your job. You always arrive at a deeper understanding when clashes break out in your family or when you receive a blow from all sorts of things happening in your life. The trials and tribulations of life are here to help you testify to the truth of your belief, because you can use the "Bhumyakramana-Mudra" (the wisdom of emptiness) in your heart to tame yourself. You will make one breakthrough after another, and you will continue to transcend your limit. To achieve a real "breakthrough", you have to ignore how you feel, ignore what you are thinking about, and ignore your dark side. All you have to do is stay calm, "settle" firmly into what is inside you, advance, and just exist. After you do this once, twice, three times, and when you keep training yourself, you will find your strength. Your life will be different. However, what is worrisome is when you don't search inside yourself to gain a deeper understanding. You think what is outside you is external to you, and it has nothing to do with what is inside you. The truth is, you cannot be more wrong. **The outside cannot be separated from the inside, because what is outside you is what is inside you, and what is inside you is what is outside you.** If you can attain inner peace, your outward appearance will also be a peaceful one. If you appear to be in a chaotic state, don't criticize yourself. Use your "Bhumyakramana-Mudra" to enter your innate self as soon as possible. Only when you go deep into yourself can you transfer from a dark, chaotic place to a tranquil place within seconds. Once peace descends on your heart, you will appear peaceful again, because you know how to gain infinite strength from your heart. This is how I have survived every test I have been put to——get back your inner peace first. Whether the emotional wounds were inflicted by my students or by the world, I always retreated to my inner self first in order to change "the setting of my interior life". And I often found that within a short period of time, all the pains were gone. Where did they go? Has there ever been any pain in the first place? No, there has not. What you have is inner peace, serenity and equilibrium, and you come to realize you have become a changed person. You should take this new self with you and keep moving forward, keep fighting, and keep facing all your problems, and you will see that whatever you cannot sort out yesterday has been resolved today, and whatever confused you a moment ago has been cleared up right at this moment.

How do you change your exterior? You don't. You have to start from the interior. You have to open up and face yourself first. This is the perfect solution and the shortest route to the answers you need, because this is the law that governs the evolution of the universe. In order to unify your divided consciousness, to help you have a clearer understanding of yourself in the process of "self-transcendence", each one of you has to know the law of the universe. No matter what happens, remember to go back to your interior life first and discover the real cause of your inner conflicts, so that you can be integrated with your heart again, and your exterior will change accordingly.

Worldliness is the process of practice

The spiritual training we have to undergo in this human world means that when each soul comes to the earth, he or she has to be very brave and choose their life's lessons. These lessons are the personal blueprints we draw up for ourselves. In these lessons, we go through different experiences and then grow up spiritually, in order to witness how great life is. In this process, we have to experience suffering first, because only after we endure suffering in life will we want to acquire a deeper understanding of the reality of life, and to see whether there are still things we don't know and experiences we haven't been through yet. Suffering can open the eye of our soul. Otherwise, we will just live our daily lives within our usual conceptual framework and repeat our inveterate habits, and the same kind of scenarios will be played out without end.

Every minute, we are creating new versions of our lives. When we encounter different events, we will experience joy, success, and perfection; or failure, aversion, and discomfort. There are always things or people we don't want to know, to hear about, or to face. Your every thought, every emotion, every tendency, every sensual experience, and every memory will be stored in your subconscious. They are collectively known in Buddhism as the "ālaya-vijñāna" (storehouse consciousness). The seeds (the impressions of our past actions) you store in ālaya-vijñāna will sprout, because consciousness is a type of vibration and it has energy. Therefore, these seeds will start to evolve, continue to germinate, to put out sprouts, and they will attract events which have the same frequency ranges. Maybe your subconscious is not aware of their existence, but these seeds, these impressions never stop moving around in your subconscious. They will keep accumulating energy until they are bursting with it, and then they will manifest themselves in everything we experience in life, so we will repeat these experiences over and over.

Consciousness has its own wave frequency. If you stick to a particular frequency range, you will keep attracting incidents that have the same wave frequencies. Therefore, negative frequencies will attract more negative incidents, and that's how someone could be so overcome with frustrations, depression, worries, and setbacks. This is what we call "karma" (your habitual thinking patterns and behaviors), and this is also the training you have to undergo in your life. What you can do now is to increase your vibration frequency. Whatever your life's lessons are, being swindled, having a difficult parent-child relationship, suffering from declining health, the person you love the most passing away, etc., the only thing you can do at moments like these is to heal yourself first. **Only when you become an integrated whole can everything be perfected.**

When you lose control of yourself, the seeds lying in your subconscious will keep manifesting themselves (subconscious means that we don't know the amount of substance it contains, but it controls 95% of our behaviors), and you are not going to be your own master. We are like bulls, and the metal rings installed in our noses are our karma. We are led around by the ropes tied to our nose rings. If the ropes are pulled to the left, we have to move to the left; if the ropes are pulled to the right, we have to move to the right. You don't have any free will, because your subconscious makes all the decisions for you.

Many people have negative opinions about karma. For example, they tend to think that karma works in this way: in the previous life, I stabbed you with a knife; therefore, in this life, I have to pay for it by letting you slash me with a sword. However, this is not the law of karma. My understanding of karma is: in your past life, you have accumulated many intense emotions, and in this life, when the time is ripe, you will experience these emotions again. When you hurt someone, what's the motivation behind it? What is the emotion that is provoked at that moment? Is it anger, being unable to forgive, thinking no one in the world truly understands you, or believing there is no justice in this world? All these thoughts and emotions will be recorded in your subconscious. Therefore, what really harms you are not the incidents that have happened to you, but your memories of them. In your next life, these "seeds of memory" you sowed in your previous lives will not simply disappear. They will stay in your subconscious. We can liken the way they work to the way a recorder works. The moment when someone presses the "play" button, the seeds of anger, distrust, and un-forgiveness will instantly turn up. The emotions you recorded in your past lives will replay themselves. Therefore, in a fit of anger, you would feel you desperately want to kill somebody. At this critical moment, if you have never learned how to deal with your emotions properly or have never had any proper instructions, you will completely lose control. As a result, time and again, you will repeat these modes of behaviors, endlessly and ceaselessly.

When karma becomes effective, can we only react by feeling helpless, by causing more sorrow, and by creating more hindrances and mistrust? Do you want to be absorbed into the force of karma? Are being worried, being furious, reprimanding someone, blaming yourself, and complaining the only reactions you can have? When the negative impressions in your subconscious start to affect your life, your emotions, your health, your mindset, or your interpersonal relationships, do you know how to explore and examine this negative energy, how to help yourself become more perceptive and introspective, so that, like peeling off all the layers of an onion, you can finally find the core of the problem? How do you face and reveal the traumas in your subconscious and learn to get along with them? How do you venture into the very depths of your heart and integrate the opposite sides and shadows lying there? How do you lead yourself and keep moving forward? If you don't have a deeper understanding of yourself, you won't be able to observe yourself from a wider perspective or from a deeper or higher standpoint inside you. Neither will you know what kind of gift these symptoms, trials, and clashes you are currently experiencing are trying to send to you. All you do is become stuck in the same frequency range, unable to free yourself.

The time to learn these lessons will come. Everyone has his or her own lessons which may concern his or her children, partners, health, career, wealth, or love life.

What is frightening is not to learn these lessons, but to be unable to tune in to a different frequency and to keep clinging to thoughts that have ossified. We will be stupid to think that we can tackle the issues we have now and find the solutions we need, with the attitude we have adopted in the past.

Osho once remarked: "When you look at your past experiences, very often you will find these four words——There Is Nothing New." You want to create new sales records, create a healthy body, and create a harmonious parent-child relationship by resorting to your past experiences, but how could that be possible? Carl Jung once said that until you make the unconscious conscious, the unconsious will direct your life and be mistaken for fate. If you can't detect how you have changed inside, if you can't restore yourself to a complete whole, if you can't heal your heart, you will never be able to escape. You must tune in to a different frequency, because tuning in to a different frequency is a process of healing yourself.

The heroic journey of transcending the self and transformation

For most people, the journey to self-transcendence is a psychological journey which looks like this——from "not knowing" to "being aware of it", and after experiencing "the awakening", finally attaining "the enlightenment".

This psychological journey one goes on, from being totally oblivious to everything to experiencing the development of one's consciousness, the awakening of one's spirituality and the realization of enlightenment is the journey you will make at SatDharma. This is how I came up with the name SatDharma. In 2007, I was on a spiritual retreat in a thousand-year-old holy site located in the Himalayas in Northern India——Gangotri. Once, when I was in very deep meditation, God sent this name to me, and to everybody.

Sat means one's supreme nature. It is the supreme nature of wisdom, unparalleled and irreplaceable. According to Lao Zi, "the way that can be spoken of is not the constant way". So, it is the constant way that cannot be spoken of. It is the great intrinsic nature of all beings, and the source of all lives. In Sanskrit, Dharma means the way, the route, or the method.

Therefore, SatDharma means: a return journey to the supreme intrinsic nature, the supreme nature of your being, and to the understanding of the supreme nature inside each one of us. It is a journey to the Truth.

We are all looking for "the silver lining" around the cloud of suffering hanging over us, looking for a way or a method that can help us put our body and mind to rest, and this particular way or method lies in the very depths of our soul, invisible to the eyes of the common people.

In his book, *The Prophet*, Khalil Gibran relates the story of a woman asking Almustafa about pain.

In this world where there is gender inequality, where the complete equality between Ying and Yang (females and males) has not been achieved, women seem to worry and suffer more, but all the worries and suffering also give them a more penetrating insight about life, and a greater power to awaken themselves. In this chapter, the prophet talks about the nature of "pain". Let's read it together.

"Your pain is the breaking of the shell that encloses your understanding.

Even as the stone of the fruit must break, that its heart may stand in the sun, so much you know pain.

And could you keep your heart in wonder at the daily miracles of your life, your pain would not seem less wondrous than your joy.

And you would accept the seasons of your heart, even as you have always accepted the seasons that pass over your fields.

And you would watch with serenity through the winters of your grief.

Much of your pain is self-chosen.

It's the bitter potion by which the physician within you heals your sick self.

Therefore trust the physician, and drink his remedy in silence and tranquility.

For his hand, though heavy and hard, is guided by the tender hand of the Unseen,

And the cup he brings, though it burn your lips, has been fashioned of the clay which the Potter has moistened with His own sacred tears." (*The Prophet*, Kahlil Gibran)

When you are going through pain in life, whether you are able to transform this pain hinges on whether your heart can accept it and endure it with joy.

Is pain merely a bitter pill to swallow, or is it actually the medicine that is good for you? Is pain the important elixir our soul needs when it is heading toward awakening? It all depends on how you understand and define it!

In chapter four of the previous book, we have talked about the father of the study of success, Dr. Napoleon Hill (1883-1970). With everything he has encountered and gone through in life in mind, at the ripe old age of 84, he wrote his masterpiece, *Grow Rich with Peace of Mind*, to provide us with a summary of his lifelong research and the fascinating experiences he has had, and also to tell us where the last piece of the puzzle about how to be "rich and content" is. In this book, he wrote: "Very few march straight to success without going through periods of temporary failure and discouragement. Yet when you are in possession of your inner self there is no such thing as a knockout blow. You may be knocked down, but you can bounce right back. You may detour on rough roads, but you always can find your way back to the paved highway". *154 After witnessing all kinds of suffering throughout his life, he shared with readers the following adage: "**Adversity? It's a tonic, not a stumbling block! Every adversity carries the seed of an equal or greater benefit**". *155

When true equilibrium descends on your heart, peace will also settle over you. Your heart is the source of all the strength you can gather to create and enrich your life. The strength you find in your heart is the armies you can command when you set out on this heroic journey to awakening. So, rather than wallow in your sorrows, you should get up and start moving forward, leading yourself to the peak of your life.

The mighty heroic journey

The great philosopher Emerson once said: "The world makes way for the man who knows where he is going!"

It seems every soul born on this planet changes from being ignorant of and indifferent to everything, to gradually understanding something, and then to seeing things with hindsight. If we want to get back our foresight, we will need to conquer one mountain peak after another in our lives.

As a matter of fact, the evolution of our soul is a heroic journey. All the pain inflicted on us seems to push us toward a journey unknown to us. We have to overcome all the obstacles before we can arrive at a better understanding of ourselves, before we know why it is necessary for us to go through these experiences, know the true meaning behind the pain, and then know where we should go.

The renowned professor of comparative mythology, Joseph Campbell (1904-1987), after conducting extensive research on ancient myths from all over the world, concluded that almost all these myths are about one thing——a hero's journey to self-discovery. In fact, according to the blueprint for our immortal soul, each one of us is an irreplaceable hero. We were born into this world to experience life and to enhance and evolve our spirituality. We are the answers to the questions about life we have been looking for, but if we want to know the answers and to uncover the mystery, we have to set out on our own "hero's fantastic journey".

Usually, in the scripts of these stories about our lives, there are three major phases. According to Joseph Campbell, they are the phrases of Separation, Initiation and Return. In his book, *The Synchronicity Key: The Hidden Intelligence Guiding the Universe and You*, David Wilcock observed, "In the early stages of our time in the magical world, we have what Blake

Snyder calls 'Fun and Games'. At this point, we get to catch our breath, temporarily distract ourselves from the intensity of the quest, and experience all the wonders and delights of this new state of existence…However, as the pages flip ahead, we increasingly find out that all is not well…we soon realize that there is a nemesis out there—a really dark, dangerous adversary who wants to terminate our quest with prejudice". Then he continued: "Joseph Campbell refers to the nemesis as the Guardian of the Threshold. This ultimately represents the part of our personality that blocks the doorway, or threshold, that leads to the fulfilment of our goal. In ancient mythologies, the Guardian of the Threshold may be a dragon, and once we cross the threshold the dragon is guarding, we find the virgin, symbolizing the virginal state of the superconscious mind; the gold, symbolizing the riches of wisdom and genius we will find when we regain contact with our higher self; and the afterlife. Campbell also demonstrated that the most important treasure is the 'Elixir of Immortality'—a magical companion, substance, or piece of knowledge that can transform the ordinary world we originally came from". *156

Does what Mr. Wilcock said here sound familiar to you? Can you see the replicas of this mythological structure in your favorite novels, stories or movies? Are these journeys similar to the journey you are making now? Then you shouldn't have any doubt anymore, because the answer is "yes". Just like what David Wilcock pointed out, it seems we are all recounting the same story in our lucid dreams. Everyone in this world is going through the same cycle, because originally we were one and the same.

In this book, we integrated the results of the research we have been conducting for many years, and divide the hero's journey into four major phases: **departure (separation), initiation, return and omniscience.** These four major phases also comprise thirteen sub-phases.

Departure——includes the sub-phases of 1. confusion, 2. predicament, 3. numbness, 4. sudden change. After your soul sets out on its journey and arrives at the earth, you may not have many strong feelings if you are still in the "consensus state". However, if you have progressed to the "individuated state" or the "spiritual state", you will feel a tremendous sense of isolation. You must feel that no one understands you, that you are "isolated from the world", and that you are unbearably lonely. Maybe deep down in your heart, you even think love (or God, or the Creator) has abandoned you. Therefore, it is very likely that you will build a fortress in your heart, building wall after wall of "defense mechanism" to protect yourself from getting scared and getting hurt. But you will also become more indifferent, and you will lose all your motivations and directions in life. Another possible scenario is that even after you have obtained everything you ever wanted, you will still feel "a sense of loss". There will be a voice in your head that keeps asking you: "Is this all?"

That's why you set out on the journey of self-discovery.

Initiation——includes the sub-phases of 5. searching, 6. trying, 7. frustration, 8. confrontation, 9. integration. As your pain and suffering increase, you finally decide not to continue your life like this, and you start praying, even though you don't believe any miracle will happen because of your praying. At this juncture in your life, even just a book, a leaflet about some courses, an email, an article, a video or a movie, a person, a sentence, or an expression of care, is likely to "push" you toward the road to awakening. But the "nemesis" will also appear, because it is the fear you have or the shadow lying in your heart. Making this long journey will make you brave and see your real strength. You will be able to walk into darkness, face your most deep-rooted attachment and flaws, and fix them. By going through this process, you will gain victory or attain enlightenment. Spiritually, you will get into the state of full realization. The real, selfless love is the "Elixir of Immortality", and after you overcome one hurdle after another, the elixir will be within arm's reach.

Return——includes the sub-phases of 10. transcendence, 11. magical effect, 12. sublimation. You will return to this world with a completely new understanding and a completely new perception of the world (panorama), as well as a completely new insight into life. You will return to the "normal life" and live as everyone else does. However, what appears to be ordinary actually holds a huge amount of love and wisdom. We should share the "Elixir of Immortality" our hearts can offer, call for the "inner revolution" to be carried out in this world, and quietly "transform" the world. Of course, this is just the beginning of a new phase, and there will be different tests and challenges lying ahead. But now you have a totally different view on everything happening in this world, and you have the magic "Elixir of Immortality". They will accompany you and other beings who were originally in "union" with you as you are marching toward the next "peak" in your life.

Omniscience——13. perfection. After you "mingle with the people of the world", *157 you will slowly approach the phase of perfection. This is a state where everything is perfect, because everyone will attain enlightenment, there will be no more worries, there will be Nirvana without remainder, there will be the accomplishment of the four immeasurables, and there will be the acquisition of all knowledge. Everything will be brought to perfection. There is no word adequate to describe this state of perfection. You will have to experience it yourself.

Now let's learn more about this hero's journey to self-transcendence, and let's go through these four major phases and thirteen sub-phases one by one.

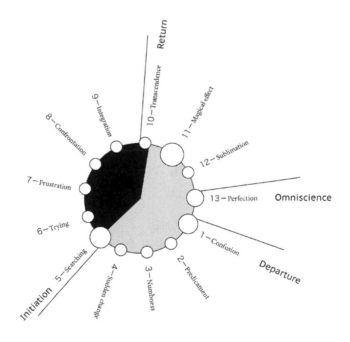

Departure

1. The phase of confusion

In this phase, you are not thinking about anything, and you don't know the meaning of your life. Although you are alive, and you eat, drink, sleep, breathe, and move every day, you are just a shell of a man without a soul you can connect with. You don't even know you have a soul or that there exists a center of higher intelligence. You only believe in the things you see happening around you every day, such as, things you have to deal with day in and day out, the household essentials, the money you earn, your career, and your family. You believe these things are the only things that actually exist, and they are what life is all about.

We now live in a society where everything is developing quickly and many people's hearts have become sick. To say one's "heart becomes sick" is to say one is emotionally wounded, unable to find the meaning and value of his life, and therefore becomes "emotionally unavailable". Many of us have lost ourselves playing all kinds of games in this world, being a workaholic, and in our troubled family relationships. Since we can find neither our true selves nor the value of life, we just muddle through and play it by ear day after day. We live in a comfort zone in the three-dimensional world, live with our basic instincts, and live with a fixation on self-identification.

You become the creation of your mind, which ceaselessly creates one version of you after another. Now you are like one of the Osho Zen Tarot Cards, "The Miser". On the card is the picture of an old lady carefully guarding all the valuables she treasures. I usually refer to this card when describing a person's mentality and psychology: clinging onto everything that was right or wrong in the past and being unable to let it go. This kind of attitude makes people intellectually poor and ignorant, because they can never see another aspect of their life, and they are unable to welcome anything new or any new possibilities.

When your heart is engulfed by how busy, ignorant, and unperceptive you are, the things you are able to care about will just be your own interests, how much money you can make, your job, your family, and your children. Day after day, your heart is trussed up by your subconscious, so your heart is closed. You are fiercely competitive and totally in lack of empathy. When you live in the phase of confusion, you are like a puppet. You have the shell of a man, but you don't have a soul. You can't make decisions for yourself because you are swayed by the the environment and circumstances you are in, and you are under the control of your subconscious and your habits.

2. The phase of predicament

In this phase, you are working very hard because you want to become a pillar of society, you want to live up to your family's expectations, and you also make a lot of effort to incorporate the mainstream culture into the creation of your new life. You hold onto your values and adhere to your beliefs. However, the impermanent nature of things will manifest itself, and the time to learn your life's lessons will come. When karma is in full operation, you choose to hand the power to change over to other authorities (such as fortune tellers or doctors) because you are seeking comfort from other people, or because you place the blame on other people. You think whatever has happened has nothing to do with you. It's all other people's faults. You are unwilling to take responsibility for your life.

Your daily life keeps repeating itself. The same problems keep snowballing. They become bigger and weightier to grapple with. You begin to wonder, "What on earth has happened in my life? Why do I keep undergoing the experiences I don't want to re-live?" Sometimes when you are implementing your plans, you will hit a "snag", which keeps popping up just when you think everything is about to be brought to a satisfactory conclusion. Because you are always in situations you don't like, you don't know what in the world has happened to you. You are stuck in a dark hole. It seems this vicious cycle will just repeat itself forever.

The inventor of the "Diamond Approach", A. H. Almaas, born Hameed Ali, also produced "the Theory of Holes". *158

We all have holes in our subconscious, but we are not aware that we are living in these holes, and we don't even know what these holes are composed of. Sometimes, you are in the hole of despair, but you are unaware of it; you are filled with anger, but you try to deny it. **When you are in a hole, the fact is, you don't have a grasp of reality. What's worse, when you look at your family, people around you, and the world from the standpoint of the hole, you are looking at them with distorted views.** It is because you are in the domain of the subconscious, which is thirty thousand times more powerful than our consciousness. No one has ever learned how to use this subconscious power properly, so you are unable to get rid of your negative energy and your twisted reflections on things. Nor can you perceive how you have been controlled by the holes.

You don't understand yourself and you don't know which hole you are currently in. But if you don't try to discover it and observe it, you will never get over the past, and you will never have anything to fill the holes. So, the first thing you need to do is to be aware of their presence. However, since you have been living in these holes for a long time, you became incapable of perceiving the condition you are in, so even if you draw the attention back to yourself, still you cannot see your true self. The theory of holes that concerns our subconscious mind corresponds to the theory about black holes in our universe. At the center of the universe there is a black hole. As black holes have enormous masses, they can suck in everything and they can warp space time. So can the holes in our lives. There are also energy fields around these holes. If we live in the holes for too long and are deeply influenced by them, the "fields" of these holes will distort our self-perception; we will forget what we originally looked like, and even lose the connection with "the center of the sacred". At that moment, all you can feel is how helpless, useless and insignificant you are. You ask yourself, "Is this how my life will be forever?"

3. The phase of numbness

There are two patterns of behaviors you might display. One is that you work hard to achieve your goals and become successful. When you finally reach the top of the hierarchy, you gradually lose yourself in what you have and no longer have. After a long while, you will become "numb" to everything and everyone around you. The other pattern is we feel so helpless about our lives that we lose our vigor and we don't see any hopes in life. We even stop making any effort, because we know everything we do will come to no fruition. Since no matter how hard we try, we are still unable to make any change, in the end we choose to give up on ourselves and forsake ourselves. Day in and day out, we allow ourselves to be snowed under with work. Gradually, we forget to listen to our "inner voices", we give up our "great dreams", and we admit that there is a gap between "ideals" and "reality". Among the students in the dynamic school of this earth, you become a dropout from life. There are also some extreme cases.

For example, as has been mentioned in the previous chapter, when some people become "emotionally unavailable," they could exhibit symptoms such as being possessive, being evil, or being in despair. Consequently, they might turn into an alcoholic, a drug addict, a sex addict, or a video game junkie, because they try to deaden their pain by being completely numb.

You want to enjoy momentary pleasures, and you are only looking for compromised perfection, so you think the material wealth you have in a three-dimensional world can fill the holes in your subconscious, and it can mend the cracks and fill the void in your heart. In fact, they are made of two completely different materials. You think the more money you earn, the stronger the sense of security you will have. You think as long as you have a happy love life, you will feel perfectly content. You think as long as you take good care of your children, you don't have to worry about their futures. However, everything turns out to be a big disappointment. It's never easy to maintain a harmonious relationship, to keep your job, to enjoy good health, or to carve out a career for yourself. Therefore, the game of "battling for energy" begins. *159 You think you are willing to make sacrifice for your family. So, when your father is in trouble, you try to sort things out for him. When your mother encounters some difficulties, you try to handle them for her. You also take full responsibility for all the problems your siblings have. When something goes wrong with the company, you never try to shirk your duties. However, you feel like an exhausted dog, because there are always issues for you to tackle. Then, you are overcome with a sense of despair, because none of the efforts you have made are being reciprocated. Your family doesn't change at all because of your hard work. Growing fatigue sets into your heart. When you can no longer tolerate the situation, you will put your "defense" mechanism to work. You choose to "run away", to be indifferent, or even to have terrible rows with others, and then simply disappear. You are drifting between two emotional extremes, either feeling everything is beyond your control or being completely numb.

As the saying goes, "Lookers-on see most of the game". Since you are not one of the lookers-on, you will find that the more you try to do, the worse the mistake you will make. Each day, you waste lots of your energy coping with all kinds of issues your life is inundated with. It seems, every day, life is trying to "hunt you down", and your life's lessons are also trying to "hunt you down". It seems you are always busy, but deep down, you feel ever more helpless and confused. Moreover, the holes in your subconscious will start to do their work on you, removing you further away from the foundation of your "heart", you feel "number" and "number" to life, you feel number and number to "hopes", and you feel numb to everything.

You think the world is just a stage for a boring play. Everything is deceitful. Everything is like those "terrible dramas that never end". You want to cry to your heart's content, but somehow you can't even shed a tear. You can only lock yourself up in this prison you built in the depths of your heart, never seeing the sun again.

In this way, you will never feel any pain, never have any worries, and never have to "see" those unacceptable things that make you feel frustrated and powerless. Over time, you won't feel any "feelings" anymore.

At that moment, you will become a solitary boat in a sea of people, an isolated island in a crowd. The emotions you are chocked with most of the time are loneliness and emptiness. Because you have never studied "spirituality and science", and you have never learned how to keep your heart company, you don't know how to make it through the long nights every day. You can only let insomnia, stress, and the feeling of being out of control devour your soul and health step by step.

The sky, the earth, and human beings all have boundless energy. But when you are in this state, it's very easy to lose your connection with the energy of the earth. *160 You also lack the inexhaustible and omnipresent energy of the Dharmadhatu *161 as your supplement. As a result, you keep turning round and round in the holes in your heart. In your daily life, you feel lost and numb. Even though you know there is a hole, you still fall into it. This is what the theory of the hole is all about.

Carl Jung once stated, "People will do anything, no matter how absurd, to avoid facing their own souls". It is true. You need to know the ways to understand yourself, to see the patterns of your life, so that you will know what you can do for your life, and how you can assume responsibility for your life. You can instill into your life a kind of new power, the power of your heart, so that you will be able to change the patterns of your life and your habits. Only through the processes of transformation and transcendence can the sun rise in your life again. However, if you think there is nothing you can do, and you are reluctant to change, those holes are only going to get bigger. When the amount of energy bottled up in your heart and your subconscious increases to the point that it "manifests" itself as different events, or when the "destructive" energy of Pluto starts to affect you, you will enter the next phase in your life.

4. The phase of sudden change———Pluto's power

You have ignored or refused to face your life's lessons, which you are supposed to learn to transcend according to the blueprint for your spirituality, or you have refused to study in order to get the credits for your life's lessons for far too long. However, every second, the evolutionary force of the universe is pushing every living being to move forward, so if you just loaf around, unwilling to make any progress, and unwilling to "see", life will remind you by resorting to things that will create greater tension, such as illness, symptoms, or the impermanent nature of all things, and shake the spiritual fortress you have been building for a long time, so you can "see" what you should have already seen.

Campbell called this kind of escape the "refusal of the call", and he pointed out that mythological stories from all over the world have already warned us that people who refused the call would pay a high price for it. As Maslow has already observed, "If you deliberately plan on being less than you are capable of being, then I warn you that you'll be unhappy for the rest of your life". *162 The unhappiness that emerges from the depths of your soul will bring about all kinds of "symptoms" of an unhappy life; for example, the "pain" we talked about in the previous section that is described in the book, *The Prophet*. You live in fear of your health being damaged, and you realize how miserable it is to be unable to "buy good health", no matter how rich you are. You may even feel you are so poor that the only thing you have is money. You don't know how to deal with it when the vicissitudes of life come as a severe blow to you. You are unable to lay a solid foundation for a happy family, for a successful career, for a good relationship with the person you love, for excellent health, and for acquiring wealth. The vicissitudes of life act like a giant monster's claw. It will destroy in an instant the "kingdom" you have been building for many years and take everything away from you. When that happens, since you are unable to compose yourself, you are unable to "see" this "doctor inside you", who is prescribing some good medicines for you. You are unable to "accept" it, unable to feel joy. You are even unable to "trust" anyone or anything. When the most important people and the most important things in your life are completely gone overnight, when you are stripped of everything, how can you appreciate these good medicines? And how can you trust anyone or anything? At this moment, your life is filled with pain, tears, helplessness, and you cannot stop wailing because you feel you are up the creek without a paddle. It seems God has forgotten about you. It seems you have been cursed by life.

Dear friends, if you are currently in this phase, please listen to me. You are now going through the most important phase in your life, the phase of "transformation". You will transform into something supremely beautiful. But now you are at a crossroads, and it is a challenge to your soul. It is not about whether you should go east, west, north or south. It is about whether you will choose to go "up". Do you want to go up and elevate your soul or do you want to go down and sink to the all-time low? Do you want to revisit the past and have your heart "stuck" there? It all depends on the decision you make now.

Do you believe that this bitter pill called "sudden change" is the "call" from your divinity?

Are you willing to believe that this is the most beautiful gift your "greater self", also called your "higher self", or your "true self", can give to your life?

I know how you will react. You will say, "How is this possible? Why do my life, my higher self, the deities, God, or all the Buddhas treat me like this? Why was I put in such an unbearable situation? Why did they make me suffer so much? Why did I 'lose everything I ever had in life'? Why did they make me feel I was on the edge of a precipice in my life, and there was no room for me to turn around, but I could only jump off it? Sometimes the pain was so terrible that I wanted to take my own life, so that I can put an end to all these suffering. Why me? Why is everything so unfair? I have never hurt anyone. I have never done anything wrong. Why? Why?"

You cannot help but let tears course down your cheeks. Only this cold space that gives you no response keeps you company. You have this feeling of instant suffocation. There is nothing you can do but to allow the pain to keep tormenting you. The infinite "black holes" of pain, and a whole series of the unknown events lying ahead, send shivers down your spine. You are gripped by great fear, and you don't know when the pain will go away. Where is your salvation? Where is the miracle? The acute sense of despair, like a sharp knife held in someone's hand, slashes at your heart ruthlessly again and again, your blood (symbolizing your vitality) drains away completely.

However, we can try to approach the situation from the opposite standpoint: is what is happening to you now everything you can have? Are there some "minor" incidents that are also taking place, but we just ignored them, or we are unable to detect them? Let's press the "pause" button now.

Please believe me. You are walking through the dark night that will appear in everyone's life. Every hero in his life has to pass through "the passage of the dark night". Though it is difficult to compose yourself, if you are reading this book, you will know that we are all here for you. Don't be afraid. We can hear you shouting. We can feel your pain, your sorrow, your loneliness, your despair, and your fear. Don't make any hasty decision now, lest you regret it in the future.

The truth is, your divinity is calling you, a brand-new life is calling you. Do you believe it? If you weren't ready yet, God would not have placed extra burdens on you. Had you not had any strength, God would not have made you learn the lessons of sudden change. These things happened so that you could see, see the broader horizons of life, see the infinite possibilities in your life, see more parts of the "love" you used to turn a blind eye to, and see your wisdom and strength.

But many souls, at this moment, will see the sudden change as a demon, or as the evil force, or they will be frightened by the experience of awakening, by their divinity and Buddha nature. They even go so far as to change their religious faith or change the organizations they used to be associated with. They will project what is in their minds onto the outside world. As a result, your family, your job, your children, the money you have, your divinity, or the awakening itself will become your fear, become the "scapegoat" lying in the shadows in your heart.

In his book, *The Hero with A Thousand Faces*,*163 Joseph Campbell cited a poem:

"I fled Him, down the nights and down the days;

I fled Him, down the arches of the years;
I fled Him, down the labyrinthine ways
Of my own mind; and in the mist of tears
I hid from Him, and under running laughter."

Campbell wrote, "One is harassed, both day and night, by the divine being that is the image of the living self within the locked labyrinth of one's own disoriented psyche. The ways to the gate have all been lost; there is no exit. One can only cling, like Satan, furiously, to oneself and be in hell; or else break, and be annihilated at last, in God". *164

A sudden change is the medicine good for our health, because it allows us to make a stop in our life's journeys, to slow down a little bit, take stock of our life and carry out some self-examination. "Willed introversion" is one of the most precious gifts God can ever give to human beings. In another part of the book, Campbell shared the following thoughts with his readers:

"Willed introversion, in fact, is one of the classic implements of creative genius…It drives the psychic energies into depth and activates the lost continent of unconscious infantile and archetypal images. The result, of course, may be a disintegration of consciousness more or less complete (neurosis, psychosis: the plight of spellbound Daphne); but on the other hand, if the personality is able to absorb and integrate the new forces, there will be experienced an almost super-human degree of self-consciousness and masterful control…"

There are deeply ingrained neural circuits within our brains that keep us alive and decide the horizons and visions of our consciousness. If there isn't any "sudden change" to "shake" these neural circuits and "break down" the structure of our consciousness, how can we see any hopes or a possible spiritual rebirth since we are so inundated with all sorts of things in our daily existence? Do you think you can withstand being devoured by a "sudden change", being devoured by "the impermanent nature of being", and being devoured by "the unknown", even though you might feel you are about to die? The great Yoga guru, Ananda Coomaraswamy, once observed, "No creature can attain a higher grade of nature without ceasing to exist".

Do you believe a "sudden change" is ripping apart your ego, forcing you to go through a conceptual "death" of your self-identity, allowing your consciousness to re-organize and re-integrate itself, and letting you enter the holy of the holies to search for the "Elixir of Immortality", enter the place where you can regain the strength to save your life?

In brief, a "sudden change" seems to be able to trigger some kind of awakening inside you, making you feel that you need to do something to change your life. It seems there really is a calling, a force that looms from inside of you, even if at the moment you are not certain about it and you are apprehensive about what the future has in store for you.

Some people will choose to go back to "the phase of confusion", lingering in the first four phases "indefinitely", until a "sudden change" occurs again to toll the funeral knell and force them to say farewell to their habitual behaviors and inclinations.

Initiation

5. The phase of searching

Campbell once remarked, "The regions of the unknown... are free fields for the projection of unconscious content". As we have talked about before, people tend to be afraid of what they don't know. But when you are willing to learn about your fear and overcome it, when you want to "see" your life, you will realize that your habitual behaviors and your modes of thought are what make you go around in circles, or make you embark on adventures only within your "safe zone". That's why you always got the same answer to questions about life. When you start to ponder the meaning of being, and when you decide to cross the border which demarcates the domain within which your rules of the game are applicable, you will enter the phase of initiation and set out on an internal hero's journey.

At this very second, it seems there is an invisible hand giving you directions. You look at the computer screen and you type the "key words" for things you have never searched before, and you check out the websites you have never thought about visiting before. Your classmates or family members who haven't contacted you for a long time unexpectedly invite you to a speech you have never heard of, "A Talk on Gentle Awakening". Or maybe you just suddenly feel downcast, so you lead yourself to a bookstore in a crowded district, and approach the shelf of books about people's different professions. A book with words of a large font size on its cover captures your attention. Though you have never read books of this kind, much to your surprise, you start a new chapter in your life because of this book.

"Valor consists in the power of self-recovery", said Emerson.

Hermann Hesse (1877-1962), winner of the Nobel Prize in Literature in 1946, is one of my favorite philosophers. He devoted his entire life to the pursuit of love and truth. He once remarked, "An enlightened man had but one duty—to seek the way to himself, to reach inner certainty, to grope his way forward, no matter where it led." To be honest, it is not easy to find the way to yourself. That is why the aphorism, "Know Thyself," was inscribed on the portico of the Temple of Apollo.

As soon as you pass through the darkness in the phase of sudden change, in a way unknown to you, the synchronicity of the universe will goad you into moving to the next phase in your life. Though it is a phase full of tests and full of the unknown, deep down you know very well that: it is the time. I should get going now. I can't waste my life tarrying forever, can I? In fact, you won't be alone on your hero's journey, because some "secret" angels, or people who are the answers to your prayers, will "turn up" to give you a hand should the need arise, or to give you some "advice" that will benefit you for the rest of your life. Gradually, you will see there is a force of "kindness", or you can call it "love", that will give you the support and help when you least expect it, when you are in the most difficult process of getting your "entry clearance" for the next phase.

"The purification of the self" is a very important process in the phase of initiation. Your soul is baptized by a sudden change and tempered by the unknown, and then gradually takes the course of "the purification of the self". The door to your "awareness" that has been asleep for a long time is opened, and light shines again when your life is in the dark. Campbell even mentioned this purifying process in this book:

"In the vocabulary of the mystics this is the second stage of the Way, that of the 'purification of the self', when the senses are 'cleansed and humbled', and the energies and interests 'concentrated upon transcendental things'; or in a vocabulary of more modern turn: this is the process of dissolving, transcending, or transmuting the infantile images of our personal past". *165

"Knock, and the door will be opened to you!" In this stage, when you are ready, the "teachers" will appear at your request. Any professional "spiritual leader" will tell you that if you want to gain strength from "the purification of the self", you have to go down to the labyrinth of your subconscious and walk through those narrow and circuitous alleys because this is the dark and dangerous "adventure" you have to embark on. Otherwise, all the spiritual training or soul searching is merely to put us in a more relaxing scenario, as if we are just a bunch of kids "playing house". It is never easy to get into the holes in the subconscious, and we have to be really lucky to find a truly professional guide or coach, and to be in a truly selfless and loving circumstance. If not, the inexperienced coach and the inexperienced you will both fall into the infinite darkness of the subconscious. You end up rousing the force of your shadow archetype, which will make you complacent, or project your self-perception onto everything, or delude yourself, or believe that you are actually making progress. You will not even have the chance to be exposed to the influence of a truly altruistic coach, a coach who can be the "necessary" crutch, the lifebelt, or the savior in your life. That is a terrible shame. We need to notice all kinds of signs in our lives to be conscious of what kind of holes we are living in. We can learn how to quiet our mind and become observant. In our day-to-day existence, we are all playing the following five roles: "those who intimidate" and "those who beseech", "those who are apathetic" and "those who interrogate", and finally "those who sit on the fence". These roles echo one another in a certain way. When you uncover the modes of thought and behaviors you have been using in your life, you need to understand that these modes are the precious footprints you have left in your life, and these are the useful clues to self-salvation. Slowly, you become more willing to follow these footprints to advance and discover the holes inside yourself. You can see how your mind has been twisted and how you have been controlled by the "false" memories from the past. You have to see it in order to overcome it. If you don't know how big the hole is, you will never pass it. We are inclined to use the image of a giant monster as the unknown darkness incarnate and are thus often defeated by our own imagination. Another tough challenge we don't want to face when stepping into the hole is a large amount of "negative emotions" we will feel. This is because we usually direct our attention to the outside world; therefore, when we suddenly turn the camera around and focus on ourselves, we start to connect with a more innate self. To be reconnected with the emotions you haven't been in touch with for a long time is a painful experience for many people. But the fact is, emotions themselves are "neither positive nor negative". The process of exploring the depth of our emotions can help us regain our strength and "see" again what those things of the past really mean to us. Only when we go deep into everything we have experienced can we bring about some transformations.

If we want to grasp the real meaning hidden behind the events occurring in our lives, behind our pain, and in the holes, we need to pass through these holes in our subconscious, through this "door of transformation", which symbolizes the spiritual training we have to undergo. The mystery of life is already imbedded in the questions you want to ask. If you want to learn, if you want to resolve the mystery and benefit from it, you have to be brave and "jump" into it. As an old saying goes, "Do you think you don't have to go through what others have been through, and can still be in paradise?" The author of *The Aquarian Conspiracy*, Marilyn Ferguson, quoted Theobald in the book as saying, "There is no riskless route into the future. We must choose which set of risks we wish to run".

How can you fill up, close, and transcend the holes in your subconscious? Love is the only answer. To really help yourself, you have to be brave enough to see these holes. If you want to help others and help this world, you must help yourself first. You must get to know these holes you are in, and then rely on love to help yourself, keep yourself company, support yourself, heal yourself, integrate the opposite sides, and finally transcend yourself.

Previously, we have mentioned this book, *Power VS. Force: The Hidden Determinants of Human Behavior*, *166 by Dr. David Hawkins. He discovered and formulated a set of consciousness levels of human beings. This discovery was even described as the unraveling of an "astonishing mystery". It is true that whether you will succeed or fail in this life all depends on your consciousness level. The level of "love" is set at 500. Here love refers to kindness, reverence, and divine providence. When you decide to "take risks", to take the first step toward change, it means you have started the journey from the level of "courage", the energy level of which is set at 200. When you pass through one hole after another and gradually feel that there are "hopes" in life, you are at the energy level of 310. Then if you keep moving, you will reach the level of "acceptance", at an energy level rated 350. Are you willing to accept a "sudden change"? Are you willing to accept your vulnerability, helplessness and fear? Are you willing to accept the fact that you have hurt others before? Are you willing to accept everything that has happened to you in the past? Are you willing to accept those who have hurt you before? With each step you take, you will transcend one thing after another, you will enter "love", experience "love", and be integrated with "love". When both your mind and body are ready, the "teacher" will lead you to the next phase.

6. The phase of trying (taking risks)

After meeting with some wonderful and miraculous "accidents", you are willing to start taking some risks. You are trying to find an exit for a life stranded in serious straits, a life that has ground to a standstill, a life that wants to find the value and meaning of its existence. By taking different spiritual courses or joining the religious groups that you think can respond to your needs, you find a harbor for your exhausted soul and provide it with a sense of security.

Whether you want to solve the predicament you are in, to tackle social issues, to cure the problems of the world, or to transcend yourself, the most fundamental and essential thing to do is to go back to visit your heart, to "understand yourself". You need to return to the origin of everything in order to learn how to love yourself. "To love yourself" are not just some empty words, but many people do not truly understand "love". To love yourself doesn't mean to be good to yourself at a superficial level, such as dressing yourself up in fine clothes, and providing yourself with delicious food. People think that treating themselves well is the only way to love themselves, but most of the time all they do is feed their egos. When life again deals them a heavy blow, or when they face some hindrances at work, because they don't have a proper understanding of themselves, because they don't know how to employ their innate wisdom to solve these problems, different kinds of energy will become entangled again.

If you have religion, or if you take courses run by certain spiritual organizations, or if you practice meditation, do yoga, or take up some independent study, indeed, it would seem like you are "trying", exploring all kinds of possibilities and examining the feasibility of all kinds of plans. But if you don't have practical methods, if you refuse to face the real origin of your internal conflicts, refuse to deal with the opposing voices inside your head, and refuse to find the crucial interior way to transform yourself, all these "exterior" ways will just bring you short-lived joy. Or maybe they allow you to temporarily "detach" yourself from these problems, to seek shelter in religion, in your spiritual self, in all kinds of courses, or in your travels. They can give you a brief respite, but they can't give you a true understanding of yourself.

At SatDharma Institute, I have met so many people who have tried countless ways and have taken countless spiritual courses. Some people also tried to meet God by becoming religious. However, after years and years of religious practices, they still haven't had any "peak experience", any "conversation with God". Nor have they attained meditative absorption (Samadhi). If you haven't truly integrated the opposing voices in your consciousness, you still haven't truly met "God" in your heart. There is also another group of people who believe they have cleansed their subconscious in many courses they took and have tackled their problems countless times. Therefore, very often they would say, "I know all of this stuff" or "I have had fun with all this stuff," etc. Or they may believe they have arrived at their "spiritual summit", they have "attained Nirvana", or they have reached one of the "four stages of enlightenment". However, all these reactions are "self-deluding".

They are just the ploys used by these people to help them hide their true feelings behind the sentence "I am fine", to provide an "accommodation" for the shadows of discriminating ideologies and opposing voices in their consciousness, and to keep up the self-deluding "appearances" of a glamorous life.

In this phase of trying, what one "tries" to do is to find an untrodden path to the domain of the divine, and to try different ways to "dissolve" the self-contradictory consciousness when undergoing the spiritual training. Here at SatDharma, we do not attempt to "kill" one's self, or to see "self" as an impediment to one's reunion with one's divinity or with one's Buddha nature. The real obstacles are the labels we unwittingly attach to our consciousness and the identity we create for our consciousness. What we need to do is to find ways to "dissolve" or "take off" these labels so that our true selves will re-emerge and display our most enchanting side. In the field of mysticism, "trying" means to enter an unimaginable, inconceivable state, to try to transcend one's consciousness and fly into the deep and mysterious space of "eternality".

In the language of mysticism, the Goddess symbolizes "the totality of what can be known", while a hero (he/she) symbolizes "the knower of the totality". These symbols function in a way very similar to some of the symbols used in the teachings of Tantra, which is one of the ancient Buddhist traditions; for example, the Yab (father) and the Yum (mother). The Yum symbolizes the immense source of wisdom: "emptiness". From "emptiness" emerges the "existence" of everything. On the other hand, the Yab symbolizes the evolution of "existence", and "upaya", the skillful means one can use in order to be integrated with this immense "emptiness". "Upaya" symbolizes "compassion". Different skillful means are devised to enable one to be unified with emptiness and with one's intrinsic nature. Therefore, "upaya" is the wisdom and compassion one has in order to help one's students learn more useful skills, in the hope that they can be integrated with their intrinsic nature.

While the hero is advancing slowly in the phase of initiation, the Goddess can serve as a symbol of the hero's (he/she) most intrinsic nature. Campbell pointed out that, "…the form of the goddess undergoes for him a series of transfigurations: she can never be greater than himself, though she can always promise more than he is yet capable of comprehending. She lures, she guides, and she bids him burst his fetters. And if he can match her import, the two, the knower and the known, will be released from every limitation". *167

Isn't this the "eternity" all the past mystics and mentors have been trying to inform us of and to help us experience?

Campbell continued in the book, "Woman is the guide to the sublime acme of sensuous adventure. By deficient eyes she is reduced to inferior states; by the evil eye of ignorance she is spellbound to banality and ugliness.

But she is redeemed by the eyes of understanding. The hero who can take her as she is, without undue commotion but with the kindness and assurance she requires, is potentially the king, the incarnate god, of her created world". *168

You will meet "the Goddess" (namely "love", the nature everyone has) after the hero inside you——symbolizing the self who wants to transcend and to discover the truth, overcomes one hurdle after another. After getting over the fantasies about the "devil", which are the projections of the "Father" and the shadow inside oneself, the hero will gradually gain a better understanding of himself, and during this process, combine the inner forces of Yin and Yang to produce fresher and more detailed insights. Finally, the hero will meet and be united with the Goddess, with his intrinsic nature. This is the test posed for any hero (someone who wants to know his true self) in pursuit of the ultimate blessing of "love". This "love" is the source of wisdom, and it also holds eternal life. In the "phase of trying", you are trying to heal yourself and pass through black holes. Your heart starts to free itself from the prison it built in order to enjoy freedom again. Because you are able to see your own reactions and how much you have twisted your mind, you are more capable of releasing and healing your heart. Only when you heal yourself first can you really feel that you are still alive. You can only slowly regain the power of equilibrium by first getting to know your heart. You will even rediscover yourself, rediscover the forces of Ying and Yang in your heart, and gradually head toward "the Goddess". At moments like these, "miracles" will start to occur for you. It is because in the ancient myths, the goddess always lives on "the other shore". Your journey to the shore will be difficult and full of crises, but "miracles" always happen on your way there. The gifts in your life will arrive one by one (successes, fortunate turns of events, happy relationships, good health, material wealth, and an affluent lifestyle, etc.) to support you. But you should never stop exploring yourself only because you have received these gifts. These "miracles" occur so that you can continue to progress toward the incredible "eternal" love. Otherwise, you will just idle away your life, which will be a real shame.

7. The phase of frustration (It is when you hit the wall. It is a phase of tough challenges)

With aspirations growing stronger, you focus on the enhancement of your spirituality, and you improve yourself by devoting yourself to your work, engaging in meaningful activities, and spreading words of love, etc. But you will hit some snags during this phase, and the ironing out of these snags is the process you have to go through in order to enhance your spirituality and transform your life

(1) After you have been putting in efforts for a while, you want to see some changes and new turns of events, either happening to you or to someone important to you. But when you realize that you or that important person hasn't actually changed, or hasn't changed as quickly as you have expected, or the situation isn't getting any better, etc., "doubts" start to arise quietly. You begin to ask questions such as "Is this really useful?" "How long do I have to keep doing this until things will be improved?" "Is this really the right way?" "Have I been deceived again?" "I don't want to do this anymore!" and so on.

(2) You develop your "consciousness" through things you learn in your life and in the courses you take. Every day, when you examine the ultimate truth of your heart, your conscious mind will be expanding; thus it will be easier for you to see the "negative" thoughts you have, a lot of imprints on your subconscious, and a lot of habits you have. Your "hidden" intentions that you can see now will provoke your strong reactions and make you reproach yourself. The eagerness to criticize yourself and the sense of shame are so overwhelming that you don't dare to advance anymore. You feel you are unworthy of it, you think you should disappear from the group, and you don't have the courage to move toward "the bright side", so on and so forth.

(3) Whether it is about your career, health, relationships, love life, or the imprints on your subconscious, no matter how hard you try, you are still unable to transcend or become enlightened. No matter how much you do, you always lag behind others. Whatever you do, you always make mistakes. You cannot catch up with others, put your finger on what is going on with you, see the core of the

problems, see your future or find any answers. It seems as if all the feelings of being helpless and powerless have come back to haunt you, and they become even stronger. In fact, these feelings are so strong that you cannot withstand them anymore.

(4) When you genuinely engage yourself in "spirituality and science" (or any other professionalfields), you will realize that there is so much you must learn. There is so much you don't understand and have never heard of before. You know "the teacher" said that you had to experience it yourself, but what kind of experience? You see the other members have all experienced something wonderful and profound, and you wonder, "Why haven't I?"

You heart is gripped by the sense of "disbelief" in yourself. You doubt whether you can ever reach the goal in this life. "Can I really make it?" Because your mind cannot stay tranquil, you cannot see the ultimate truth about your heart, you cannot experience deep meditation, you cannot attain "meditative absorption", and finally, you cannot even do the basic spiritual practices you are supposed to do every day. The thought of beating a retreat and of giving up keeps popping into your head. You feel you are so far away from your "destination", and you doubt that you are ever going to make it.

(5) It seems you have arrived at some new understanding. You feel you have obtained some insight. However, after sharing your experience with the "teachers", *169 after discussing with the senior teachers in the group, you realize that your knowledge is still very superficial. Or you feel that the moment in which you have just made a breakthrough was also "the moment" in which the universe has sent you another "test". As expected, you failed the test. Immediately, you were defeated. You cannot help but once again allow yourself to sink into the scenario in which you are defeated and frustrated.

(6) You see your old partners, members of the same spiritual group, your family, and the seniors from the school you went to, all going around in circles. You see very clearly how obstinate and unyielding their consciousness is. There are even some who have decided to quit. You feel very disheartened. It seems there is nothing you can do to help them. You are very anxious, but you don't know what to do. After a long while, you feel even more frustrated, and you

no longer know how to keep advancing. The sense of helplessness and powerlessness sharpens. You don't have the motivation to do anything. At a moment like this, it seems no matter what kind of "mindset" you used to have, it vanishes completely. Your life becomes even more tedious, and you are simply at a loss.

(7) You are faced with your comrades whose hearts have also gone astray, or you are keeping them company. Therefore, you have to endure many of their negative comments, their criticisms, the stress they feel, their high-strung temperament, and so forth. You feel so powerless because you can't change them, and you don't know what else you can do.

You can't trust your teammates. You don't have any support. You feel no one really understands you. You feel unable to move forward anymore. You don't even know how to handle yourself. Finally, grief-stricken, you have no other choice but to bow out.

Darkness, heavy blows, all the negative voices in your head, and your mistrust, these are all the "shadows", the imprints that hide in the greater depths of your consciousness, and they will re-emerge in this phase. You know that, like an athlete who is training to build up his muscle strength, at some point "fatigue" will set in. He will feel he has hurt himself, and his passion will wane. But to learn what this "failure" symbolizes is actually a very important process to go through during this phase. It will train you to have stronger resolve, more intense meditative absorption, higher spirits, and deeper concentration. It gives you a softer heart and makes you humble so that you have a more profound understanding of what it means to be accepting and be receptive, what it really means to "suffer", and what it means to trust "love". Will you be able to be impervious to the influence from other people, your surroundings, darkness, and all the adversities, and fully concentrate on what's inside you? You should focus your attention on "the resolution to meet 'the Goddess'", on "the goals in your life", on the determination that, "no matter what happens, I will keep soldiering on". Therefore, you will be willing to calm down, trying to keep yourself company; or you may choose to just let it go, allowing yourself to be immersed in the "feminine" energy, to be caressed by love, to fill your heart with love, and to continue to move forward alongside love.

You used to be able to feel your inner love and the light inside you. However, one day, all of a sudden, you just "hit the wall". It feels like you are "running into an invisible obstacle". As a consequence, love disappears. The light disappears. You can no longer feel the energy of your innate divinity, nor can you feel the mentor's love or detect their vibration frequency.

During this phase, the "love" and wisdom you used to experience simply disappear without a trace. At a time like this, whom can you depend on? What can you depend on? What can you do? In this moment, something that will also symbolize "failure" will be you being led to a different direction by your negative desires. Here, we can try to gain more detailed knowledge of the "seven deadly sins" in Catholic theology *170: **pride, envy, wrath, sloth, greed, gluttony and lust.**

At this point in your hero's journey, it would seem there is a rope made of strings of rubber bands that is tied to you and is pulling you towards the opposite direction. Now you are faced with a great inner struggle. When your heart is trussed up by the seven great forces and the 26 "enemies" born out of them, it will fall into another "dark" abyss, and you would think, "Rather than buck myself up and move on, not knowing where the destination is and feeling that I am heading toward the terrifying 'unknown', it would be better to follow the order of these seven voices so that I can have an 'easier' life".

For me, these seven forces are like seven angels hidden in the depths of your heart. When your mind is in chaos and your nerves are shattered, they will come out to get some fresh air. They are the extension of the shadow inside you, and they are the "planktons" that make you temporarily lose your way. *171 When your soul is taking a small detour, your heart will be radically affected. In the middle of a quiet night, you will feel ever more powerless and helpless. You know very clearly the direction you should be heading in, but you are being pulled by a reaction force towards another direction. You feel totally defeated, and you want to find the strength to "support" yourself. Therefore, you start to look for "kindred spirits", people who are stuck in the same situation, to seek their empathy and approval.

Very often, you will meet people like this in your psychiatrist's office, in your doctor's consulting room, when you are with your therapist, or in some courses you are taking. When you go through these experiences of losing your emotional balance once again, either in your dreams or when some symptoms have started to arise, layers and layers of your ignorance will be unraveled, and you will find what hides behind all these symptoms——your vulnerability. Psychiatrists, clinical psychologists, the clergy, priests or pastors, mentors or the teachers in spiritual courses often carry out the redemptive function of the role of "monks who enlighten others". They redeem people and forgive their "sins". If there are also shadows in the hearts of these "monks who enlighten others" that haven't been properly integrated, the monks will transform themselves and play the role of "the savior" whom people can rely on. People will believe that only these monks, as "the saviors", can protect their vulnerable souls. Because "the savior" is here, these people no longer have to face the real, innate problems. They don't have to deal with the sense of frustration and the shadows in their hearts. They don't have to "grow up". They don't have to be "compelled" to move forward.

If there are "teachers", spiritual groups, doctors or educators who genuinely want to help these people grow up, let them see the opposing forces inside themselves, see the real cause for their problems; or if they genuinely want to keep these people company on their hero's journeys, they will be treated as "Aunt Sally". They will either be subject to attacks or choose to leave voluntarily. This is what happened to Osho, and George Gurdjieff, who came up with the "Fourth Way".

As far as I am concerned, it is much easier to leave any center of spiritual practices in the outside world than to walk the inner path towards awakening. But, do giving up and leaving mean that you don't have to face yourself anymore? Don't be silly. It's like the presumption of some people when they change their jobs or get a divorce without any hesitation. In the end, you must still face yourself. The time to learn your life's lessons will still come. Everything is still impermanent. Your life will keep waking itself up. No matter where you are, nothing will stop happening. The fact that you choose to leave a group of spiritual practices in the outside world doesn't mean that the sun in your life will never set again. It doesn't mean that from now on, only daytime exists and night will never come. That's impossible. If you are unable to feel real love, no matter where you go, your mind will never be at ease. You will still be gripped by great fear. Your heart will still be filled with fierce criticisms or distrust. You think you have been redeemed. However, when the time comes to learn the "lessons", all the secrets you have put behind you and the weak and vulnerable sides you try to hide from others will come back and devour you at this very moment. How do you face what is happening to you right now? If you can't feel love, how can you believe in love? When you can't see what's in front of you, will you still have the confidence in yourself and continue to advance? When the voices in your head keep criticizing others, criticizing your mentors, criticizing your fellow members who are learning together with you, and criticizing the whole world, can you still believe in love? Can you still trust your own heart?

Guru Nanak once said, "By conquering your mind, you conquer the world!"

In fact, now that you have reached this stage, do you know these seemingly "negative" experiences are but the "illusions" you have when going through this process?

In *The Hero with a Thousand Faces*, there is a story about the five sons of the Irish king Eochaid, who, "having gone one day hunting, they found themselves astray, shut in on every hand. Thirsty, they set off, one by one, to look for water. Fergus was the first: 'and he lights on a well, over which he finds an old woman standing sentry. The fashion of the hag is this: blacker than coal every joint and segment of her was, from crown to ground; comparable to a wild horse's tail the grey wiry mass of hair that pierced her scalp's upper surface; with her sickle of a greenish looking tusk that was in her head, and curled till it touched her ear, she could lop the verdant branch of an oak in full bearing; blackened and smoke-bleared eyes she had; nose awry, wide-nostrilled; a wrinkled and freckled belly, variously unwholesome; warped crooked shins, garnished with massive ankles and a pair of capacious shovels; knotty knees she had and livid nails.

The beldame's whole description in fact was disgusting.

'That's the way it is, is it?' said the lad.

And 'that's the very way,' she answered.

'Is it guarding the well thou art?' he asked.

And she said: 'it is.'

'Dost thou licence me to take away some water?'

'I do,' she consented, 'yet only so that I have of thee one kiss on my cheek.'

'Not so,' said he.

'Then water shall not be conceded by me.'

'My word I give,' he went on, 'that sooner than give thee a kiss I would perish of thirst.'

Then the young man departed to the place where his brethren were, and told them that he had not gotten water.'

Olioll, Brian, and Fiachra, likewise, went on the quest and equally attained to the identical well. Each solicited the old thing for water, but denied her the kiss.

Finally it was Niall who went, and he came to the very well.

'Let me have the water, woman!' he cried.

'I will give it,' said she, 'and bestow on me a kiss.'

He answered: 'forby giving thee a kiss, I will even hug thee!'

Then he bends to embrace her, and gives her a kiss. Which operation ended, and when he looked at her, in the whole world was not a young woman of gait more graceful, in universal semblance fairer than she: to be likened to the last-fallen snow lying in trenches every portion of her was, from crown to sole; plump and queenly forearms, fingers long and taper, straight legs of a lovely hue she had; two sandals of the white bronze betwixt her smooth and soft white feet and the earth; about her was an ample mantle of the choicest fleece pure crimson, and in the garment a brooch of white silver; she had lustrous teeth of pearl, great regal eyes, mouth red as the rowanberry.

'Here, woman, is a galaxy of charms,' said the young man. 'That is true indeed.'

'And who are thou?' he pursued.

'"Royal Rule" am I,' she answered, and uttered this: 'King of Tara! I am Royal Rule...'

'"Go now,' she said, 'to thy brethren, and take with thee water; moreover, thine and thy children's forever the kingdom and supreme power shall be...And as at the first thou hast seen me ugly, brutish, loathly—in the end, beautiful—even so is royal rule; for without battles, without fierce conflict, it may not be won; but in the result, he that is king of no matter what shows comely and handsome forth"'. *172

44

Did you see it?

It turns out, that ugly "hag" is the challenges and clashes you are currently facing. You can even say it is the "manifestation" of the shadow. Moreover, the "royal rule" is the mystery of life. If you cannot "kiss" the repulsive, ugly "problem" or shadow, you will never "see" the eternal "royal rule"; the "water" they are asking for symbolizes the wisdom with which you can solve the problem. By being engaged in the fierce battles and struggles in your heart, you are willing to "kiss", to embrace, and to love the problem, and then you will obtain the wisdom to resolve the problem and see the eternal life.

In this stage, the toughest test you must face is whether you are able to transcend your current beliefs. Can you let it go and stop being attached to your ego? All your beliefs or the values you deem "correct" are not working for you now. If you still try to hold onto the values you assert, you will only see the ugly hag, you will never get the water, and you will never get to know the eternal law.

The renowned Hindu monk, Shankar Acharya, *173 once uttered an aphorism about self-transcendence: "So long as man has any regard for this corpse-like body, he is impure, and suffers from his enemies as also from birth, death, and disease; but when he thinks of himself as pure, as the essence of good and immovable, he assuredly becomes free from them…"

In this stage, you will be knocked down, be defeated by your attachment, your ideology, and the values you have been so proud of. But can you co-exist with "the poison", with "the problem", with "the enemy"? Here, "the enemy" symbolize the seven deadly sins we talked about earlier. It also symbolizes the most formidable obstacle you are encountering now. It can be someone, something, or even the shadow in the deepest recesses of your heart. To transcend dualism, break the mold, be brave, and take necessary actions, these are the most essential tasks you have to take on.

During the process of your self-integration, you must remove, one after another, the masks you have been wearing for a long time, but the defense mechanism in your subconscious will start to do its work.

There will be voices in your head telling you to resist any change. However, even if you are undergoing changes and experiencing the fear of the unknown, you must keep going, and you must understand why it is necessary for you to learn these lessons, so that you can truly take full responsibility for yourself. When you are in the process of constantly healing your heart, you will become more sensitive, your awareness will be heightened, and you will be more perceptive about yourself. But when you try to make changes, you will also feel that all the past thoughts, ideas, and habitual patterns are being discharged from your subconscious. That's why no matter how hard you have been trying, you still made very little progress. You will suffer from the pain caused by thoughts such as "everything I have been doing is useless", "everything I have been doing is wrong", and "everything I said was wrong". You feel as if your original self is about to break down.

When we want to make changes, to improve ourselves, to be awakened; when we make up our minds to embark on an internal journey; and when we try to be our own gurus, our own "torchbearers", there will be more obstacles that we will have to overcome. When we try to move forward, a lot of voices will start to pop up in our heads; when we try to transform ourselves, our bodies will start to disobey us; when we make a solemn vow to obtain Bodhicitta, the enlightened mind, things will seem to become more unpredictable, more chaotic, and more uncontrollable. When we rise to our feet and are ready to move forward, the boulders in our way will become bigger, the number of obstacles will increase, the mountains we have to climb will become higher, and the darkness we will be plunged into will become deeper. What can you do under circumstances like these? What can you do when you feel too weak to proceed? What can you do when darkness falls all around you and you can't see your future? There are so many negative voices in your head. All that you ever did was vow to become a "torchbearer". However, it seems darkness suddenly gathers around you, and you are about to be devoured by it. You feel as if you have fallen into the hole again. It is pitch black all around you. It is so dark that you can't see your hand in front of you, you can't see anything, and you can't feel anything. Time goes by very slowly when you are in a dark place. You even begin to doubt whether you can make it through these times. But one day you will bounce back, you will see hope again, and you will meet your higher self, your original self in your higher consciousness, because you are on your way to gradual awakening, and you are going through the process of creation.

Your life wants you to go through this process because this is a wonderful test. When you can't feel anything, when you are thoroughly defeated by yourself, when you are confused by what you used to believe, you still may have the resolve to venture into the inside of yourself. When you are examining the ultimate truth of your heart, just make sure you can persevere; make sure you choose to trust yourself, and remain seated. Ignore all the voices in your head. Don't pay too much heed to whether you can detect the energy that comes from your heart, from love, and from your mentor; whether you can feel the blessing from God; or whether you can transcend yourself. Nor should you care whether God can see you, hear you, and love you. Let go of all these thoughts, no matter how many there are in your mind. They have enormous power to tear you apart. When they keep pulling and dragging you this way and that, just ignore them and remain seated.

"Innocence" and "gentleness" will be the most important tools for you to pass through this phase.

8. The phase of confrontation--"the demons that lie within" vs. "archetypes"

Whether in mythology or in the field of transpersonal psychology, "confrontation" carries significant meanings. "Confrontation" is also the shortest and most direct route to self-transcendence. To help you understand the challenges a hero must face and the life transformation he has to undergo in order to reach this phase, we have to mention Carl Jung's idea about the archetypes of our collective unconscious and Dr. Carol S. Pearson's book, *The Hero Within: Six Archetypes We Live By.*

Archetypes are the fundamental concept in Jungian psychology. There are four kinds of archetypes:

- The Self: the Self is the center of one's soul, and it is also the totality of one's soul.
- The Anima: Anima is the feminine inner personality and image as present in the unconscious of the male. It can be negative or positive.
- The Animus: Animus is the masculine inner personality and image as present in the unconscious of the female. It can be negative or positive.

47

- The Shadow: Shadow is the unconscious aspect of personality that is opposite the image of one's ego.

Archetypes are the more central part of the collective unconscious. They are a psychological archive that belongs to the entire mankind. They are not what human beings acquired through learning. They are passed down from generation to generation through our collective unconscious. They are not set in a particular type or image, but they can emerge one by one through all kinds of imprints or the complexes one has hidden in one's subconscious.

Professor Yu Dehui from National Dong Hua University once remarked, "From Carl Jung's point of view, our archetypes are all carefully hidden deep in our subconscious. It's difficult for us to detect them." Carl Jung also told us, "Until you make the unconscious conscious, it will direct your life and you will call it fate."

Dr. Carol Pearson, the author of *The Hero Within: Six Archetypes We Live By*, expounds six different archetypes in order to help us see segments of the abstruse, inscrutable subconscious. In the book, she wrote, "Each archetype projects its own learning task onto the world.

People governed by an archetype will see its goal as ennobling, and its worst fear as the root of all the world's problems". *174

She continued, "Each archetype moves us through duality into paradox. Within each is a continuum from a primitive to a more sophisticated and complex expression of its essential energy". *175

These six archetypes are: the Innocent, the Orphan, the Wanderer, the Warrior, the Martyr, and the Magician.

Dr. Pearson stresses that, "the archetypes discussed in this work are those important to the hero's journey, that is, a journey of individuation. These are the archetypes manifested in our daylight worlds that help us define a strong ego, and then expand the boundaries of the ego to allow for the full flowering of the self and its opening up to the experience of oneness with other people and with the natural and spiritual worlds". Besides, "the journey described here is more circular or spiral than linear. It begins with the complete trust of the Innocent, moves on to the longing for safety of the Orphan, the self-sacrifice of the Martyr, the exploring of the Wanderer, the competition and triumph of the Warrior, and then the authenticity and wholeness of the Magician". *176

These six archetypes all have their "inherent" fears. The fears, which can be fully manifested through their shadows, are suppressed and hidden in the subconscious.

For Jung, a person's shadow aspect testifies to the contradictory nature of human beings. For example, if the dominant personality traits in one's consciousness point to the East, then the recessive personality traits in one's subconscious that complement the dominant ones usually point to the West. The shadow aspect can also be positive or negative. The positive side of a person will have a negative shadow aspect, and vice versa.

All kinds of shadows that haven't been properly integrated with one's other personality traits and have been repressed will be "projected" as "the demons that lie within us". These "demons" will hamper our progress, make us want to turn back before reaching the destination, unable to trust others, and even "project" our demons onto others. Carl Jung has already shared with us his wisdom by stating that "[a]s long as we confront the demons that lie within, and accept them as part of ourselves, on a global scale, they won't be projected on to the real world".

In world mythologies, a hero during the confrontation phase will meet his "father". Campbell describes this encounter as the "atonement with the father". This "father figure" has all kinds of negative aspects projected onto him by the hero's shadows. The hero's original self, through the manifestation of his archetypes and shadows, is trying to help him go through different experiences and have his personality traits well integrated.

In the process of integration, he will experience a more "complete" self.

In many ancient myths, a "father" represents the archetype of a horrifying demon. In many religions, God is believed to have the potential for destruction. The archetype of "the father" that a hero harbors is now possessed by the demons that lie within him, namely, his shadows. What he is unable to penetrate and thereby transcend are these demons, namely, the archetype of "the father". Another explanation is that the hero feels as if he doesn't deserve the encounter with "the father". We tend to blow up the gruesomeness and cruelty of the demons many hundreds or even thousands of times. Consequently, we are left incapable of confronting the demons, and we worry that we will have to tackle the crisis of being devoured or possessed by them.

Three Turns Around the Hero's Wheel

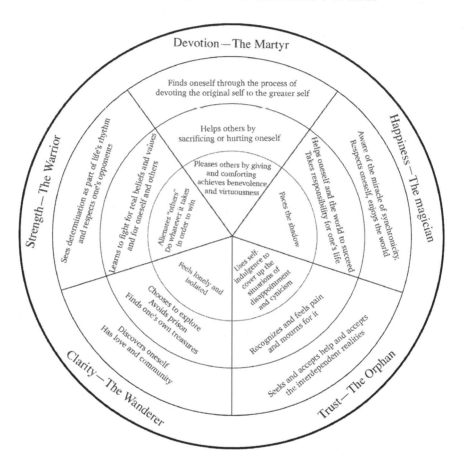

Campbell wrote: "For the ogre aspect of the father is a reflex of the victim's own ego—derived from the sensational nursery scene that has been left behind, but projected before; and the fixating idolatry of that pedagogical nonthing is itself the fault that keeps one steeped in a sense of sin, sealing the potentially adult spirit from a better balanced, more realistic view of the father, and therewith of the world. Atonement (at-one-moment) consists in no more than the abandonment of that self-generated double monster—the dragon thought to be God (superego) and the dragon thought to be Sin (repressed id). But this requires an abandonment of the attachment to ego itself, and that is what is difficult. One must have a faith that the father is merciful, and then a reliance on that mercy. Therewith, the center of belief is transferred outside of the bedeviling god's tight scaly ring, and the dreadful ogres dissolve". *177

Besides, "…if it is impossible to trust the terrifying father-face, then one's faith must be centered elsewhere (Spider Woman, Blessed Mother); and with that reliance for support, one endures the crisis—only to find, in the end, that the father and mother reflect each other, and are in essence the same". *178

When we are under the influence of the archetypes and shadows of the unconscious and the collective unconscious, it becomes very easy for us to magnify all the negative emotions.

Marie-Louise von Franz (1915-1998), Carl Jung's most important assistant, wrote in *Man and His Symbols*, "When an individual makes an attempt to see his shadow, he becomes aware of (and often ashamed of) those qualities and impulses he denies in himself but can plainly see in other people—such things as egotism, mental laziness and sloppiness; unreal fantasies, schemes, and plots; carelessness and cowardice; inordinate love of money and possessions—in short, all the little sins about which he might previously have told himself: 'That doesn't matter; nobody will notice it, and in any case other people do it too'". *179

Usually, people don't really want to confront their inner shadows or archetypes, so they can only avoid them by resorting to other methods, such as taking different courses, chanting Buddhist sutras, saying Mass for people, repenting of what they have done, going to church, praying and consulting fortune tellers, asking doctors to prescribe them medicine, or trying any other ways to numb themselves. They will do anything as long as they don't have to confront "the demons that lie within" themselves. However, our shadow sides are the manifestation of our true selves and are our intrinsic nature. Through the exploration of our id ———our intrinsic nature, the shadows could help us evolve, so long as we face them and get them well integrated. In this process, what are usually considered our common "flaws" or "negative characters" will become the "important footprints" which lead us to the answer about whether we will discover our shadows and our archetypes.

Six Hero Archetypes

	Orphan	Martyr	Wanderer	Warrior	Magician
Goal	Safety	Goodness, Care, Responsibility	Independence, Autonomy	Strength, Effectiveness	Authenicity, Wholeness, Balance
Worst Fear	Abandonment Exploitation	Selfishness, Callousness	Conformity	Weakness, Ineffectuality	Uncentered superficiality, Alineation from the self, others
Response to Dragon	Denies it exists or waits for rescue	Appeases or sacrifices self to save others	Flees	Slays	Incorporates and Affirms
Spirituality	Wants deity that will rescue and religious counselor for permission	Pleases God by suffering, Suffers to help others	Searches for God alone	Evangelizes, converts others, Spiritual regimes, disciplines	Celebrates experience of God in everyone, respects different ways of experiencing the sacred
Intellect /Education	Wants authority to give answers	Learns or forgoes learning to help others	Explores new ideas in own way	Learns through competition, achievement, motivation	Allows curiosity, learns in group or alone because it is fun
Relationships	Wants caretaker(s)	Takes care of others/ sacrifices	Goes it alone, becomes own person	Changes or molds others to please self, takes on Pygmalion projects	Appreciates differences, wants peer relationships
Emotions	Out of control or numbed	Negative ones repressed so as not to hurt others	Dealt with alone, stoic	Controlled, repressed to achieve or prevail	Allowed and learned from the self and others

Physical Health	Wants quick fix, immediate gratification	Deprives self, diets, suffers to be beautiful	Distrusts experts, does it alone, alternative healthcare, enjoys isolated sports	Adopts regimes, discipline, enjoys team sports	Allows health, treats body to exercise, good food.
Work	Wants an easy life, would rather not work	Sees as hard and unpleasant but necessary, works for others' sake	"I'll do it myself," searches for vocation	Works hard for goal, expects reward	Works at true vocations, sees work as its own reward
Material World	Feels poor, wants to win the lottery or inherit money	Believes it is more blessed to give than to receive, more virtuous to be poor than rich	Becomes self-made man or woman, may sacrifice money for independence	Works hard to succeed, makes system works for self, prefers to be rich	Feels prosperous with a little or a lot, has faith will always have necessities, does not hoard
Task/ Achievement	Overcoming denial, hope innocence	Ability to care, to give up and give away	Autonomy, identity, vocation	Assertiveness, confidence, courage, respect	Joy, abundance, acceptance, faith

The Innocent is not included on the chart because it is not a heroic archetype. When we live in paradise, there is no need for goals, fears, tasks, works, and so on. The Innocent is both pre- and post-heroic.

Source of reference: *The Hero Within: Six Archetypes We Live By*, written by Carol Pearson, translated by Zhu Kanru, Xu Shenshu, and Gong Zhuojun, published by New Century Publishing Co., Ltd., p.28.

The real challenge posed to the hero here is whether he will be brave enough to walk into the "father's" house, meet with the "father", and be unified with the "father". "Whether the shadow becomes our friend or enemy depends largely upon ourselves", said Marie-Louise von Franz. "The shadow becomes hostile only when he is ignored or misunderstood".

This is the darkest period before the real integration with one's intrinsic nature. Only by going through the toughest "test" and by being "reborn" from the deepest darkness can we stand a chance of being truly enlightened, and only then can our divinity and Buddha nature really spread their wings.

Otherwise, all of these are just "fake enlightenment". They are incomplete.

If you have continued reading this book until now, are you still terrified by the demons that lie within you, by the shadow, or by the father figure?

As a matter of fact, we need their help, because only when they are manifested as "symptoms" can we see them. To face them and to integrate with them is the only way to salvation. They are like the creature, Gebbeth *180, that petrifies the protagonist in the film, *Legend of Earthsea*. The Gebbeth, clearly intent on killing the protagonist, never stops chasing him. None of the magicians can escape from its clutch. At first, the protagonist was scared, but then it dawns upon him that "it's useless to run away. The only solution is to confront it directly". From that moment on, his fear gradually subsides, and he starts to "face" the situation and to look for the Gebbeth. Eventually, he meets the Gebbeth and merges with it. It turns out that the Gebbeth is part of his inner strength. Only when he faces it with eyes open can he create a real union with it. When you embrace your shadow, the two of you become coalesced immediately, and what is dualistic will be transformed into a single "whole". When two opposing forces bring forth even greater forces, you come to feel that you are a more complete person.

What happens in a movie is usually a vivid portrayal of what happens in real life. If you want your conscious mind to return to its original "neutral" state, holding onto a dualistic concept will become a major obstacle for you. However, if you are willing to confront and then embrace your "Gebbeth", then it will no longer be an impediment, and you will thus become a cohesive "whole". How can you embrace your greatest pain, embrace the bitterest criticism against you, embrace your deepest fear, and embrace your deepest attachment to your "profession"—what you do to make a living? What has been giving you the strength to keep going for 50, 40 or 30 years? Some people rely on their families. Others rely on their careers. Ask yourself: what do you rely on to continue living in this vast world?

If you can understand the logic behind these questions, you will be able to regain a very simple state of mind. You will even direct the attention back to yourself and be united with your inner self. That is how you will become the richest person in the world, because you will have everything you need inside you. We must first complete our world on the inside before we can complete the world on the outside. Otherwise, the world on the outside will still be broken and fragmented.

To take a different point of view, we can say the "Gebbeth" is what our mind really wants (even though it is desperately trying to run away from it). Our mind is like a "demon" (here it refers to the dualistic nature of our consciousness). For example, you always regard yourself as someone who "seeks justice", but in your subconscious mind, what you really want is to rule the world. However, since in this life you are playing the role of the justice seeker, you hide your desire to "rule the world" in your subconscious so that you don't have to face it. Other people see you as justice incarnate, a person who always steps up and makes sure justice is served, but they can't see your shadows.

Normally, if other people step on our shadows, we tend to blow a fuse immediately, and we apply some logic to defend ourselves, claiming that we are not the kind of person others think us to be. Nevertheless, Ying and Yang are inseparable, so if you play the role of "Yang", you will also bring forth "Yin"; if you play the role of "Yin", you will also bring forth "Yang". So, how can you integrate them? You must face and embrace your own "Gebbeth". First, see clearly what it looks like. If you are too afraid to look at it, you will never see the other side of yourself. Maybe you will achieve a lot in this life, maybe people will extol you for your great accomplishments, but your subconscious will always try to drag you to the other side. When you are willing to be less obstinate about what you think is "correct", when you are ready to accept and embrace its opposite, you will become a cohesive "whole". When you are able to perceive and understand, your world will become complete. This is how easy spiritual practices are. They are not complicated at all. We are to blame for making them complicated.

Many things that seem reasonable are usually proved to be bogus. Many worldly renowned "masters" or "gurus" have their own shadow archetypes. Though we are under the impression that they are praised and worshipped by others, below the surface, they might have very different archetypes. The "subtle" distinction between what's on and below the surface, which many people are unconscious of, is what we should actually investigate. However, the more dazzling and glamorous these masters' lives are, the less they care about this subtle distinction, because they believe they have achieved "the supreme", "the ultimate".

However, the truth is they don't have the courage to look at their own Gebbeth. I used to be in the same situation many years ago, and I have thoroughly examined myself. I asked myself why I wanted to undertake spiritual practices. Why did I want to spread the message of love? What was my real intention behind this? Did I want to be a master? Did I keep trying to recruit disciples in order to prove how valuable I was? I had to see my "Gebbeth" to understand what I was really looking for. Did I want everyone to agree with me? Or did I want to become a "demon"? (It means: I didn't have to abandon my dualistic way of thinking. The only thing I had to do was to manipulate people who desire salvation.) What on earth was my "Gebbeth"? When I reached that stage, I looked at myself with a very incisive mind. I didn't show myself any sympathy. During the 10 years from 1999 to 2009, I made a lot of mistakes (here it refers to what is considered "wrong" by the general public), and I fell. But each time I fell, I forced myself to look at the real "Gebbeth" behind my mistakes so that I can understand myself better, so that I can regain more of my strength. Otherwise, we will always be "threatened" by the secrets we hide in the darkness, in our shadows, and we will always see or reveal only one side of our divided selves.

We have to learn to embrace our own "Gebbeth", to transform what is dualistic into what is united, and we have to accomplish this task from the inside out, so that we will not fixate on certain doctrines or certain phenomena. Go back to "the center of the sacred"—where your Svabhava is, where neutrality exists, and you will feel completely free and at ease. It has nothing to do with religion, nothing to do with doctrines. Our Svabhava has always been there, and it reminds us that from the very beginning, we have always been Buddhas, and we have always been Jesus Christ.

Maybe you didn't know the "Gebbeth" existed, but now you must get to know it. At first, you will feel scared, so you can only take a little peek at it. Gradually, you will be able to look it in the eye; gradually, you will be able to embrace it; gradually, you will be able to integrate with it. This is the track of spiritual practice that you are on. The progress everyone has made is different; therefore, everyone enters different stages at different times. Some people might have undergone similar experiences in their past lives, so now they are able to embrace their "Gebbeth" straightaway, while others are still terrified. There is no right or wrong approach to one's "Gebbeth", and you don't need to compare yourself with others. Do you really need to experience the opposite side of your current self in order to make yourself a complete person? No. An experience like that could cause havoc in your life, in your body, and in your mind; many people will take a backward step because of this. In order to avoid going through what's at the other end of the spectrum in your real life, we devised these programs to help you undergo the experience in your conscious mind. When you embrace the "Gebbeth" and get into the "Gebbeth" in your conscious mind, you will be integrated with another side of yourself, and you will complete yourself.

In fact, a "Gebbeth" is also one of the faces of a "father" figure. Therefore, after we integrate our dualistic nature, we will be able to "meet the father" with a bigger heart.

The key issue in a hero's encounter with the father is whether he can "open his heart, and transcend his fear".

From the moment the universe began until now, all the complexes and inherent contradictions we have are the original mysteries of "the father" and the infinite creative power of "being". If we can open our mind, transcend our fear, and find courage to integrate with it, then we will be mature enough to understand that in this immense universe, which seems both indifferent and affectionate, all the human tragedies that have ever been or are currently being staged have real value and meaning. Campbell told us that "[t]he hero transcends life with its peculiar blind spot and for a moment rises to a glimpse of the source. He beholds the face of the father, understands—and the two are atoned".

When we can face the shadow lying in the depths of our subconscious, then we will get closer to the source and the truth we have been trying to discover.

It seems all the torment we have endured in the past would "disappear" after we are united with our true selves, and during this process, we will be rewarded with deeper insight, which allows us to see everything, including the shadow, the archetypes, or "the father" from a new perspective. The meaning of life will seem clearer to us. We will be able to understand why we have to come to this earth to go through these experiences and embark on this unique hero's journey. Nothing can replace these astonishing experiences and discoveries. Campbell shared with us his similar views, "Ultimately, there is no way to avoid the hero's quest. It comes and finds us if we do not move out bravely to meet it. And while we may strive to avoid the pain, hardship, and struggle it inevitably brings, life takes us eventually to the promised land, where we can be genuinely prosperous, loving and happy. The only way out is through".

In this phase, we will have a better understanding of life, and we will not be as scared as we used to be. From this moment on, it seems we can instill stronger determination and faith into our life, and we will become more comfortable and at ease with life. These benefits are just like what we have learned from the story of the "Gebbeth". Campbell wrote, "For the son who has grown really to know the father, the agonies of the ordeal are readily borne; the world is no longer a vale of tears but a bliss-yielding, perpetual manifestation of the Presence". *181

Here is a ballad originating from the deprived Jewish slums in Eastern Europe. It teaches us that when it seems as if all hopes are gone, when it seems as if God has forgotten us, we can still adopt a different point of view to uncover the truth behind all the miseries.

"Oh, Lord of the Universe
I will sing Thee a song.
Where canst Thou be found,
And where canst Thou not be found?
Where I pass—there are Thou.

Where I remain—there, too, Thou art.
Thou, Thou, and only Thou.
Doth it go well—'tis thanks to Thee.
Doth it go ill—'tis also thanks to Thee.
Thou art, Thou hast been, and Thou will be.
Thou didst reign, Thou reignest, and Thou wilt reign.
Thine is Heaven, Thine is Earth.
Thou fillest the high regions,
And Thous fillest the low regions.
Wheresoever I turn, Thou, oh Thou, art there." *182

All the emotions, thoughts, ideologies, and all the occurrences we believe to be true are recorded in our energy fields; thus we are tightly tied to these heavy burdens. However, when you can clearly see the patterns and configurations of your life, and when you are able to find the root cause of the problems and their solutions, it means you are ready to untangle your heart from the burdens it is bound to in order to let it heal. It means you have started to face the shadow, the holes and the defense mechanism inside you, and you have started to wipe off the imprints that weigh so heavy on your heart. You have allowed light to pour in, to brighten every dark corner of your life.

You walk to the inside of yourself and trace every stage of the development of your life in order to examine all the obstructions and obstacles you have encountered. You strip yourself of layers after layers of personas you have adopted so that you can become transparent and clear to yourself once again.

Your present life is the summation of everything that has happened in all your previous lives. We tangled our consciousness up in all kinds of relationships in each of our past lives, so we produced the consequences that we must bear now. Our life's "lessons" provide excellent opportunities for us to learn and transcend ourselves. However, to shoulder one's responsibility doesn't just mean to show repentance. What the book, *Zero Limits: The Secret Hawaiian System for Wealth, Health, Peace, and More*, demonstrates is a complete process we should go through: we should learn to say "I am sorry. Please forgive me. I thank you and I love you!" Some emotional stirrings may start to emerge from the depths of your heart, and you want to say, "Thank the universe for completely unfolding itself so that I can go through these experiences. I am willing to take full responsibility for everything I have experienced in life. I love you and I love all the experiences!" Only when you face yourself bravely can you see through yourself and then regain your courage, wisdom, strength, and love. This is a very beautiful process.

Darkness is not terrifying. What terrify us are our discriminating ideologies and our fears. For example, in the film *The Lovely Bones*, after the girl, Susie, is murdered, she seems to have this unidentifiable power that always enables her to see the killer's house. But she is too afraid to push the door open and walk into it. She doesn't have the courage to confront the dark imprints in the very depths of her heart.

Being unenlightened means no light is shed on us. To be unenlightened in our past, present and future lives means we will never be able to see the light. However, as long as you can find the courage to walk into darkness and bring light into darkness, it will be "brightened up". Therefore, later on in the film, Susie plucks up her courage, opens the door, and walks into the house. She can even see the "safe" where her body is hidden. At first, the shock she felt was tremendous, but she must walk into the house on her own, for only when she walks into it can the darkness naturally reveal itself to her.

Finally, she opens that fearsome "Pandora's box" where her soul is locked. Once the "safe" is open, she realizes there is nothing inside except for a beautiful red camellia flower. When you choose to walk into the darkness, you will bring light into it, and naturally there will be no longer any dark places in your life. You will become used to what you are "re-united" with ——"love". At that very moment, you will gradually let go of the dualistic consciousness, you will receive that "precious gift" life wants to give to you, and, with "love", you will be able to march forward bravely and transcend yourself.

When you begin to face yourself, you will see the viewpoint you have adopted and the masks you have been wearing in order to live in "the seven quadrants". *183 When you are playing the role of a son or a daughter, you have to wear the son or the daughter's mask; when you are being a mother, you have this role to play, this mask to wear, and these values to hold onto. In a workplace, there are roles for you to play, and the masks for you to wear, depending on the position you occupy. For each role we play, there is a mask that we must wear. We tend to cut our lives into pieces, without realizing that all these pieces are inseparable, because each one of them is an integral part of ourselves. Isn't it true? Only after we have gained some truly deep and penetrating insights into ourselves can we see our habits, the tricks we play, and the way we maneuver others. Our mind is very clever because it will protect us from answering many questions. It knows that we are very sensitive, and we don't want to hurt ourselves. Our subconscious will set off reactions before anyone can press our buttons. We will assume our "professional" personas to prevent people from climbing over this wall of our self-defense. If you have come to realize how much you have become used to playing these tricks, you must make up your mind to debunk yourself. As long as you are still wearing masks, you will be unable to see the beauty of the naked truth. The quality of this beauty is something you can easily and effortlessly enjoy. This beauty is "Zen". When you are willing to walk into the holes and get to know yourself, you are experiencing "Zen", and you are creating "heaven" for yourself.

9. The phase of integration

When your soul experiences a strong sense of "frustration", it may drop onto the ground and pound its head on the floor (like the emoticon "orz" denotes), but if you survive this toughest test, stand up to your inner "demon" (the shadow, the imprint), and become integrated with it, you will turn into a completely different person.

"'Let the light penetrate the darkness until the darkness shines and there is no longer any division between the two", says a Hasidic passage, "The *sadik* in the Hasidic tradition…has allowed the light to enter him and shine out into the world again". *184

When the light passes into the darkness, the darkness will not be dark anymore. Nor will the light be light anymore. What emboldens one's soul to get into "the darkness", penetrate "the darkness", and conquer "the darkness" is the power of ——"love".

The power of "love" is truly incredible. "Love" can indeed transform what is dualistic into "oneness". It can transform Ying and Yang into "oneness". It can transform the whole world into "oneness".

"So when you ask what love is", said Krishnamurti, "you may be too frightened to see the answer...you may have to shatter the house you have built, you may never go back to the temple!" *185

"Love" is regarded as a cultural symbol that is different in Eastern and Western mythologies. In the West, "love" symbolizes the Blessed Virgin Mary; "love" is the symbol of God; God is "love". In the East, "love" symbolizes the compassionate Avalokitesvara, a name that is familiar to all. This bodhisattva empathizes the whole of mankind that is suffering from the delusion of believing in our "actual existence" in this world. When we were on our spiritual journey to Tibet, every child we saw, either in the cities or in the countryside, chanted "Om mani Padme hum," the mantra associated with Avalokitesvara. The literal meaning of this mantra is "the Mani jewel in the lotus flower". Its implication is: one's most intrinsic nature blossoms like a lotus flower. The Mani jewel located in the depths of the lotus flower is the symbol of the ultimate wisdom. It is the eternal "Elixir of Immortality".

The power of Avalokitesvara's vows and love cannot be limited by anything. Avalokitesvara will answer the prayers of whoever prays to it. Its power to hear everyone's crying and to alleviate our misery has left a profound impression on people in the East.

To illustrate my point, I would like to quote two paragraphs from "The Universal Gateway of Guanyin Bodhisattva Sutra", which composes part of *The Lotus Sutra:*

"[I]f hundreds, thousands, millions, or a countless number of sentient beings who suffer a myriad of afflictions heard of Guanyin Bodhisattva and single-mindedly recited his name, the Bodhisattva would immediately perceive their calls and deliver them from their suffering", and then, "if there were sentient beings beset by excessive lust and cravings, who constantly revered and recited the name Guanyin Bodhisattva, they would be freed from such desires. If they were filled with anger, by constantly revering and reciting the name Guanyin Bodhisattva, they would be freed from anger. If they were filled with foolishness and ignorance, by constantly revering and reciting the name Guanyin Bodhisattva, they would be freed from ignorance".

According to *The Flower of Compassion Sutra*, eons ago, Amitābha was a king named Wuzheng Nian. He had one thousand sons. The eldest one was named Bu Xun. After he was ordained as a Buddhist monk, his monastic name was "Avalokitesvara" (also known in Chinese Buddhism as Guanyin Bodhisattva). In the distant future, after Amitābha had attained Nirvana, he would take his place and become "the Thus-Come-One of Omnipresent Light and Mountains of Great Merits". The story in the second scroll of "The Flower of Compassion Sutra" tells us that the birth name of Avalokitesvara is Bu Xun. Numerous eons ago, he was the first child of the wheel-turning king named Wuzheng Nian. He made the following vow in front of the Buddha of the Treasure Store, "As I am pursuing the Bodhisattva Path, any sentient being who experiences pain and fear, who loses the faith and strength to follow the true teachings, who is plunged into deep darkness where no light shines, who is anxious, worried, lonely, or poverty-stricken, who has no one to turn to for protection, or who has no one to lean on and no roof over his head, if he evokes my image and chants my monastic name, my deva-ears will hear his cry for help, and my deva-eyes will see his misery. Therefore, I give my promise to all the suffering sentient beings: 'if I cannot deliver every one of you from your pain, I will never attain the complete unsurpassed enlightenment'".

The Buddha of Treasure Store thus prophesized that he would attain enlightenment in the future: "Good man, you have seen all the sentient beings on earth, in heaven and in the three evil paths. They evoked your great sympathy, so you vowed to remove all their worries and help them live in happiness. Good man, I therefore prophesize that you will one day become Avalokitesvara". In summary, this story narrates how Bodhisattva, because of the great compassion he feels for all living beings, declares that he will end their suffering and bring true joy to them; thus the Buddha of Treasure Store gives him the name Avalokitesvara, a bodhisattva who embodies the compassion of all Buddhas.

In *Dale Jingang Bu Kong Zhenshi Sanmei Ye Jing Boreboluomiduo Li Qu Shi* (in Sanskrit, Prajñāpāramitā-naya-śatapañcāśatikā; Adhyardhaśatikā prajñāpāramitā), a sutra of Esoteric Buddhism translated by Amoghavajra, it is claimed that in the Western Pure Land, Amitayus, also known as "the Thus-Come-One who has obtained the originally pure intrinsic nature" or "the Thus-Come-One who contemplates at ease", is the Buddha incarnate. However, in the evil world of the five kinds of turbidity, Amitayus will become incarnate as a Bodhisattva.

In the passage from "The Universal Gateway of Guanyin Bodhisattva Sutra" we just cited, if we replace Guanyin Bodhisattva with "the love of great compassion," the whole passage will read like this: "[I]f hundreds, thousands, millions, or a countless number of sentient beings who suffer a myriad of afflictions heard of 'the love of great compassion' and single-mindedly recited this phrase, 'the love of great compassion' would immediately perceive their calls and deliver them from their suffering". In addition, "if there were sentient beings beset by excessive lust and cravings, who constantly revered and recited the phrase, 'the love of great compassion', they would be freed from such desires. If they were filled with anger, by constantly revering and reciting the phrase, 'the love of great compassion', they would be freed from anger. If they were filled with foolishness and ignorance, by constantly revering and reciting the phrase, 'the love of great compassion', they would be freed from ignorance".

When you enter the field of "the love of great compassion" and "become" He——Being itself, you will truly be able to achieve the ultimate liberation.

It is because, as we have mentioned in the last chapter, "the love of great compassion" is the "essential nature" of all living entities. He is a field that has a "mind" of His own. He also symbolizes everyone's potential for becoming a Buddha.

In *The Flower of Compassion Sutra*, when Guanyin Bodhisattva, during his final life on earth as a human being, shattered the bounds of the last threshold for himself, he paused. He made a vow that before he "attained the unsurpassed, perfect enlightenment", he would guard the heart of every sentient being without exception, and he would lead all creatures to enlightenment. Since then, He has revealed Himself as an omnipresent being whom all the sentient beings rely on for their salvation. The divine grace of (or the field of) His powerful good wishes fills the void of the whole Dharmadhatu. Just like the Buddha and other mentors, this great being that once manifested itself in this human world is the human hero who can transcend the ultimate ignorance, fear and darkness.

Campbell wrote, "When the envelopment of consciousness has been annihilated, then he becomes free of all fear, beyond the reach of change".

This accords with what the Buddha and other mentors have pointed out: "All beings have the Buddha nature". Or, in Campbell's words, "this is the release potential within us all, and which anyone can attain— through herohood". Accordingly, we are all capable of attaining "the perfect enlightenment" we have never experienced before.

"The world is filled and illumined by, but does not hold, the Bodhisattva (he whose being is enlightenment)", said Campbell, "Rather, it is he who holds the world". The concept of duality doesn't enclose him; the wind blowing from eight different directions doesn't sway him; pain and pleasure do not affect him. He leaves duality behind; he returns Yin and Yang to their proper places. He creates everything out of emptiness, but he is not bound by the images of things he created. He is the real image of our existence, and the state of being we can all get into.

In the "phase of integration", because we all feel "love" deeply, we become "love" itself. All the pairs of opposites begin to dissolve in love. Manas-vijnana (the mind-knowledge) is transformed into the equalizing wisdom. Even Yin and Yang are fused together in love.

Through his study of mythology, Campbell discovered that, be it the masculine Avalokiteshvara, the feminine Guanyin, or the androgynous deities from all over the world, they all represent the cabalistic phenomena that have existed since the beginning of time: the process in which one is divided into two, and two is divided into multiples, as well as the process in which two is combined into one to create a "new life".

This process is also an illustration of the three stages described in the ancient Egyptian funeral text, *The Book of the Dead*——death, rebirth, and creation.

In **the phase of confrontation**, one confronts death. It is the collapse and death of one's original self.

In **the phase of integration**, one experiences rebirth. All the opposites are dissolved and integrated into oneness. A new life emerges——this is the rebirth.

In **the phase of transcendence**, creation begins. Because one has penetrated duality, one is able to take actions through inaction, and create everything.

Real love is selfless and unconditional. It is the power bestowed upon us by God. It is what Jesus admonished us to do in the Bible:

"But I tell you who hear: love your enemies, do good to those who hate you, bless those who curse you, and pray for those who mistreat you. To him who strikes you on the cheek, offer also the other; and from him who takes away your cloak, don't withhold your coat also. Give to everyone who asks you, and don't ask him who takes away your goods to give them back again.

"As you would like people to do to you, do exactly so to them.

"If you love those who love you, what credit is that to you? For even sinners love those who love them. If you do good to those who do good to you, what credit is that to you? For even sinners do the same. If you lend to those from whom you hope to receive, what credit is that to you? Even sinners lend to sinners, to receive back as much. But love your enemies, and do good, and lend, expecting nothing back; and your reward will be great, and you will be children of the Most High; for he is kind toward the unthankful and evil.

"Therefore be merciful, even as your Father is also merciful.

Don't judge, and you won't be judged.

Don't condemn, and you won't be condemned.

Set free, and you will be set free.

"Give, and it will be given to you: good measure, pressed down, shaken together, and running over, will be given to you. For with the same measure you measure it will be measured back to you." *186

During the phase of integration, because one gets to be reborn after stepping into "the darkness", one can testify to the existence of the all-embracing love; so can one transcend the division between races, religions, countries, ethnic groups, and cultures as well. One is also able to overcome one's prejudices and find in oneself the love that is genuine and boundless. All things in this world are the children of God, including the heretics. Why are we so unwilling to transcend ourselves, overcome our prejudices, and bring forth the real, transcendent peace, so that the real, universal love can permeate the world?

Campbell stated in a mocking tone that if one doesn't attain "the highest enlightenment", the aggressive preaching style one may worship cannot really solve any problem, because one's ego doesn't disappear. On the contrary, it becomes bigger. If one cannot live and behave in accordance with one's true self but allows oneself to become the victim of political maneuvering, consequently, one would engulf the world in the crime of plundering and religious wars. It would be ridiculous. One would realize it is just an act of self-delusion, if one tries to compare the chaos in the world we live in with the wisdom passed down to us from our ancestors and with the glorious achievements of the greatest heroes in the history of humanity.

To illustrate his points, Campbell mentioned two hymns composed by the poet-saint, Jetsun Milarepa (1052-1135). They were completed around the time when Pope Urban II was calling on all Christians in Europe to launch the First Crusade against the Muslims (1096-1099).

"Amid the City of Illusoriness of the Six World-Planes
The chief factor is the sin and obscuration born of evil works;
Therein the being followeth dictates of likes and dislikes,
And findeth ne'er the time to know Equality;
Avoid, O my son, likes and dislikes.
If ye realize the Emptiness of All Things, Compassion
will arise within your hearts;
If ye lose all differentiation between yourselves and others, fit
to serve others ye will be;
And when in serving others ye shall win success, then shall ye
meet with me;
And finding me, ye shall attain to Buddhahood".

The chaos in our heart is caused by the "prejudices" we hold as a fortress to defend ourselves. In order to secure their own "territories", people tend to regard any "outsider" not protected by the divine beings they worship as someone "sentenced to death" by the "dogmas" or "God" (or we can also call it the Highest God) they believe in. Campbell's words explain the contradiction we are confronted with in this world: "Instead of clearing his own heart the zealot tries to clear the world".

Can you see his point here? It seems, as long as people belonging to any organization (including the spiritual ones), religion, and country do not enter the darkness inside of themselves and clear their own hearts, they will inevitably use "the truth" they believe in as the weapon to conquer others, and as the most convincing excuse to "cultivate" the "uncivilized" people and modernize the places these people live in. This, however, only makes this world more chaotic. Everywhere we go, there are always antagonism and power struggles among different groups of people, and even things as ridiculous as wars can break out because of the fights between people.

If you really want to help yourself, help others, and help the world, the only way you should pursue is to achieve the "true integration" of your heart.

Once you understand what "emptiness" is, compassion will arise from the bottom of your heart. When your dualistic consciousness is dissolved into "emptiness" and is transformed into "oneness" by love and compassion, real wisdom will "be born". Only by reaching this stage can you really "serve" other people without sensing the difference between "yourself and others".

All the sentient beings have a heart that harbors "the love of great compassion". Its intrinsic nature is always clean and perfect.

The hero will uncover a great, astonishing secret at this moment: the love of great compassion, the love that doesn't discriminate one against another, not only fills the void of the whole Dharmadhatu, but also exists in everything. It brings into existence all sentient and insentient beings, and even erases the boundary between them. In this vast realm of great love, darkness and light, oneness and diversity, and Yin and Yang, they all appear to be in a new state of "oneness", shining the light of infinite luminosity.

Therefore, Campbell wrote in his book, "The perennial agony of man, self-torturing, deluded, tangled in the net of his own tenuous delirium, frustrated, yet having within himself, undiscovered, absolutely unutilized, the secret of release: this too he regards—and is".

From now on, pain won't just be pain, and happiness won't just be happiness. The one who is suffering inside us is actually the great "Being". Moreover, the existence of darkness and madness in this world is actually due to the existence of that unique "love". We and the Lord of All Things, we and the Father, are actually "one and the same", just as what Jesus Christ said, "I and the Father are one". This is the "redemptive insight" the hero will obtain during this phase. We will no longer be misled by the dualism in nature and in consciousness. Though everyone, as a private individual, is ignorant, arrogant, self-contradictory, limited, prone to projecting his feelings and views onto others, prone to defending himself, prone to experiencing all kinds of suffering, and always feeling as if he is under the "threat" from the impermanence of life and from other possible enemies, he still has a deep insight into life which tells him, "That being or the impermanent nature of all things is actually God".

In the end, we realize the secret he (the hero) has been attempting to uncover is himself. This is the profound meaning of enlightenment. The Six Patriarch once admonished people to "think of neither good nor evil," because when you can see the world with your heart, the appearance of everything, as well as all your thoughts and your consciousness, will transcend the division between "good" and "evil". As a matter of fact, we can all merge into the Lord, into our intrinsic nature, just as all the deities, Bodhisattvas, and Buddhas have merged into all the sentient and insentient beings. If this is how things are supposed to be, why should we be afraid of ideas such as "impermanence", the existence of "hell", the existence of "demons", and "reincarnation"? "Affliction is Bodhi"; "mundane dharmas are the same as supra-mundane dharmas", and they are "neither produced nor destroyed"; they are "neither the same nor different"; they are "neither permanent nor impermanent"; and they are "neither coming nor going". What we should learn is "Reincarnation is Nirvana". As of this moment, the hero can stay far away from delusional dreams. When he has no fear, he will be in the state of happiness.

Now, let's see Campbell's response: "Come, let us return to the Lord. He has torn us to pieces but he will heal us; he has injured us but he will bind up our wounds. After two days he will revive us; on the third day he will restore us, that we may live in his presence. Let us acknowledge the

Lord; let us press on to acknowledge him. As surely as the sun rises, he will appear; he will come to us like the winter rains, like the spring rains that water the earth." Campbell told us, "This is the sense of the first wonder of the Bodhisattva: the androgynous character of the presence. Therewith the two apparently opposite mythological adventures come together: the Meeting with the Goddess, and the Atonement with the Father...And in both cases it is found (or rather, recollected) that the hero himself is that which he had come to find".

What a beautiful hero's journey it is. All the "trials and tribulations" one encounters on this journey, the test of the terrifying darkness, and the inexplicable spiritual suffering are all given the most beautiful and most obvious meaning.

In the same vein, in his book, *Buddhism and the Art of Psychotherapy*, Hayao Kawai, the first Japanese Jungian analyst and a renowned clinical psychologist, mentioned *The Avatamsaka Sutra* (volume 34) when describing how the Bodhisattvas establish themselves on the "Ground of Happiness":

"I feel deep happiness because I have turned away from the mundane world.

I feel deep happiness because I continue to draw near all the Buddhas.

I feel deep happiness because I am no longer concerned by the affairs of ordinary people.

I feel deep happiness because I am approaching the realm of wisdom.

I feel deep happiness because I have left behind all the evil destinies forever.

I feel deep happiness because I am whom all the living beings can place their reliance.

I feel deep happiness because I see all the Thus Come Ones.

I feel deep happiness because I can live the experiences of all the Buddhas.

I feel deep happiness because I have obtained the impartial nature of all the Bodhisattvas.

I feel deep happiness because I have distanced myself from anything that is alarming, hair-raising, and terrifying".

When the entire world is gripped by the fear that the radical terrorism ISIS represents, when it has infiltrated into Syria, when people even started to give Islam a wide berth and put away the Qur'an, which teaches people to worship Allah, how can we feel deep happiness? How can we be integrated with the world?

A passage from the book, *The Synchronicity Key: The Hidden Intelligence Guiding the Universe and You*, provides us with another point of view on this issue. Lex Hixon, a scholar of Islamic studies, stressed in his English translation of the Qur'an, *The Heart of the Qur'an*, that "[t]he Qur'an repeatedly emphasizes living a life of modesty, gratitude, honesty, justice, compassion and love. More than any outward signs of piety, it sees these qualities as identifying the real Muslim, the person surrendered to the One Reality..." *187

Therefore, no matter how chaotic the outside world is, let what is inside us become "an integrated whole," because originally we were all united as "one".

To become "an integrated whole" carried a significant meaning in the ancient alchemy. Concepts such as "the integration of mercury and sulfur", the integration of Yin and Yang, "a sacred marriage", "the meeting of the clear sight of a mother and that of her child", and so on, are all part of the "mystic experience", or what Carl Jung called the "numinous experience". *188

In this phase, when it comes to Jung's idea about the individuation process, nothing is more important than the "numinous experience". When we are going through this sacred "numinous experience", our consciousness can thus be transformed into a higher state of being, or even into "the origin of the sacred" ——our Svabhava.

In *Why God Won't Go Away: Brain Science and The Biology of Belief*, another book focused on the inner world of those who believe in mysticism, the author remarked, "In her book *Mysticism* (mysticism, in Chinese transliteration, "xuanmi zhuyi", is sometimes also translated as "shenmi zhuyi" or "miqi zhuyi") a preeminent study of mystical spirituality, author Evelyn Underhill calls the term *mysticism* 'one of the most abused words in the English language...But for Underhill, there is nothing vague or confused in mystical thought. Mysticism, she says, 'is not an opinion: It is not a philosophy. It has nothing in common with the pursuit of occult knowledge...

It is the name of that organic process which involves the perfect consummation of the Love of God: the achievement here and now of the immortal heritage of man. Or, if you like it better—for this means exactly the same thing—it is the art of establishing his conscious relation with the Absolute". *189

"According to the fourteenth-century German mystic John Tauler, for example, the mystic's soul becomes 'sunk and lost in the Abyss of the Deity, and loses the consciousness of all creature distinctions. All things are gathered together in one with the divine sweetness, and the man's being is so penetrated with the divine substance that he loses himself therein, as a drop of water is lost in a cask of strong wine'". *190

In another paragraph, the authors quoted Hallaj Husain ibn Mansur, the Sufi master and a resident of medieval Iraq, "describing the intimate intermingling of the mystic and his Lord:

I am He Whom I love, and He whom I love is I:
We are two spirits dwelling in one body.
If thou seest me, thou seest Him.
*And if thou seest Him, thou seest us both". *191*

Moreover, "the medieval Catholic sage Meister Eckhart, writing from the cooler climes of Germany, had similar words to say on the very same subject: *'How then am I to love the Godhead? Thou shalt not love him as he is: not as a God, not as a spirit, not as a Person, not as an image, but as sheer, pure One. And into this One we are to sink from nothing to nothing, so help us God'".* *192

"[A]nd in the plain-spoken insights of Black Elk, the Oglala mystic and shaman:
'Peace comes within the souls of men
*When they realize their oneness with the universe'".*193*

It seems feeling peaceful is a common experience during the phase of "integration". Fourteen years ago, I led my first group of students to Guoxing Township in Nantou for a month-long spiritual retreat. The training I provided was the toughest one, as we aimed to get into the state of "emptiness" right away. Everyone had to endure great pain. It was not easy for us to move through many psychological stages, move past the imprints in our consciousness within a short period of time, and suddenly go into the state of "emptiness" in order to gain a thorough knowledge of "emptiness". It posed a real challenge to me and my students. Fortunately, we managed to open a window onto our spirituality, so today we are able to testify to this sweet "ecstasy" we are now savoring. At this moment, we are in a mental state which "cannot be described in words." Many years ago, when I seriously got into this tranquil state that "cannot be described in words", I found that "being quiet and still" seemed to be a better interpretation of this state. In addition, this state comprises four degrees of "quietude": **quiet, very quiet, extremely quiet, perfectly quiet.**

We have had some initial discussions about this topic in *The Age of New Awakening*. When our consciousness gets into the state of quietude, the experience is simply too marvelous for words.

To try to give an account of this experience, let's cite two passages from *Dao De Jing*:

"The way is so vast that when you use it, something is always left.
How deep it is!
It seems to be the ancestor of the myriad things.
It blunts sharpness
Untangles knots
Softens the glare
Unifies with the mundane.
It is so full!
It seems to have remainder.
It is the child of I-don't-know-who.
And prior to the primeval Lord-on-high." (Chapter four)
"Effect vacuity to the extreme.
Keep stillness whole.
Myriad things act in concert.
I therefore watch their return.
All things flourish and each returns to its root.
Returning to the root is called quietude.
Quietude is called returning to life.

Return to life is called constant.
Knowing this constant is called illumination". (Chapter sixteen)

In the state of quietude, everything returns to its root, and returning to the root is called returning to life. This is where life "was born," and this is the real "eternal Way".

Only when you have a true understanding of this "eternal Way" can you gain a "thorough knowledge" of it, and this is fundamentally what we consider real wisdom.

In *Why God Won't Go Away: Brain Science and the Biology of Belief*, the authors observed, "Virtually all mystical traditions identify some sense of union with the absolute as the ultimate spiritual goal. Correspondingly, nearly all those traditions have developed rigorous systems of training and initiation, designed to help the devoted reach that rarefied state. In Zen, nonsensical koans were used to loosen the grip of the conscious mind, and open the doorway to the spirit. Kabbalistic Jews performed complicated mental manipulations of numbers and images to reach the same end. Christian mystics relied upon intense contemplative prayer, fasting, silence, and various forms of mortification to free their minds from mundane matters and focus more intently upon God. These disciplines emerged independently, but all are based on a common insight: The first step in attaining mystical union is to quiet the conscious mind and free the spirit from the limiting passions and delusions of the ego".

"The same ideas...also lie at the heart of Western schools of mysticism, and are echoed in the following words from the Hebrew mystic Rabbi Eleazar: *'Think of yourself as nothing and totally forget yourself as you pray. Only remember that you are praying for the Divine Presence. You may then enter the Universe of Thought, a state of consciousness which is beyond time. Everything in this realm is the same—life and death, land, and sea...but in order to enter this realm you must relinquish your ego and forget all your troubles'*". *194

As a matter of fact, "self-transcendence" has long been the ultimate goal for all mystics: "Greek Orthodox mystics in the fifth century also came to believe that God could only be known by a mind that has been cleansed of all distracting thoughts and images. The Orthodox mystics called this stillness of mind *hesychia*, or inner silence, and taught that it was the only way to open the door to a mystical union with God". *195

"In her book, *A History of God*, religion scholar Karen Armstrong explains that the goal of Greek mysticism was to gain 'a freedom from distraction and multiplicity, and the loss of ego—an experience that is clearly akin to that produced by contemplatives in nontheistic religions like Buddhism. By systematically weaning their minds away from their 'passions'—such as pride, greed, sadness or anger which tied them to the ego—hesychiasts would transcend themselves and become deified like Jesus on Mt. Tabor, transfigured by the divine 'energies'". *196

In the chapter "The God of the Mystics", Armstrong pointed out, "The first of these 'drunken' Sufis was Abu Yazid Bistami (d. 874)... As he approached the core of his identity, he felt that nothing stood between God and himself; indeed, everything that he understood as 'self' seemed to have melted away:

I gazed upon [al-Lah] with the eye of truth and said to Him: "Who is this?" He said, "This is neither I nor other than I. There is no God but I." Then he changed me out of my identity into His Selfhood...Then I communed with him with the tongue of his Face saying: "How fares it with me with Thee?" He said, "I am through Thee, there is no God but Thou".*197

For these mystics, God has no "objective existence". He is "no external deity 'out there', alien to mankind: God was discovered to be mysteriously identified with the inmost self".

When one is going through the most wonderful mystical experience, the distance between mankind and God will be reduced to naught. The only thing you need to do now is to be brave, get into that state, and enjoy that experience.

Armstrong remarked, "It would be the end of separation and sadness, a reunion with a deeper self that was also the self he or she was meant to be. God was not a separate, external reality and judge but somehow one with the ground of each person's being". *198

In his book *The Varieties of Religious Experience*, William James, the prominent American psychologist, referred to the theory proposed by Canadian psychiatrist R. M. Bucke when talking about the difference between "cosmic consciousness" and individual consciousness: "The prime characteristic of cosmic consciousness is a consciousness of the cosmos, that is, of the life and order of the universe. Along with the consciousness of the cosmos there occurs an intellectual enlightenment which alone would place the individual on a new plane of existence—would make him almost a member of a new species. To this is added a state of moral exaltation, an indescribable feeling of elevation, elation, and joyousness, and a quickening of the moral sense, which is fully as striking, and more important than is the enhanced intellectual power. With these come what may be called a sense of immortality, a consciousness of eternal life, not a conviction that he shall have this, but the consciousness that he has it already". *199

"In Paul's language, I live, yet not I, but Christ liveth in me. Only when I become as nothing can God enter in and no difference between his life and mine remain outstanding". *200

"'The overcoming of all the usual barriers between the individual and the Absolute is the great mystic achievement,' said William James in *Varieties of Religious Experiences*.

*'In mystic states we both become one with the Absolute and we become aware of our oneness. This is the everlasting and triumphant mystical tradition, hardly altered by differences of clime or creed. In Hinduism, in Neoplato-ism, in Sufism, in Christian mysticism...we find the same recurring note, so there is about mystical utterance an eternal unanimity which ought to make a critic stop and think, and which brings it about that the mystical classics have, as has been said, neither birthday nor native land. Perpetually telling of the unity of man with God, their speech antedates languages, and they do not grow old". *201*

In addition, James mentioned some mystical experiences recorded in the dharma-lineage of the highest order that has been preserved in the Himalays for centuries, about how one can become God: "He who would hear the voice of Nada, 'the Soundless Sound,' and comprehend it, he has to learn the nature of Dharana....When to himself his form appears unreal, as do on waking all the forms he sees in dreams; when he has ceased to hear the many, he may discern the One—the inner sound which kills the outer....For then the soul will hear, and will remember.

And then to the inner ear will speak THE VOICE OF THE SILENCE....And now thy *Self* is lost in SELF, *thyself* unto THYSELF, merged in that SELF from which thou first didst radiate.... Behold! thou hast become the Light, thou hast become the Sound, thou art thy Master and God. Thou art THYSELF the object of thy search: the voice unbroken, that resounds throughout eternities, exempt from change, from sin exempt, the seven sounds in one, the VOICE OF THE SILENCE, *Om tat Sat*".

This dharma-lineage that has been around for thousands of years is "the Light of Jesus," and it is also the method we have been teaching in our courses on "the transmission of mind". Moreover, it is also the dharma of enlightenment recorded in the chapter, "On the Bodhisattva's Attainment of Perfect Absorption Through Hearing Practices", from *The Shurangama Sutra*: "Then Avalokitesvara Bodhisattva rose from his seat, prostrated himself with his head at the feet of the Buddha and said: 'World Honored One, I remember when, as many eons ago as there are sand grains in the Ganges, there was a Buddha named Avalokitesvara appearing in this world. It was under that Buddha that I made the Bodhi-resolve (Bodhicitta). That Buddha taught me to enter Samadhi through a process of hearing (sounds) and reflecting (on what I heard). Initially, I entered the flow of emptiness and forgot about the objective reality. Since what came into my ears was quieted, for me, what was moving and what was still did not exist anymore".

In this passage, we learn that Avalokitesvara Bodhisattva is asking for the Buddha's advice, and the Buddha responds by suggesting three stages of practices: to hear, to reflect, and to practice until the practices are proved effective, as a way to achieve Samma Samadhi, or right concentration. At the initial stage, it is indicated that when one's ears hear anything, one can try to enter the flow of one's Svabhava, a mental state where the sounds that the ears pick up have no real existence. The meaning of "the flow of emptiness" is further expounded in the following paragraph: "Since what came into my ears was quieted, for me, what was moving and what was still did not exist anymore. As I gradually advanced in this process, the hearing of the sounds and the sounds that were heard both disappeared. Once I stopped hearing anything, there was nothing for me to rely on, and my sense of being aware of the objects and the objects I was aware of also became nothing but emptiness. When the emptiness of awareness was in a state of perfection, emptiness itself and what had become empty also ceased

77

to exist. When nothing was formed and nothing was lost in my mind, the state of still extinction thus manifested itself to me". This is how one can transcend both the mundane and the supramundane worlds and how one can reap two great benefits. First, one can be united with the wonderfully enlightened mind of all the Buddhas in "the ten directions" (the entire universe). Secondly, one can be united with all the sentient beings in the six paths and show equal concern for all these sentient beings. Now, you should have realized that this mystical experience of "integration" can transcend religion, race and any other kind of division.

This is also similar to what Maslow proposed in 1969 as a supplement to his previous theory: there is a need above the need for self-actualization. It is the ultimate metaphysical need ——the most deeply ingrained need for a "transpersonal" (transhuman) psychology. Maslow observed, "It will center in the cosmos rather than in human interests and needs. It transcends human nature, one's ego and the idea of self-actualization, and so on. Without the transpersonal, we get sick, violent; we tend to hurt ourselves or others; or else we become nihilistic, lose hope (hopeless) and become apathetic. We need 'something greater' than ourselves, something that stimulates awe and that we can dedicate ourselves to." He also notices that "when you open the door to value and to value experiences and peak or transcendent experiences, a whole new level of possibilities is open to investigation".

This is the basic human right for each of us. This is also the key to the door to the realization of our "potential for divinity" that is hidden in the innermost part of our soul. Now, the key is in our hands. It is waiting for us silently to use it to open that door to the divine mystery. Once the door is opened, everything else in the world will be open to our exploration.

In this three-dimensional world, we all live in the holes in our subconscious mind, a situation that can be referred to as our collective consciousness. In the 1990s, when our collective consciousness started to surpass the energy level of 200, why did people of great vision become so excited? Because anything which is beyond the level of 200 points to courage, it means we would be able to "face" ourselves more candidly, and it means we would become more capable of unlocking our potential for divinity and getting ready for the unknown future. You must be willing to step into the darkness, step into those holes, and allow the light to penetrate you, until the holes you are in begin to shine; then, there will be no difference between the light and these holes, and that's how you will be able to brighten up the whole world: "It's better to light a candle than curse the darkness". The candle here represents light, and this saying implies that you must be brave and take with you your self-consciousness, love, and light when you walk into your holes. Because you are the only person who can save you. This is how people work wonders in this world. When you are trying to save yourself, you are also shedding light on the collective consciousness of mankind, and you are also saving (changing) the world.

At the time when we are trying to enhance our spirituality, there will be "chaos", but "chaos" can give our brain positive stimulation. It is because our intelligence is connected to our synapses, and it is associated with our intuition and the scope of our perception. We develop certain habits when cranial nerve nuclei are formed around the synapses, and these nuclei shape our personalities, our way of thinking, and our behavioral patterns. If our brains are not strongly stimulated, no new synaptic communication will be established.

Our brains need to be stimulated. However, most of us are afraid of pursuing any kind of stimulation. When we finish school and start working, we start to suppress the "naughty" part of our nature, so much so that if you at some point demonstrate your more naïve side, people will stare at you and even criticize you according to their own opinions and ideologies. Our brains need to be stimulated, and chaos can be a kind of stimulation, so can fear or dancing. All kinds of emotions, or even a vacuity of emotions, can act as a stimulus. When the synapses are stimulated, the cranial nerve nuclei around them will also change, and that's how the normal modes can be broken. One's personality will also change accordingly. This is how changes come about. These changes will make you more mature and mellow. You will become a new self. You will begin to display the unique characteristics of your spirituality and become a genius in the field you choose.

This is the reason why we started to work in this unique and professional field of science and spirituality, because we want to help everyone enter that sacred sanctuary step by step. "Integration" is a wonderfully divine experience we can enjoy; it is also the core value when it comes to the discussion about how to "transcend ourselves". If we can learn to "transcend ourselves", we will have a more satisfying life and a healthier interpersonal relationship. We can extend the influence of our love and compassion over different races, countries, cultures, the whole world, or even the universe. "Integration" makes us more aware of and responsible for the cultivation of the entire mankind and the flourishing of everything in the universe.

But remember, this is just a new beginning. This is not the end of the journey. It's really a shame to see how many people thought they have already obtained "the Elixir of Immortality", that they have "arrived at" the destination, so it's no longer necessary to make any further progress. There are still more incredible realms in your hero's journey waiting for you, to discover and to be surprised by them.

Return

10. The phase of transcendence

Toward the end of the phase of integration, when our consciousness is about to return to "the origin of the sacred", there is one last barrier we must overcome.

Some mystics described this as the darkest "night in our soul". It is like hours of the deepest darkness before the dawn breaks. Maybe the hero has been in many situations where he felt "death would be a relief". However, once the hero has surmounted the difficulties, he will be able to see "the light at the end of the tunnel" once again. However, this moment we are talking about is the darkness of darkness, where we come face-to-face with the archetype "Satan".

During this phase, there is the subtlest "benightedness", which nonetheless is interspersed with the most dazzling "brightness".

SatDharma's spectrum of consciousness shows us that the hero has come to the momentous stage, the "peak of the two realms". *202 The hero is about to move onto "the third realm". "The two realms" manifest themselves as the whole "Dharmadhatu" we see now. It is a "world full of causes and effects". Here, we must "take" and "complete" all the "lessons" we are supposed to learn in every one of our reincarnations.

When an individual soul is about to descend to the three-dimensional earth to embark on his "hero's journey," he will choose and design his "lessons" beforehand, and make plans for the "credits" he has to take in the field of life sciences, in the academy of the Earth. Sometimes, there are some "lessons" we were unable to complete in our former lives, so we have to "combine" them with other lessons we are learning in this life. The superior guiding spirits, in order to help us "complete" the "lessons" in this life, will predispose us to the "archetypes" in our consciousness that we have unwittingly "used" before. There are positive archetypes and negative ones. Therefore, when the hero is on this journey, on the one hand, he must "face" the challenges lying ahead, while on the other, he must also "face" the inner "conflicts".

This is also "the principle of karma" that underpins the operation of our Dharmadhatu. According to this principle, we have "the drive for creation" which enables us to completely harness the power of the archetypes in our consciousness. This "drive" is also the "records" of the credits we must take or the challenges we must face in these two realms and in the Dharmadhatu. Besides, it is the "records" of the thoughts we have and the actions we take under the influence of these "archetypes", as well as all the emotions we experience and the tension that has an impact on the seed of each of our ideas.

Now, it is the time for us to earn all the "credits" we have to take in the Dharmadhatu. All the negative archetypes we must face will "come swarming" to us during these final hours. We can regard them as the "final exams" that our conscious mind must pass.

A classic example I can give will be the story about how the Buddha encountered the personification of his main "antagonist": Kama-Mara, when sitting under the Bodhi tree.

The literal meaning of Kama-Mara is: Desire—Hostility, or Love and Death. It can also mean our most dangerous illusion——Maya.

The "chief examiner" for this last and most difficult test, the "Threefold Fire" we have to walk through at this final stage, is also the biggest "shadow archetype" in the depths of our soul. He is the "final threshold guardian to be passed by the universal hero on his supreme adventure to Nirvana".

Campbell wrote, "Having subdued within himself to the critical point of the ultimate ember the Threefold Fire, which is the moving power of the universe, the Savior beheld reflected, as in a mirror all around him, the last projected fantasies of his primitive physical will to live like other human beings—the will to live according to the normal motives of desire and hostility, in a delusory ambient of phenomenal causes, ends and means. He was assailed by the last fury of the disregarded flesh. And this was the moment on which all depended; for from one coal could arise again the whole conflagration". *203

This personification of Kama-Mara is not only the biggest shadow archetype in our hearts, but he is also our "other selves". Therefore, he is very clever, and he knows very clearly what "our biggest weakness" is. The imprints of our archetypes and of our habitual patterns that have been accumulated for the many lives we have lived can become the "ember" smoldering in every corner of our consciousness and arise the conflagration of the Dharmadhatu inside us. Here, the clarity of the hero's mind will be put to the most severe test. If the hero still believes the ember of desires in his consciousness is something "real," then everything he is going through now will appear more "real" than "what is actually real". If the hero understands that the ember of all the darkness, shadows, and imprints in his consciousness is but "the manifestation of love," just a coat that covers the august and dignified "ultimate intrinsic nature," the hero will put himself in a "completely different" situation. At this moment, the hero will either, together with "Mara," be burned into ashes by the conflagration and then fall into the dark illusion in the very depths of his unconscious mind; or the hero will have "the Midas touch", he and Mara will pass the final threshold of delusory fire, and turn it into a pennant of victory that emblematizes the glory of the absolute stillness.

"As in the stories of the cannibal ogresses," said Campbell, "the fearfulness of this loss of personal individuation can be the whole burden of the transcendental experience for unqualified souls. But the hero-soul goes boldly in—and discovers the hags converted into goddesses and the dragons into the watchdogs of the gods". *204

The Buddha's mind was clear enough now to face the abhorrent Mara created by his delusions. He made the "Bhumyakramana-Mudra" (the earth-touching gesture) with great elegance, anchoring his heart to "the origin of the sacred"——the pure land of Svabhava. As the Buddha's mind was in a state of absolute immutability, he showed no regard for the "kaleidoscopic forms" of these delusions. For him, they were like the dazzling light emitted from the precious diamond that was one's intrinsic nature, and no matter how horrible or tempting the final delusions were, what actually shone forth from them was still the pureness of one's intrinsic nature.

The ultimate light of wisdom gives us a dramatic manifestation of the original form of the infinite consciousness, from which we learn that: I am also He, the Buddha is Kama, Kama is the Buddha, the delusions are the clear mind, and the clear mind is also the delusions. The light of Svabhava shines in a multitude of forms, and these multitudinous forms are all Svabhava. Svabhava is all the sentient beings, and all the sentient beings are the "manifestation of the purity" of Svabhava.

Karma works in the same way as these delusions do. Svabhava produces the wheel of karma. When the wheel turns, all the human dramas in the Dharmadhatu will begin to unfold. No matter how one's karma changes, no matter whether it is manifested as something "evil", something "horrific", or something that makes one "sad and morose", all these faces of karma are also the "display of the primitive form" of Svabhava. Karma is Svabhava. Karma is the ultimate liberation. If you can understand the logic behind these statements, then from now on, you will see that "affliction is Bodhi," and you will stop discriminating one thing from another. You won't even have the concept of "non-discrimination" in mind. Everything in the Dharmadhatu will "reveal its true nature and attain liberation naturally"; everyone who is ignorant will "reveal his/her true nature and attain liberation naturally"; and all things will "reveal their true nature and attain liberation naturally". Therefore, there will be no ignorance and no extinction of it, and so forth until there is no old age and death, and no extinction of them.

The "Bhumyakramana-Mudra" turns everything back to its pure original nature. Even Kama is the manifestation of the pure original nature of the "Bhumyakramana-Mudra". This mudra of ultimate purification is not made to subdue the "demon" outside oneself, but to help one fully realize that everything is the manifestation of the "demon inside"—— therefore, originally, everything is "pure by nature". If you understand this, you will be able to enter the state of real "integration", where the clear light of the wisdom of non-discrimination shines through the immense void of the Dharmadhatu. This is the light of the diamond that is our consciousness, the light that penetrates even the finest particles that compose the delusory inner demon dwelling in our hearts for the many lives we have lived.

At this stage, you should understand all the absolute truths without knowing what "the absolute" is. You should understand everything, without knowing what "to understand" means. Everything that has existed since time immemorial seems to be waiting for this moment to come, the moment when you arrive at a "clear understanding" of life. This is "the world of Nirvana" no words can describe. In the end, "that shore of salvation" exists everywhere. It has already existed in every living entity, in every particle, in every moment we live, and in the Dharmadhatu. Even the "Dharmadhatu" and the "world of mankind" are themselves "that shore of salvation".

When you reach this stage, you also reach what in the SatDharama's spectrum is called the Third Realm (the Realm of the Absolute Truth).

What I have illustrated so far is the "experience of spiritual awakening" that I have been through in 1999. The "state of clear understanding" that cannot be described in words is originally part of the "inner state of self-cognition" of all being. Whichever way you want to describe it, you will be "wrong", because the Way that can be described in words is not the Eternal Way. What I can do is lead all of you to the "entry" to that state, and then you will have to "experience" it yourself.

However, another challenged is posed to the hero here.

If everything is "pure by nature", everything "originally neither exists nor ceases to exist", everything is "already consummate by nature", and everything will "reveal its true nature and attain liberation naturally", then everything in the Dharmadhatu, including the Dharmadhatu itself, has already been "purified". Our "ignorant" soul has been "purified". "Ignorance" existed in the past, so there is "enlightenment" in the present. If everything is already purified by its nature, then why do we need to "do" anything at all?

Is there anything left for us to "do"?

After becoming enlightened, the Buddha was about to enter the state of Nirvana. As he knew all the sentient beings had their Buddha nature, so they too could become enlightened without his help. However, due to some predestined causation, the Buddha decided to join mankind's world once again. Ever since then, he has lighted up the world with his wisdom and has kept walking with all the sentient beings, and he will continue to do so until everyone attains enlightenment.

Campbell wrote, "When the hero-quest has been accomplished, through penetration to the source, or through the grace of some male or female, human or animal, personification, the adventurer still must return with his life-transmuting trophy. The full round, the norm of the monomyth, requires that the hero shall now begin the labor of bringing the runes of wisdom, the Golden Fleece, or his sleeping princess, back into the kingdom of humanity, where the boon may redound to the renewing of the community, the nation, the planet, or the ten thousand worlds". *205

At this point of the journey, the hero must return to the world and share with everyone "the Elixir of Immortality", the new value of life he has gained after going through the transformations. Nonetheless, this "Elixir of Immortality", this state of "the ultimate Nirvana", is too alluring. Besides, since everything in the world is "pure by nature," some heroes will be faced with the struggle of the "refusal of the return".

"The hero may have to be brought back from his supernatural adventure by assistance from without", said Campbell. *206

"That is to say", Campbell continued, "the world may have to come and get him. For the bliss of the deep abode is not lightly abandoned in favor of the self-scattering of the wakened state. 'Who having cast off the world,' we read, 'would desire to return again? He would be only *there*.' And yet, in so far as one is alive, life will call. Society is jealous of those who remain away from it, and will come knocking at the door". *207

Now, the vow of "love" that the hero made in his heart has woken him up——the Bodhisattva has arrived.

The Bodhisattva is a sentient being who has become enlightened and who has thus gained deep insight. Any Bodhisattva has the great compassion Guanyin Bodhisattva has. In his last reincarnation in the world of human beings, when a Bodhisattva is near the end of his hero's journey, when he is about to pass the final threshold composed of the delusions he has to smash into pieces before he can attain Buddhahood, suddenly he sees all the other sentient beings. He sees them as if they are the cells and photons he is made of. He knows they may be attired in ignorance, but in their intrinsic nature there lies hidden the absolute pure light of Svabhava. So, he pauses. He immerses himself in the ocean of the infinite power of great compassion and makes another vow: he vows that before he enters the world of the Buddhas——the realm of the supreme perfect enlightenment, he will help all the other sentient beings become fully enlightened "without any exception."

This is the manifestation of a Bodhisattva's "great love", his "sacred love", and his "boundless love that cannot be described in words". The Buddha's heart is a heart of great compassion. This is the true heart all Buddhas have. It is manifested as the wisdom of dharma nature which is marked with no action, no cognition, no attainment with nothing to attain, and complete equality. Therefore, the Bodhisattva lets all the sentient beings discover their intrinsic nature by themselves and uncover the mysterious realm where they can "reveal their true nature and attain liberation naturally" on their own initiative.

"The Bodhisattva, however, does not abandon life. Turning his regard from the inner sphere of thought-transcending truth...outward again to the phenomenal world, he perceives without the same ocean of being that he found within", wrote Campbell. Accordingly, everything is "neither the same nor different" for the Bodhisattva. At this moment, the Bodhisattva experiences within and without a deep sense of tranquility——the stability and peace that come from the absolute stillness. So, he rises and "returns to them". He chooses to walk toward the world of human beings. On the inside, he has achieved complete liberation. On the outside, he embodies the core value of selflessness. He lives in this world with all the sentient beings. The light of his compassion catches the truth: this world is Nirvana. "Waves" of great compassion go out from this precious mentor, this saint, as a "gift" to celebrate the awakening of all of us, so that everyone can achieve liberation in this life. What he teaches us is very practical: this worldly life itself is "the center of the sacred"——"the great game" played by our intrinsic nature. What we see, hear, smell, taste, and touch is all Nirvana itself, not the slightest distinction existing between them.

Campbell observed, "And so it may be said that the modern therapeutic goal of the cure back to life is attained through the ancient religious discipline after all; only the circle traveled by the Bodhisattva is a large one; and the departure from the world is regarded not as a fault, but as the first step into that noble path at the remotest turn of which illumination is to be won concerning the deep emptiness of the universal round".

The Bodhisattva's wisdom is so profound that the ordinary people cannot even fathom it. Campbell remarked, "Those who know, not only that the Everlasting lives in them, but that what they, and all things, really are *is* the Everlasting, dwell in the groves of the wish-fulfilling trees, drink the brew of immortality, and listen everywhere to the unheard music of eternal concord". *208

In *The Divine Comedy*, Dante also unlocks for his readers the mystery of the phase of transcendence——"so it is that when Dante had taken the last step in his spiritual adventure, and came before the ultimate symbolic vision of the Triune God in the Celestial Rose, he had still one more illumination to experience, even beyond the forms of the Father, Son and Holy Ghost...he (Dante) writes, 'made a sign to me, and smiled, that I should look upward; but I was already, of myself, such as he wished; for my sight, becoming pure, was entering more and more, through the radiance of the lofty Light which in Itself is true. Thenceforward my vision was greater than our speech, which yields to such a sight, and the memory yields to such excess".

"There goes neither the eye, nor speech, nor the mind: we know It not; nor do we see how to teach one about It. Different It is from all that are known, and It is beyond the unknown as well".

"This is the highest and ultimate crucifixion, not only of the hero, but of his god as well", said Campbell. In the realm that transcends everything known and unknown, "the Son and the Father alike are annihilated". *209 All the images of the multiple universes displayed in the Dharmadhatu, including everything that is high or low, secular or sacred, everything that is made manifest seems to reflect that mystic power that is eternal and unfathomable. Henceforth, everything "reclaims" its sacred radiance. This is all "God", and "God" is "love". "Love", all the more so, is the intrinsic nature of all the material forms we see in the universe. This "center of the sacred" that "transcends" everything is the spring of life. It is within and without, but it is neither within nor without as well. It is beyond all we can think and conceive. This "mystery" is the center of the sacred inside each individual——it is their intrinsic nature. Everything surrounding this center is made manifest, and everything that is made manifest is also the revelation of "the center of the sacred". There is no distinction between them at all.

A maxim from *The Quran* admonishes us, "Unto Allah belong the East and the West, so wherever you turn, there is the face of Allah!"

From now on, the enlightened one will have this "deep insight" with him when he returns to mankind's world, and he will see two as one, because this is what the Absolute is, and this is what Nirvana is.

You feel like waking up and getting up from the deep abode in your consciousness, just like you are woken up from a very deep sleep. You arrive at a kind of understanding. You experience a kind of spiritual awakening. "While you are still asleep", you are in a state of ignorance and the world is an unknown place to you. However, when you actually wake up from the source of your consciousness, a mental state so profound that your senses cannot even tell you what it is, you will have a very deep insight, and you will experience a dawning realization, which will lead you to the discovery of an entirely new aspect of life and the acquisition of an entirely new knowledge of life. You, however, will just observe everything that is happening to you "with perfect composure".

Now you have arrived at God's residence, namely, the Brow Chakra. When you get into this state, you will gain more profound insights and more comprehensive viewpoints. That is what true wisdom is. It is completely different from your usual thought process. You will come to know that everything you are experiencing now is a delusion, and everything your heart desires is also a delusion. You used to regard these delusions as something real, but now that you are awake, you are able to transcend your last desire and overcome your ultimate fear. You will become more complete and more at ease with yourself. You will feel free and unconstrained in life, so you can begin to exploit your potential, develop your creativity, and showcase the unique charm of your spirituality.

You no longer see everything in this world from the perspective of dualism, so you no longer have any attachment. Your original self has died, which means you have let go of all the ideologies you once had. You have moved from the first three layers of the human aura to the dimension of higher consciousness. You have broadened the scope of your intuition, so you are able to receive more profound messages that come from the source of your consciousness. You will have deeper insight into life and will observe life more closely. Regardless of how the outside world changes, regardless of whether things are permanent or impermanent, what is inside you will never change again. You will see everything objectively, calmly and with a clear mind. When you realize everything is but the creation of your intrinsic nature, your heart will become purer, because you will no longer be bound by any ideologies. The day you accomplish these spiritual goals will be the day you celebrate your life.

In the phase of integration, you will be elevated from the position of "enlightening yourself" to that of "enlightening others", and from "benefiting yourself" to "benefiting others". You will be able to "put yourself in other people's shoes".

This is a demonstration of your big Bodhi heart. You are willing to extend your love to other sentient beings. You are willing to love all living entities in the world.

During the phase of transcendence, to enlighten yourself is the same as to enlighten others, and to benefit yourself is the same as to benefit others. Therefore, whatever you do, you are enlightening both yourself and others, and you are benefiting both yourself and others. It is because whatever you see, whether they are people you know or people you don't know, whether it is an animal, a tree or a blade of grass, you see it through your intrinsic nature, when you are in perfect meditation. Therefore, even in excrement you can see the Buddha. You have completely understood that everything, including the Buddha, all living creatures, and emptiness, is neither the same nor different, and there is no need to distinguish one from the other. The moment you enter the phase of integration is the moment you start to pursue the Bodhisattva path. It is a process during which you have to proceed from stage one to stage seven, so you will obtain greater wisdom and compassion, and you will realize everything within and without is neither empty nor not empty. In the phase of transcendence, when you reach stage eight, you will realize that all your dualistic views are created by your mind, and that reincarnation is Nirvana. Everything in the Dharmadhatu is the Absolute. Everything is either empty or not empty, neither empty nor not empty. Your innate love and wisdom will keep growing because they keep interacting with the material world, and thus produce more beautiful blossoms.

11. The phase of magic effect

After seeing "the face of God" and completely understanding the mystery of "becoming one with God", the hero returns to the common run of mankind and comes to the painful realization that people are indulging themselves in the hustle and bustle of the world, thus not in the least interested in "the mystery of the sacred".

Besides, human languages and intelligence are so limited that it is impossible to describe even one percent of what "the origin of the sacred" is. Dionysius the Areopagite, a Christian mystic who lived in the first century, once said, "The truth so infinitely excels all things. It is above them".

Eckhart, a German mystic who lived in the Middle Ages, "tells of the still desert of the Godhead: 'where never was seen difference, neither Father, Son, nor Holy Ghost, where there is no one at home, yet where the spark of the soul is more at peace than in itself'". *210

So, how can we unravel to the world the great mystery of everything and anything? This would be a series of "impossible missions". This would be the challenge the hero has to take on after going back to the world. As Campbell observed, "The returning hero, to complete his adventure, must survive the impact of the world". *211

Though everything in this world is the manifestation of God and the manifestation of one's pure intrinsic nature, for the mundane people, "the two worlds, the divine and the human, can be pictured only as distinct from each other—different as life and death, as day and night", said Campbell.

The great Indian mentor Kabir, in one of his poems, warns us of how ignorant we could be:
"Along the path pearls are scattered,
Ignorant the blind passes on;

90

So without inward light of God,

Man through this world hopping on".

The challenge posed to the hero here is: how to become the master in these "two worlds"?

There will always exist the inexplicable and confusing contradiction between the mainstream values, namely, what is considered reasonable in our collective consciousness, and the knowledge of the mystery of immortality the hero has acquired when he returns from his journey to the divine. The fact that dominant values of a society hold sway over the general public means no matter what kind of divine gift the hero has brought back from the depths of the transcendent consciousness, it will soon be justifiably "replaced" by all kinds of distractions and diversions that enjoy great popularity in the kingdom of humanity.

Things that "didn't exist" before may pose a "threat" to us, may cause "excitement" among us, or may bring forth something so "absurd and bizarre" that we simply cannot comprehend. Thus, "the need becomes greater for another hero to refresh the world", wrote Campbell. *212

Jesus, however, once taught us something different:

"Don't think that I came to send peace on the earth. I didn't come to send peace, but a sword. For I came to set a man at odds against his father, and a daughter against her mother, and a daughter-in-law against her mother-in-law. A man's foes will be those of his own household. He who loves father or mother more than me is not worthy of me; and he who loves son or daughter more than me isn't worthy of me. He who doesn't take his cross and follow after me isn't worthy of me. He who seeks his life will lose it; and he who loses his life for my sake will find it.". *213

But Campbell asked, "How teach again, however, what has been taught correctly and incorrectly learned a thousand thousand times, throughout the millenniums of mankind's prudent folly? That is the hero's ultimate difficult task. How render back into light-world language the speech-defying pronouncements of the dark?" *214

Granted, Jesus has taught us something that transcends this world. However, if we don't have the determination to wish to see our intrinsic nature——to see God, if we cannot transcend our love for our family, then how are we going to prostrate ourselves in front of the most sacred and most mystic Svabhava and savor the sweet dew of the Elixir of Immortality?

The taste of the sweet dew is the taste of the wine of divine love described by Kabir in one of his poems about divinity:

"The wine of divine love
The more you drink
The better it tastes
But it is something hard to get
Because the wine merchant—
Oh, Kabir,
He asked you to exchange your head for it!"

In short, how can you reveal to mankind something that doesn't exist in this world, something that is hidden in the mystic? It is as difficult as trying to explain to those who live in a two-dimensional world what the third dimension is, or trying to represent to people in a three-dimensional world the image of a five-dimensional world.

Campbell has the same concern: "How translate into terms of 'yes' and 'no' revelations that shatter into meaninglessness every attempt to define the pairs of opposites? How communicate to people who insist on the exclusive evidence of their senses the message of the all-generating void?" *215

Almost all the prophets, mystics, positivists, and mentors must deal with the same difficulty. This world is unwittingly hurtling toward the realm of ignorance and destruction. When someone who is awake is trying to deliver a message to wake up other people in a system that is asleep, he is usually treated as a lunatic or a fraud. Many prophets and mentors in human history had made some heavy sacrifice for the attempt. They were either beaten to death, or nailed to a cross, or banished from their home countries. The truth is, people of this world have been accustomed to living in a long dream, and any fool who tries to wake us up or disturb us when we dream will either become the target of severe criticisms and be ruthlessly lambasted, or be thrown into prison, languishing away in darkness for the rest of his life.

Campbell, again, gave us some powerful descriptions of what the returning hero has to struggle with: "Many failures attest to the difficulties of this life-affirmative threshold. The first problem of the returning hero is to accept as real, after an experience of the soul-satisfying vision of fulfillment, the passing joys and sorrows, banalities and noisy obscenities of life. Why re-enter such a world? Why attempt to make plausible, or even interesting, to men and women consumed with passion, the experience of transcendental bliss? As dreams that were momentous by night may seem simply silly in the light of day, so the poet and the prophet can discover themselves playing the idiot before a jury of sober eyes. The easy thing is to commit the whole community to the devil and retire again into the heavenly rock-dwelling, close the door, and make it fast". *216

Campbell also mentioned another interesting story, the dream of Rip Van Winkle, to explain the fascinating contradiction that confronts the returning hero. He reminded us rhat Rip moved into the adventurous realm unconsciously, as we all do every night when we go to sleep.

But though we are refreshed and sustained by these nightly visits to the source-darkness, our lives are not reformed by them; we return, like Rip, with nothing to show for the experience (of "traveling through time and space") but our whiskers. After Rip returned, "he found an old firelock lying by him, the barrel incrusted with rust," as if it has been lying there for centuries. "As he rose to walk, he found himself stiff in the joints, and wanting his usual activity…As he approached the village, he met a number of people, but none whom he knew; which somewhat surprised him, for he had thought himself acquainted with every one in the country round. Their dress, too, was of a different fashion from that to which he was accustomed. They all stared at him with equal marks of surprise", as if he was from a different world. When Rip stroked his chin, "to his astonishment, he found his beard had grown a foot long….He began to doubt whether both he and the world around him were not bewitched…"

Everyone looked at this person who had a "strange appearance". Soon, an "army of women and children…had gathered at his heels," and he "attracted the attention of the tavern politicians. They crowded round him, eyeing him from head to foot with great curiosity. The orator bustled up to him, and, drawing him partly aside, inquired on which side he voted. Rip stared in vacant stupidity". He still cannot get his head around all that had happened.

"Another short but busy little fellow pulled him by the arm, and, rising on tiptoe, inquired in his ear whether he was a Federal or a Democrat. Rip was equally at a loss to comprehend the question, when a knowing, self-important old gentleman in a sharp cocked hat made his way through the crowd...his keen eyes and sharp hat penetrating, as it were, into his very soul—demanded in an austere tone what brought him to the election with a gun on his shoulder and a mob at his heels, and whether he meant to breed a riot in the village. 'Alas! gentlemen,' cried Rip, somewhat dismayed, 'I am a poor, quiet man, a native of the place, and a loyal subject to the King, God bless him!'"

"Here a general shout burst from the bystanders: 'A Tory, a Tory! A spy! A refugee! Hustle him! Away with him!' It was with great difficulty that the self-important man in the cocked hat restored order". (*Rip Van Winkle*, Washinton Irving, 1819)

After the hero returns and faces with these pointless inquiries or even attacks, these usual sorrows and joys of the mundane world, how can he still keep the world-transcending wisdom intact in that moment?

"The taste of the fruits of temporal knowledge", wrote Campbell, "draws the concentration of the spirit away from the center of the eon to the peripheral crisis of the moment. The balance of perfection is lost, the spirit falters, and the hero falls". *216

It is not something new to see how the returning hero is defeated by the world. People's focus will always be on their personal interests. As long as we are so short-sighted, we will be unable to turn our attention away from the chaos of the world to the origin of the eternal firmament.

Do you remember Campbell's statement: "The returning hero, to complete his adventure, must survive the impact of the world"?

The hero is destined to become the loneliest soul in the world. That is the curse put on him once he has returned. No one can see what is in his mind. It may seem to him that everyone is 'sober' and only I am still 'drunk.' His clear mind, however, will be harshly judged by those who can distort facts as if it is part of his original sin. But his unforgettable experience with love, his touch with God in that mystic land, means he will never lose his mind again. Not only can this awakened mind detect what Rip had failed to notice, but it can also see the truth deep in his soul, the truth that cannot be concealed by or submerged in the reality created by the day-to-day life people are used to living.

This is a very important lesson the hero must learn: he must integrate the two worlds, be wise enough to become the master of the two worlds, and have the infinite wisdom to show that these two worlds are originally one and the same world.

"Symbols", which can also be called "dharmas", are only the vehicles of communication between these two worlds, as Campbell observed. "They must not be mistaken for the final term, the *tenor*, of their reference. No matter how attractive or impressive they may seem", *216 they are still "the finger that points to the moon", not the moon itself.

"For then only do we know God truly", wrote Saint Thomas Aquinas, "when we believe that He is far above all that man can possibly think of God".

When you experience something unsurpassable, you will know better how to become the "bridge" between these two worlds and how to engage them in "dialogues" with each other. However, as human beings, if we want to truly understand the existence of something sacred, we still have to abandon all our ideologies.

"My desire-body is dying and it lives", said Kabir.

In the Hindu epic, *Bhagavad Gita*, Lord Krishna once delivered to Arjuna a discourse on truth: "but only by devotion to Me may I be known in this form, realized truly, and entered into. He who does my work and regards Me as the Supreme Goal, who is devoted to Me and without hatred for any creature—he comes to Me".

Only when one is willing to come to the true self inside oneself—Svabhava—can one comprehend Jesus' words: "...whoever will lose his life for my sake will find it" (World English Bible Matthew 16:25).

"The meaning is very clear; it is the meaning of all religious practice. The individual, through prolonged psychological disciplines, gives up completely all attachment to his personal limitations, idiosyncrasies, hopes and fears, no longer resists the self-annihilation that is prerequisite to rebirth in the realization of truth, and so becomes ripe, at last, for the great at-one-ment...he no longer tries to live but willingly relaxes to whatever may come to pass in him. Many are the figures...who represent this ultimate state of anonymous presence", said Campbell. No matter how absurd and tumultuous the outside world is, these great, anonymous souls always know the place of perfect safety and absolute stillness where their mind can dwell securely in the realm of the unexcelled, where they can conceal the light of their brilliance from the crowd. "The sages of the hermit groves and the wandering mendicants…..'Sometimes a fool, sometimes a sage, sometimes possessed of regal splendor; sometimes wandering'", sometimes as demure as a maiden, sometimes as quick as a rabbit, "sometimes wearing a benignant expression", sometimes as enraged as a devil; "sometimes honored, sometimes insulted", sometimes famous, "sometimes unknown—thus lives the man of realization", regardless of his role as a butcher, a mendicant, a connoisseur or a king, "every happy with supreme bliss", as if nothing happening in the outside world will ever disturb his heart of eternal tranquility.

"So is the perfect knower of the Imperishable always the Imperishable, and nothing else", wrote Campbell.

The Noble Sutra of the Explanation of the Profound Secrets,*217 an important sutra of the Yogacara School, also gives us a detailed description of the ten grounds (stages) Bodhisattvas have to go through before attaining the ultimate realization.

"The explanation of profound secrets" means the unravelling of deep mysteries.

There exists an uncanny parallel between the hero's journey and the thirteen stages a Bodhisattva must reach. Stages eleven, twelve and thirteen are respectively the stage of perfect enlightenment, the stage of marvelous enlightenment, and the stage of Buddhahood.

During the phase of integration, the ecstasy you will be filled with after experiencing the eternal Svabhava is called "the Very Joyous". It marks the beginning of a Bodhisattva's journey to enlightenment. Stage one to stage seven in the Bodhisattva path correspond to different degrees of one's integration with one's intrinsic nature ——one's divinity, during the phase of integration. During the phase of transcendence, one reaches and verifies the true existence of the eight stage in the Bodhisattva path, the stage of the Immovable. During the phase of magic effect, one can reach and realize stage nine and even stage ten; the state of Great Bodhisattva, to wit.

Stages eight, nine, and ten correspond to the third realm in SatDharma's spectrum of consciousness. During the phase of transcendence, one reaches the stage of perfect enlightenment, which corresponds to the fourth realm. Finally, one enters the phase of perfection—perfect enlightenment, the true state of God, the state which Amitābha, the one who has reached the perfection of enlightenment and practice, has achieved, and it corresponds to realm five.

These "ten stages" are formulated as the efficient means a Bodhisattva can use to attain enlightenment, as even a Bodhisattva still has to overcome some minor hindrances to wisdom. A Bodhisattva, during his hero's journey, will gradually remove these minor defilements of ignorance, and then enter the "realm of ten knowable characteristics". The "stages" that constitute the Bodhisattva path carry many different meanings, but the core meaning is "reliance". In the process of attaining enlightenment, a Bodhisattva relies on completing these stages to earn all kinds of merits. Therefore, as a saying goes, "to reach a stage means to earn one's merits". The essential nature (intrinsic nature) of the "stages" can help one obtain the wisdom of non-differentiation in order to bear witness to the reality of Dharmadhatu. All the merits earned are the manifestation of the dignity of the disciples surrounding a Bodhisattva in each of the "stages". When we think about the intrinsic nature of Dharmadhatu, we should know that the only reality of Dharmadhatu is that there is no difference between the concepts one has and the mental state one is in. Absolute equality is part of the original enlightenment, part of our intrinsic nature, and it means we see the first stage the same as the tenth stage. The tenth stage can be likened to the traces left by the birds flying across the sky. It is something difficult to conceive and difficult to comprehend. Therefore, these ten stages, formulated as the skillful means, can explain the processes during which a Bodhisattva must surmount all kinds of obstacles and learn to perceive the subtle differences between intrinsic nature and one's true self, as he ventures down to great depths to explore the ultimate realm of Svabhava.

Due to the limited space in this book, we will begin our discussion with the eighth stage during the phase of transcendence.

The eighth stage—one realizes the reality of Dharmadhatu, which is, "(dharmas) neither increase nor diminish". This is the state a Bodhisattva attains after desisting from "the ignorant acts of attaching to formlessness". To further illustrate stage eight, we need to go back to stage seven, where a Bodhisattva, after desisting from "the ignorant acts of attaching to the subtle marks in the manifested activities," realizes that "there is no difference in the meanings of all dharmas".

Here, the "subtle marks in the manifested activities" refer to "the perceptible forms" of all kinds of dharmas which the Thus-Come- One teaches and which a Bodhisattva who has entered stage six still "apprehends". In short, it means a Bodhisattva in stage six, though having testified to the purity of one's intrinsic nature, still commits the infractions of attaching to the subtle differences between "the manifested activities" of the truth and those of the non-truth. After a Bodhisattva enters the seventh stage, he will desist from fixating on these subtle differences and on the manifestation of the truth. From then on, what a Bodhisattva sees in everything is but their "formlessness". Thus, there will be no difference between one's intrinsic nature, the Buddha, all sentient beings, and the world of all sentient beings. A Bodhisattva will only contemplate the "formlessness" of the Buddha, the Buddha's teachings, all the sentient beings and the self, because they are all the manifestation of one's intrinsic nature. Everything is manifested as emptiness. Furthermore, since a Bodhisattva has gained a thorough understanding of all the dharmas the Thus-Come-One has taught, he no longer perceives the differences in these dharmas, and the non-differentiable nature of these dharmas is the reality of Dharmadhatu he has come to realize.

However, even though a Bodhisattva in stage seven can contemplate "formlessness" as the essence of everything, he still cannot desist from noticing their "functions". That means that after reaching the seventh stage, a Bodhisattva has understood that there is no difference in all the "dharmas", including the revealed and the unrevealed ones, including the mundane and supramundane ones, and therefore, these "two worlds" or "two states" are almost identical to one another. However, even so, there are still subtle differences in the functions of these "dharmas". After completing each stage, a Bodhisattva can thus attest to dharmas' different functions, and how these dharams function in different ways to guide different sentient beings. Because of the attention paid to the essence of formlessness and to these different functions, a Bodhisattva encounters the obstacle that will prevent him from realizing the nature of "effortlessness", meaning the ultimate reality is beyond the volitional effort of human beings, or what is attained by one's volitional effort is not yet the ultimate reality. As this realization must be accomplished during stage eight, a Bodhisattva thus has to get rid of the subtle body in our consciousness still clinging onto these differences in functions, so that he can desists from "making volitional effort," and recognize that "nothing really arises or perishes". This shows a Bodhisattva has thoroughly understood that all dharmas neither increase nor diminish, because all of them—wholesome, unwholesome, revealed, unrevealed, mundane, and supramundane are but the manifestation of one's intrinsic nature. Therefore, since everything is neither the same nor different, nothing arises, and nothing perishes, the hero has completely desisted from perceiving any subtle difference between these "two worlds" and thus becomes the true master of these two worlds. Whatever is revealed or unrevealed to him is pure by nature.

A Bodhisattva who has completed the practices in stage eight should attain "maya-upama-samadhi" (a state of meditative absorption in which one acquires an illusory body). Thus, he encounters no obstacles when examining all dharmas, and whatever he wants to see will appear. This is called "the dependence on the unhinderedness of (conceptualizing) forms". He will also be able to see the multiple worlds in all Dharmadhatus. Whatever the land he wants to bring into existence, he can conjure it up with ease. This is called "the dependence on the unhinderedness of (conceptualizing) land".

The ninth stage—this is the entry to the phase of magic effect. To reach stage nine, a Bodhisattva must elevate himself from what he has achieved in stage eight. During stage eight, though a Bodhisattva is filled with the great joy by realizing that reality is formless or markless, he still has slight attachment to this marvelous state where everything is formless and quiescent. Therefore, he is yet able to benefit all the sentient beings without making any volitional effort. Only when a Bodhisattva takes and acts on the Buddha's wise advice about the purity of all things can he rise from deep meditative concentration to perform altruistic deeds for more people. It is because he has understood that all sentient beings are the manifestation of our intrinsic nature, so all the sentient beings are us. After deepening his understanding of intrinsic nature, a Bodhisattva knows he should start from knowing himself, from knowing his intrinsic nature, and through the light of Svabhava, arrive at bringing benefit to all the sentient beings without making any volitional effort. As of this moment, a Bodhisattva sees through everything, overcomes this great obstacle, and enters the ninth stage where there is no form and no volitional effort.

Now a Bodhisattva is able to remove the obstacle of making volitional efforts; therefore he can acquire four kinds of unhindered understanding. He will enjoy total freedom when teaching dharmas, and he will enter the state called "the dependence on the unhindered understanding".

The tenth stage—it is the latter stage during the phase of magic effort. A Bodhisattva desists from "the ignorant acts of not being free from all dharmas", and enters the realm where he can have "a strong dependence on the freedom from karmas, Dhāraṇī (long mantras), and a strong dependence on the enjoyment of freedom in meditative absorption".

To sum up, a Bodhisattva who has reached stage ten has learned all dharmas by heart. He sees clearly the nature of everything as merely the manifestation of one's intrinsic nature, including all dharmas and non-dharmas, revealed and unrevealed dharmas, as well as all the mundane and supramundane phenomena. Therefore, under any kind of circumstances, a Bodhisattva can enjoy the acquisition of a thorough knowledge of his intrinsic nature and relish the freedom that comes from it. It doesn't matter whether he is a prostitute (such as Vasumitra mentioned in *The Flower Garland Sutra*), a pimp, a beggar set upon by dogs, or a hero worshipped by everyone. "Just as an actor is always a man", said Campbell, "whether he puts on the costume of his role or lays it aside", nothing will change the bliss and freedom he has achieved inside.

He has completely "isolated" himself from all the karmas generated by his actions. He has used the flame of the wisdom of truth to burn out the ideas that are about to sprout from somewhere deep in his heart, ideas about everything good and bad, about Yin and Yang, about the wholesome and the unwholesome, as well as the revealed and the unrevealed dharmas.

Though there is just one tiny obstacle about the "ignorant act of slightly attaching to forms produced by forms" he hasn't quite overcome, nothing will ever have any impact on his "imperishable nature".

In many myths, "the battlefield is symbolic of the field of life," wrote Campbell. In this battlefield, "the weak are always the prey of the strong". Every living creature feeds on one another. The business world is a battlefield; life itself is a battlefield. It seems everywhere in this world is a battlefield. Once you have a deep insight into this real "sin" that none of us can avoid, how will you present yourself? How will you demonstrate your inner equilibrium? How do you prove that you have the wisdom to live your life properly? Maybe after seeing the grim reality of this world, many people would feel unable to accept it, disgusted by it, and they would either choose different masks to wear, or desensitize themselves by convincing themselves that "other people also live an ugly life like me".

Campbell discovered some psychological pitfalls that haven't been overcome yet. Even during the phase of integration, it is likely that some people may attain "fake enlightenment". They "pretend" they have fully understood the supreme truth, and they choose to delude themselves and the world. Campbell observed with a heavy heart,

"Like most of the rest of us, one may invent a false, finally unjustified image of oneself as an exceptional phenomenon in the world, not guilty as others are, but justified in one's inevitable sinning because one represents the good. Such self-righteousness leads to a misunderstanding, not only of oneself but of the nature of both man and the cosmos". *218

As the quote from Huston Smith's *The World's Religions: Our Great Wisdom Traditions* we used in chapter one says, "The only thing good without qualification is not as Kant argued the good will—a will can mean well within terribly narrow confines. The only thing good without qualification is extended vision, the enlargement of one's understanding and awareness of what reality is ultimately like". *219

Smith's words completely correspond to not only the ultimate understanding the hero arrives at through the training in spirituality and science, but also the ultimate goal of the myth pointed out by Campbell: "The goal of the myth is to dispel the need for such life ignorance by effecting a reconciliation of the individual consciousness with the universal will. And this is effected through a realization of the true relationship of the passing phenomena of time to the imperishable life that lives and dies in all". *220

It seems no matter which fields people work in, great minds think alike, regardless of whether they are talking about "good", "justice", or "redemption".

Maybe you are raising the flag of "legitimacy", fighting hard against what you deem as "the evil", but you are running the risk of "justifying" the evil as something yourself or the group you belong to cannot avoid, because you haven't gained a true understanding of your intrinsic nature, of your consciousness, of the volition of the universe, and of the important connection between all things in the world and your intrinsic nature, your divinity. Therefore, you see yourself as the embodiment of justice, and it is your duty to "attack" the "opposite side" of you—your enemy.

Even during the phase of integration, there is still a risk that an "opposite" like this may exist. It is because when you regard yourself as "the exception", or think you are already "enlightened", or you invent an image of yourself as someone who has received "the divine mandate", you are unable to see the true value of the "opposite". An "opposite" exists so we can welcome "integration" in the future. It exists so we can arrive at a full understanding of everything. "Opposite" is the manifestation of "love". If we only think about getting rid of "opposites", we have a kind of "ignorant desire" about life, and it will only breed more evil, more "opposites". But we can "escape" from this predicament, if we can discover the value of "the Imperishable" that lies in all the perishable "opposites" such as Yin and Yang, and if we can see how closely the opposites are related to each other.

We should also stress that it is very important for the hero to get to know his imperishable nature after he passes the phase of transcendence.

12. The phase of transcendence (the fourth realm—the stage of perfect enlightenment—the manifestation of madness)

"The universe came into existence because of the ignorance of the true self,

And it will disappear because of the knowledge of the true self". (*Yoga Sutras of Patanjali*, 5-11)

When two opposite worlds are almost fused into one, it is time that one enters the phase of transcendence.

In SatDharma's spectrum of consciousness, entering the phase of transcendence means entering the fourth realm——the absolute "darkness".

Here, "darkness" doesn't have the same meaning as it does in the material world. It means that all "light", upon reaching this realm, will completely melt into "darkness". All "love", upon reaching this realm, will melt into "darkness" as well. The "love" that fades away in "darkness" is the "love" that ordinary people have difficulty in perceiving, as if it has never existed before.

It reminded me of the concept of "the golden mean", which many people in the modern world have misunderstood.

The Buddha provided us with a clear explanation of "the golden mean" in the *Kātyāyana Sutra*:

"Oh, Kātyāyana,

'Yes' is at one extreme, and 'no' is at the other extreme.

The golden mean is impalpable, and incomparable; it is nowhere to be found; it is not manifested; and it is incomprehensible.

Oh, Kātyāyana,

This is what the golden mean is, and this is what the truth is".

During the phase of integration, we have started to experience "the unification of the dichotomy". We will arrive at a true and deeper understanding of the fact that "the nature of dichotomy is unity" when we are in the phase of transcendence—the eighth stage.

In the phase of magic effect—stage nine to stage ten, we will be able to proficiently utilize both love and wisdom, both intelligence and knowledge, which are derived from the understanding that two is one (Yin and Yang are one; two worlds are one world).

During the phase of transcendence, all our wits, as well as everything we have come to realize and have validated, become utterly useless here. It seems we are now preparing for the dignifying entry to "the phase of perfection". We want to let the self who is in the phase of magic effect "die" again, let our whole selves go back to square one, and enter the state of "chaos" that precedes our return to the origin of everything.

The origin, or the source of the beginning, has its own "evolutionary" order. Every living creature learns to go with this orderly ebb and flow of life—rising and falling.

Campbell wrote, "As the consciousness of the individual rests on a sea of night into which it descends in slumber and out of which it mysteriously wakes". *221

Just like everything that abides in it, the universe itself was born out of the state of eternal silence and keeps existing in this silence until the "time" comes, and it will "melt" into nothingness.

"To melt away" is an extremely beautiful condition and state. In this state, there is no consciousness, no "oneness", no physical bodies, no soul, no individual thoughts, no divisions, and no universe. From the ultimate stillness in the oldest of the oldest times, everything was born, and when the time is right, everything will "dissolve", melt away and eventually return to "chaos".

We should make use of the clear and orderly flow of the power of this origin to restore our bodies, our minds, and our spirit to the state of "order", of vigorousness, of waking, and of perfect health.

"The philosophical formula illustrated by the cosmogonic cycle", wrote Campbell, "is that of the circulation of consciousness through the three planes of being.

The first plane is that of 'waking experience': cognitive of the hard, gross, facts of an outer universe," the facts that are "common to all".

The second plane is that of 'dream experience': cognitive of the fluid, subtle, forms of a private interior world". It is like the ādāna-vijñāna, the appropriating consciousness proposed by the Consciousness-Only School of Chinese Buddhism.

The ādāna-vijñāna manifests itself as naturally as a waterfall pours down. By nature, it is the same as the mental state people are in when they are asleep and dreaming.

The third plane is that of 'deep sleep': dreamless", sober, and "profoundly blissful".

In the first plane, we encounter the dualistic experiences of life.

In the second plane, whether the experiences are positive or negative, they "are digested, assimilated to the inner forces of the dreamer".

In the third plane, in this vast zone of unconsciousness, "all is enjoyed and known unconsciously, in the 'space within the heart,' the room of the inner controller, the source and end of all".

The cosmogonic cycle repeats itself in the same order.

It is "to be understood as the passage of universal consciousness from the 'deep sleep' zone of the unmanifest, through 'dream'", creating ether, "to the full day of waking", when it "sees" everything; "then back again through dream to the timeless dark".

"The Hindus represent this mystery in the holy syllable AUM. Here the sound *A* represents waking consciousness, *U* dream consciousness, *M* deep sleep. The silence surrounding the syllable is" the knower who "witnesses", and "the unknown: it is called simply 'The Fourth'", said Campbell.

"The syllable itself is God as creator-preserver-destroyer, but the silence is God Eternal". Its absolute purity makes sure that everything which "flows" out of it is absolutely pure as well.

Campbell wrote, "'The Aged of the Aged, the Unknown of the Unknown, has a form and yet has no form,' we read in a cabalistic text of the medieval Hebrews. *222 'He has a form whereby the universe is preserved, and yet has no form, because he cannot be comprehended'". *223

In his research, Campbell explained: "This Aged of the Aged is represented as a face in profile: always in profile, because the hidden side can never be known. This is called 'The Great Face,' Makroprosopos; from the strands of its white beard the entire world proceeds.

'That beard, the truth of all truths, proceedeth from the place of the ears, and descendeth around the mouth of the Holy One; and descendeth and ascendeth, covering the cheeks which are called the places of copious fragrance; it is white with ornament: and it descendeth in the equilibrium of balanced power, and furnisheth a covering even unto the midst of the breast. That is the beard of adornment, true and perfect, from which flow down thirteen fountains, scattering the most precious balm of splendor. This is disposed in thirteen forms...And certain dispositions are found in the universe, according to those thirteen dispositions which depend from that venerable beard, and they are opened out into the thirteen gates of mercies".

For me, the most amazing illustration of this face is what Campbell continued to write: "The white beard of Makroprosopos descends over another head, 'The Little Face,' Mikroprosopos, represented full face and with a beard of black. And whereas the eye of The Great Face is without lid and never shuts, the eyes of The Little Face open and close in a slow rhythm of universal destiny. This is the opening and closing of the cosmogonic round. The Little Face is named 'God,' the Great Face 'I AM.' Makroprosopos is the Uncreated Uncreating and Mikroprosopos the Uncreated Creating: respectively, the silence and the syllable AUM, the unmanifest and the presence immanent in the cosmogonic round". *224

I am
(svabhāva/ original enlightenment)

I am God
(God/ deepening consciousness)

(Yin and Yang)

(Universe)

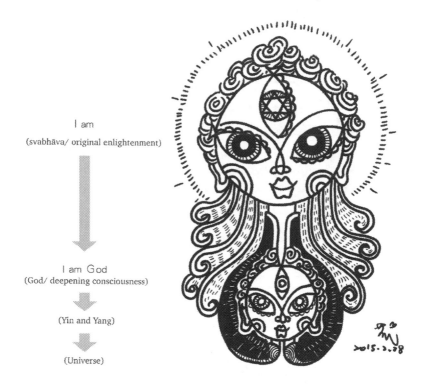

I could only marvel at Campbell's discovery. In the ancient sutras of the Yogachara school of Buddhism and the teachings of the Buddha—the Tathāgatagarbha sutra, we can also find the philosophy which, to our amazement, echoes Campbell's research outcomes.

To put it simply, "The Great Face"—"the Uncreated Uncreating", corresponds to the initial "wisdom of original enlightenment"— cognition and its objects, while "The Little Face"—"the Uncreated Creating", corresponds to "the acquired wisdom"—consciousness and its objects; everything in this Dharmadhatu, or even in the entire

106

universe, is "all the games" played by our cognition and its objects, and by our consciousness and its objects. Cognition and its objects— "The Great Face", is the dharma-body of the Thus-Come-One, and consciousness and its objects—"The Little Face", is "the merit of the dharma-body" of the Thus-Come-One. To utilize both the wisdom of original enlightenment and the acquired wisdom means to utilize both our intelligence and knowledge. Therefore, we will see that "The Great Face" and "The Little Face" are one and the same. This is the true realization of our Buddha nature.

It seems that, during this phase, the understanding of the truth brings our consciousness back to the plane of "dream experience". Though it may mean to return to the timeless dark, consciousness itself can emit the light of "the imperishable", giving us a more illuminating insight into the order and wisdom with which things in the universe and in the Dharmadhatu evolve and melt away. Moreover, it also sheds light on the state the collective consciousness is in when it is in the plane of "dream experience".

The phase of transcendence is so incredible that it seems identical with the mental state the Buddha has achieved, namely, the full realization of our Buddha nature. It is the same as what God was at the beginning of time. As this state is so inconceivable that human languages can barely describe what it is, Campbell opted for myths to give it a more apt depiction. However, in the end, it still comes down to each individual who has to experience it themselves, so that they would know why there have been heroes in each generation who are willing to embark on this adventure to no man's land, in order to see with their own eyes the very beginning of all the beginnings—all the mysteries about God.

This state is close to the state one attains when, after all the wishes have been fulfilled, everything will come to an end: the realm of sentient beings will be no more; the world will be no more; emptiness will be no more; Dharmadhatu will be no more; Nirvana will be no more; the Buddha will be no more; the wish to acquire the profound wisdom of the Thus-Come-One will be completely fulfilled; the realm of mental factors will be no more; and the wish to have the Buddha's profound wisdom in order to spread the teachings of the Buddha will be completely fulfilled. In short, everything will be fulfilled and then vanish. Therefore, we can fully understand why "The Little Face" represents all the mysteries about consciousness and its objects, while "The Great Face" represents the absolute pureness of cognition and its objects. The boundary between "The Great Face" and "The Little Face" gradually dissolves in this pure, absolute "darkness". We can no longer tell which one is which. The wisdom of original enlightenment and the acquired wisdom as well as one's cognition and one's consciousness all become indistinguishable. However, since its nature never changes, we cannot say that He is, in all respects, "one".

Comparison of the States of Consciousness Occurring in Shamanic Journeys, Advanced Yogic and Buddhist Meditation, and Schizophrenia Source of reference: *Paths Beyond Ego: The Transpersonal Vision*, written by Roger Walsh and Frances Vaughan, translated by Yi Zhixin and Hu Yinmeng, published by PsyGarden Publishing Company, p.82.

During the phase of transcendence——the fourth realm, we still can't completely desist from "the ignorant acts of perceiving the extremely subtle marks in the objects of the world". It means, in the realm of "The Great Face"—cognition and its objects and "The Little Face"—consciousness and its objects, the light of omniscience hasn't fully shone through. Therefore, the subtlest differences between objects still exist. When even these subtlest differences can completely "melt away", we will attain "perfect enlightenment", the state of the Buddha, the state of God at the beginning of time.

13. The phase of perfection--perfect enlightenment—one has perfect enlightenment and perfect practice and thus one's life is in the ultimately perfect state

There are no words, absolutely no words, to describe this state. Unfortunately, most of us do not understand what "Buddhahood" really means.

This is how Bodhidharma described it in "Bodhidharma's Bloodstream Sermon":

"The mind is the Buddha, and the Buddha is the mind. Beyond the mind, there is no Buddha and beyond the Buddha there is no mind...

If you think there is a Buddha beyond the mind, where is he? There is no Buddha beyond the mind, so why envision one? ...People, though, are deluded. They are unaware that their own mind is the Buddha. Otherwise they wouldn't look for a Buddha outside the mind.

Buddhas don't save Buddhas. If you use your mind to look for a Buddha, you won't see the Buddha. As long as you look for a Buddha somewhere else, you'll never see that your own mind is the Buddha. Don't use a Buddha to worship a Buddha. And don't use the mind to invoke a Buddha. Buddhas don't recite sutras. Buddhas don't keep precepts. And Buddhas don't break precepts. Buddhas don't keep or break anything. Buddhas don't do good or evil. To find a Buddha, you have to see your nature. Whoever sees his nature is a Buddha. If you don't see your nature, invoking Buddhas, reciting sutras, making offerings, and keeping precepts are all useless. Invoking Buddhas results in good karma, reciting sutras results in good memory, keeping precepts results in a good rebirth, and making offerings results in future blessings—but no Buddha.

...

A Buddha isn't one-sided. The nature of his mind is basically empty, neither pure nor impure. He's free of practice and realization. He's free of cause and effect. A Buddha doesn't observe precepts. A Buddha doesn't do good or evil. A Buddha isn't energetic or lazy. A Buddha is someone who does nothing, someone who can't even focus his mind on a Buddha. A Buddha isn't a Buddha. Don't think about Buddhas. If you don't see what I am talking about, you'll never know your own mind. People who don't see their nature and imagine they can practice thoughtlessness all the time are liars and fools. They fall into endless space. They're like drunks. They can't tell good from evil".

As *The Sutra of Perfect Enlightenment* tells us, during the phase of perfection, even one's lust, wrath, and delusion are the manifestation of one's Buddha nature, are "The Great Face"—the manifestation of the pureness of cognition and its objects.

However, the more we talk about it, the more mistakes we will make. When the hero hasn't attained the mental state of "non-differentiation", it is pointless to talk about it, and it won't benefit anyone.

"The Buddha" is an ordinary person, a stupid person, an omniscient person, a person who has achieved perfect enlightenment, but also a person who knows nothing. This state is so normal and common that there is nothing worth discussing.

The mystery we have been trying to unravel in this section has already existed in everyone's mind, in the entire universe, and in the Dharmadhatu. It is everything and everywhere. But before our apperception is fully developed, the mystery will only be used as a tool to win a debate between different conscious minds.

As one of the heroes, when you arrive at the border of this state and intend to "melt" into this state, if it is indeed our destiny, we will pass to you, face-to-face, everything you need to know about the mystery. It will be transferred from one mind to another, and you will need to investigate it carefully in order to verify it. There is nothing and no one else you can resort to.

The heroic journey brings the awakening power for life

"If I speak in the tongues of men and of angels, but have not love,
I am only a noisy gong or a clanging cymbal.
If I have prophetic powers and understand all mysteries
and all knowledge, and if I have all faith, so as to remove mountains
but have not love, I am nothing."
--1 (*New World Bible,* Corinthians 13:1-2)
"So faith, love, hope abide, these three;
But the greatest of these is love."
--1 (New World Bible, Corinthians 13:13)

The unknown force in one's life propels him to embark on a journey to the unknown.

Life itself is the big unknown, but it holds some magic mystery. I often say that life is our most valuable teacher. However, because we don't tend to develop our consciousness, we fail to grasp all kinds of "gifts" and mystery life wants to impart to us. Life itself, the existence of a vast amount of beings, is by definition a wonderful "hero's journey".

Through what we experience and learn on this "hero's journey", we will be able to see the "gifts" that life intends us to discover: the turning points in life and the wisdom or "love" that comes after our transformation.

We all live as an integrated whole, but we need to go deep into life itself, be brave and transcend ourselves, and realize what love—the love of our true self, of our intrinsic nature, is. Otherwise, we will still be torn apart by the force of the dual opposites in our consciousness.

It seems life itself provides us with a "game" to play, a "game" by playing which we can finally realize that we are the mystery we want to penetrate. At each stage of the development of our consciousness, we will realize and understand more things about life, and we will grow spiritually, so that eventually we will be able to see the "gifts" that are right before our eyes but so far we haven't been able to see.

In *The Hero Within: Six Archetypes We Live By*, Dr. Pearson wrote, "as long as we are not all taking our journeys, finding our voices, our talents, and making our unique contributions to the world, we start feeling less and less alive, even the most privileged among us. No one can truly profit for long at another's expense". *225

There is a great force lying within each one of us, waiting for us to "redeem" ourselves, and we must release that force.

All the shadow archetypes we encounter during our hero's journeys are there to point out a fact to us: we must face, accept, transform, penetrate and integrate these shadows so that we can be someone different. This is pertinent to every aspect of the existence of all beings, and it is about whether the development of one's personality can provide one with the values that transcend contemporary ideologies and predicaments.

Campbell said, "The hero of yesterday becomes the tyrant of tomorrow, unless he crucifies *himself* today". *226

What he meant to say is if the hero hasn't completely integrated the opposite sides of his innate shadow archetype, and hasn't crucified the idea of "ego", so that he can melt into everything, and then be "resurrected", but instead he is already planning about "saving" the world, it's very likely he will run the risk of falling into the trap of these opposite sides and becoming the tyrant of tomorrow. However, even if that is the case, the hero is still on a unique journey to the discovery of something deep and profound.

Dr. Pearson said, "Heroism…is a matter of… becoming more and more themselves at each stage in their development. Paradoxically, there are archetypal patterns that govern the process each of us goes through to discover our uniqueness, so we are always both very particularly ourselves and very much like one another in the stages of our journeys". *227

Being unique is the value every living being has. It is also the characteristic of our soul that lies deep inside each one of us. It will never be replaced by another being, and there will never be the risk of having it "surpassed" by other beings. It is because the "sin" we all have committed is to conceal our intrinsic nature under a glowing coat. Therefore, we have to take the coat off and reveal our uniqueness by revealing our archetypes, so that we will know ourselves better and feel more positive about ourselves. On our own unique hero's journeys, we will realize that every individual must pass through the darkness in his consciousness, break free from the stranglehold of his archetypes, in order to gradually build up his own unique strength. When we are getting more intimate with our own hearts, we will be surprised to find out that we are also getting more intimate with other people, other lives, and the world. We will see that everyone is on his own hero's journey to self-realization. No one is faster or slower at making the journey. The slogan, to triumph over your worse self, turns out to be the best medicine for our soul, because it is the mental attitude that best resonates with everyone in this world. When we gain a deeper understanding of ourselves, our deep sympathy will be gradually extended to other human beings, other races, other countries, and even to all the living creatures.

Love is the only way home. It is also the brightest spot in our hero's journeys.

Because love can transform the discriminating consciousness of our archetypes, for the first time, we will become aware that the real goal in our lives is not to pursue victory, but to learn more about ourselves.

If more and more people can gain a deeper understanding of themselves, I think, as of this century, there will be a very different fate that awaits mankind.

Dr. Pearson wrote, "Heroism is redefined as not only moving mountains but knowing mountains: being fully oneself and seeing, without denial, what is, and being open to learning the lessons life offers us". *228

She cautioned us: **while the hero in the past was always acting alone, the hero in this day and age is no longer one person. "We all need to be doing so".**

"Heroism for this age requires us to take our journeys, to find the treasure of our true selves, and to share that treasure with the community as a whole through doing and being fully who we are. To the degree that we do so, our kingdoms are transformed". *229

"As we change, however, reality changes, too. The more we have the courage to be ourselves, the more chance we have of living in communities that fit for us". *230

The mission for the hero today is no longer to highlight or prove his heroic spirit or value, let alone to prove who he is. The real lesson for the hero is to let himself become who he truly is, and to be that true self. When the aim the hero pursues becomes something internal, it will kindle a great spark of wisdom about life, and the spark will open the door to a new world. As people are encouraged to make each other's lives brighter, they will produce dazzling light of life that shines on a new milestone that the global consciousness will strive to reach.

All the heroes will also be encouraged to take up the position most unique to themselves, so that they can keep injecting incredible new life into anything that passes away from dying cultures and ossified dogmas.

The Heroic Mission

"Our greatest admiration for truth is to fulfil it in a down-to-earth way".—Emerson

From the moment the hero ignites the innate light of wisdom and returns to this world, he is destined to break the mold that constrains his contemporaries so that he can transcend the scope of their vision.

Campbell believes a hero is someone who can understand, accept, and overcome the challenge posed by his fate.

"The hero-deed is a continuous shattering of the crystallization of the moment", wrote Campbell, especially to slay "the monster of the status quo".

Because the hero has become his original self, and has transcended the vision of his contemporaries, he can see the full picture of the real obstacle that prevent people from bringing about changes at the moment.

The hero has penetrating insight and will jump into action, so that he can clear away or change the obstruction in the road, and thus the evolutionary energy can keep pushing life to move forward.

The primeval energy that has been propelling the world to continue to evolve seems to be completely "integrated" with the hero at this point, and the two of them become the mystery of life itself. This extraordinary hero will keep circulating the energy within the universe. Moreover, because his innate eye of wisdom has been opened, when people are in danger, racked with great pain caused by the impermanence of life, indulged in all kinds of pleasures the world can offer, or overcome with grief, the hero can balance the opposing forces and assure people of the existence of their intrinsic nature.

In the chapter "The Hero as World Redeemer" in *The Hero with a Thousand Faces*, Campbell wrote: "Two degrees of initiation are to be distinguished in the mansion of the father. From the first the son returns as emissary, but from the second, with the knowledge that 'I and the father are redeemers, the so-called incarnations, in the highest sense".

As I stated before, whether it is the first or the second degree of initiation, one is not better or worse than the other. The position each hero takes up entails the most important job he has to do.

They have to present their original selves, but the direction they are heading in and their power to bring about changes in the world will not change. Through overcoming the inner obstacles posed by their archetypes, the heroes can effect wholesale changes and inject energy and new life into all the restricting, ossified, and rigid cultures.

When it comes to the implication of the myths, Campbell said, "Stated in direct terms: the work of the hero is to slay the tenacious aspect of the father (dragon, tester, ogre king) and release from its ban the vital energies that will feed the universe". *231

This is the basic mode the hero uses to display his power. Through the father, the symbol of the "entirety" of a culture, all the opposites the father presents, and everything people hold fast to, the light of the hero's wisdom shines. The hero thus is able to discover the nature and value of life, and the real power that can help him transcend any pairs of opposites.

Because the hero has acquired the wisdom that allows him to have a clear understanding of immortality, he will remove, one by one, the fantasy obstacles that prevent people from seeing the reality of life, so that everyone can kindle their sparks of wisdom about life. Campbell wrote, "The mission of today's hero is to create a symbolic system that transcends those man-made divisions between different races, countries, religions, cultures and societies, so that the deeper meaning behind life can be revealed. No doubt this will require the collective effort of people living in the present era".

This is the effort we have kept making so far. Transpersonal experiences, as well as spirituality and science, can bring all the heroes to: love.

Love is the only way home. Because of love, the heroes are readier to take up their unique positions; because of love, the heroes are more willing to demolish the boundary fences between different ideologies, races, religions, countries, societies, and cultures, so people can move to a higher spiritual sphere to contemplate the meaning behind immortality.

Love makes all the imagined opposites melt away and makes the hero's mission more relevant to the contemporary world.

The hero today will have more courage to respond to the calls issued by love, and he is more willing to begin a new journey in life. He will bring about an integration greater than anyone could imagine, for people living in this century, and for the beginning of the era of Aquarius.

Because of love, the hero is able to strive to transcend his personal limits, geographical boundaries, and the past, and work together with other people to create a new era, a different future.

Regardless of the stage of life the hero is in, he should completely trust his own being and his intrinsic nature, and follow the inner path to progress everyday toward something incredible.

When the world is undergoing transformation, no matter how great the challenges we must face and how great the pain we must endure, the status quo will not change. Nor will the world rid itself of pride, fear, battles that bring people to the edge of death, evils that are legitimized, and misunderstanding about the sacred and the divine.

Come on, all the heroes—people living in the modern world, we should all together withstand the "dark" archetypal energies that will be released when the world is about to transform and reverse all the opposites. Here, "dark" doesn't mean "darkness" itself. It means all our intelligent power that is projected onto it. Only through the light of the pure and eternal "love" in the hero's heart can the dark energy return to one, because it is originally a part of one.

Let's endure together the extreme pain humanity must suffer when undergoing transformations, so that the world will move forward more quickly. When more and more people are willing to set out on their hero's journeys to bring together the opposite sides within themselves, they will understand that the true victory doesn't come at the moment of brightness and glory. On the contrary, we claim victory if we still have the courage to keep going even in the most despairing times, the darkest hours in our lives. Let's ignite the flame of "love" in our hearts, understand the value and meaning of the lessons we must learn in life, and emit the light of our intrinsic nature, the light that is unparalleled, that is eternal, and that doesn't discriminate but shines equally on all things.

Chapter 6

"Seeing" is the Great Awakening

The Profound Wonder of the Omniscient Eye

"As long as you still feel the stars as something 'above you,' you have not yet acquired the gaze of a man of deep understanding."
-Friedrich Nietzsche

The True Meaning of "Seeing" and Discernment

"If you close the door to all mistakes, the truth will remain outside."
-Rabindranath Tagore

"God would not under any circumstances fetter his creations with shackles; instead, He inspires them by frequently bringing about changes in their lives."
-Rabindranath Tagore

"I am convinced that human consciousness is the ultimate answer to all questions."
-Drunvalo Melchizedek (*Living in the Heart: How to Enter into the Sacred Space within the Heart*)

July 13, 2014 – I am sitting on a plane heading for Jordan as part of our once-a-year spiritual trip. Our destination this time is Egypt. First we will fly to Petra, Jordan, and then make our way to Egypt. My diary reads: "Plane is preparing to take off from Hong Kong. We'll fly for three hours to Thailand, rest an hour, and fly another nine hours to Jordan." The notes on page 374 show my thoughts and all the recordings I made in my diary. As the "Awakening Summit" *232 is set to be held in September, I can use my time on the plane to meditate.

The act of "seeing" is itself an awakening. It is just that most people do not know where to go to "see," not to mention what they should be "seeing." This is alluded to in the following paragraph from the book *The Healing Power of Illness: The Meaning of Symptoms and how to Interpret Them*:

"On the path to self-discovery, "seeing" is a grand and miraculous criterion. By simply "seeing," one can change the nature of the object being seen, as the very act of "seeing" injects light (consciousness) into the darkness. When we come across something that is difficult to comprehend, our habit is to try and change it. In actual fact, all we need is the ability to perceive."

This single paragraph perfectly encapsulates the nature and value of "seeing."

Simply "seeing" is enough to change the nature of the object being seen (the "creation," in other words). This is precisely the "truth" discovered by quantum physics: that the observer is also in fact the observed, and can affect the results of observation. Indeed, in the Buddha's teachings, the watching and the watched are one. The deeper one experiences this, the greater his ability to affect the result.

When we are troubled by life's myriad problems (such as illness, viruses, money, relationships, and so on) and feel overwhelmed by the high-risk society we ourselves have built, practically everyone looks only to the surface of the problem, to the fear, anxiety, and pressure; how to quickly solve these façade-level issues. It is rare that people are able to "see" the true crux of the problem or the truth lying behind the dilemma.

When you learn how to "see," to really peer into the core of the "seen," the objects being seen begin to miraculously transform.

"Unless people learn to seek answers outside the obvious, surface-level causes, they will continue to be trapped in old patterns born of insufficient self-knowledge" *233 wrote Dr. David R. Hawkins.

Indeed, we must learn to rediscover ourselves in every object and every moment. As we do not have a deep grasp of ourselves, we cannot have a true understanding of the world. When we are constrained by the mindset of the material world, the mindset of binary opposition, we move farther and farther from the truth, which only breeds more opposition and attachment. Does this really solve our problems and create a better future for ourselves and the planet?

Do you Really Want Life to Be Different?

Human consciousness has gradually moved from the Age of Pisces into the Age of Aquarius. A so-called "age" refers to a significant period in the orbital cycle of the universe. One such cycle lasts 25,920 years, hence it takes the sun 2160 years to slowly rotate in a backward procession through a single constellation of the zodiac. These 2160-year periods are known as "Ages," and each age features different energies, beliefs, zeitgeists, and development trajectories.

1.Wanting Something Different
is the Start of Change!

【Kindling desire】

Do you want something different? Pisces Vs Aquarius
Is there a master key for life?

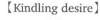

2."Seeing" New Opportunities!

【Breaking free from the
habit of left-brain thinking】

How does one truly "see" new opportunities?
Activate the right brain, train your spiritual power,
and meditate with neutral serenity.
Activate the pineal gland, the gateway to Divinity.

3.Gaining New Insights

【Creating a new mental
pathway (from the heart)】

How do we change the prejudices that reside in our subconscious minds?
Utilize the invisible power and restore your ability to "see." By expanding
your consciousness, you can view with fresh insight your life, career, family,
relationships, and finances.

4.The Power of Stillness

【The power of stillness】

Meditation: Stillness gives rise to peace;
peace gives rise to wisdom; wisdom gives rise to all things.

5.The Compassion, Wisdom,
Strength, and Beauty of the Divinity!

【The mysterious power of prayer】

Getting to know one's true self – the real self.

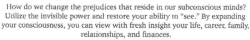

The Age of Pisces is a time in which the material and spiritual are in mutual opposition. In this age, a primary focus is on discovering the value of the dark side, yet there is also an emphasis on sacrifice, service, devotion, forgiveness, tolerance, compassion, suffering, and atonement. This spirit is best represented in the form of Christianity. In the Age of Pisces, people work in order to survive; they diligently strive to make their dreams come true and become role models for others. On the flip side, prevalent traits include disapproval of oneself, self-orientation, the repression of thoughts and emotions, and believing oneself to be trivial or insignificant. As for attitudes held by religious adherents, many simply follow religious conventions, observe doctrines, and believe in the power of God. They view everything as being determined by external beliefs, that all happenings are the will of "God;" but they misconstrue the true meaning of God and the Buddha. Education is skewed toward science and the development of left-brain cognition, with a focus on rational thinking, rigorousness, and criticism. Whether it be on issues of one's tribe, country, religion, or gender, people are locked into clearly-defined and mutually opposing positions, which produces continuous jostling and arguing. And given the highly advanced nature of modern technology and the prosperity of industry and business, people are more indifferent and aloof in their everyday interactions.

The Age of Aquarius is an information age, the eleventh of the 12 houses of the zodiac. The number 11 is formed with two equal-length strokes, implying that the age of equality is already upon us. This "equality" is true equality in a broader sense of the word: an age where the barriers between humans come tumbling down, the distinctions between superiors and subordinates, higher and lower status, disintegrate; where differing viewpoints are accepted, the self is not as pronounced and group interests come first; where humans enjoy closer bonds and greater mutual respect.

The Age of Aquarius is an age for pursuing ideals, showcasing the self, and resisting authority. It places greater emphasis on freedom, cultivation, intuition, insightfulness, and a deeper confidence in unlocking even more life potential and mustering the ability to physically heal oneself. In this age, people do not work to simply survive, but instead to manifest and express their "selves," and even to raise themselves spiritually. In the Age of Aquarius, people have a deeper connection with their own minds and with universal consciousness. Thus, the definition of "religion" will be re-examined.

So-called "faith" involves exploring within for the existence of a greater spiritual realm, to understand the divinity inside. We all have the divine spark of God within us, so there is no need to try and emulate others. This way, moreover, spiritual drills become far more varied and lively. And despite the "side effects" of technology - increased distance between one another, heightened indolence - the wide array of incidents that occur in society serve to awaken human consciousness and dissolve unnecessary boundaries. The myriad concepts prevalent in the Age of Pisces – with its 2,000 years of predominantly masculine (*yang*) energy and a materialistic focus – are now evaporating and disintegrating. We are gradually entering into the Age of Aquarius, an age characterized by feminine (*yin*) energy and a focus on the spiritual. Thus, a host of new elements are slowly emerging and taking shape, such as new values, new energies, new mindsets, new economies, and new types of lifestyles.

The convenience of the internet, communications technology, and transport has turned the phrase "a global family" into reality. Our mutual bonds and the impact we each assert have grown. For instance, when something happens in one region or country it affects the development trajectory of the entire globe, whether it be in the area of politics, economics, the military, climate, natural catastrophes, or disease. In the future, even more attention will be given to issues such as life sustainability, environmental awareness, the spirit of humanitarianism, spirituality, and holistic health for the body, mind, and soul.

Pisces is a water sign, and water is an element that denotes feelings and emotions. It is a sign that points toward Divinity, an age in which karmic patterns will highlight the various contradictions and oppositions that exist between human nature and the Divine. It seems almost as though this age is preparing people spiritually for the Age of Aquarius. After all, it is only through a deep understanding of the dark side that one can truly harbor love. Aquarius is a wind sign, and wind is the element of wisdom. It entails a deeper and more nuanced exploration of spirituality and the awakening of the intuition. In this age, the drive to pursue a spiritual path and seek out truth will be stronger. Indeed, 2,000 years of this perpetual pull-and-push battle between two polarities (the material versus the spiritual) will prompt consciousness in this new age to move from duality to unity. It is an age in which people will crave for more harmony and wisdom. As a consequence, education in the Age of Aquarius will comprise a more holistic focus, with emphasis on whole brain development and the synthesis of mind and brain. There will also be a greater synthesis between several opposing polarities, be it emotion and reason, intuition and intelligence, logic and mystery, the secular and the spiritual, and material and spirit, each of which will develop simultaneously.

The Age of Pisces and the Age of Aquarius possess a different character and energy. From the perspective of unconsciousness, the Age of Pisces draws out and illuminates the shadow of human nature's dark side, leaving humans no option but to face the dark side and try to integrate it. This is the perfect prelude to the Age of Aquarius, which ushers in an age of more subtle mind movement and elevated consciousness. Thus, you could say it is an age defined by the internal exploration of the self and enlightenment. We should count ourselves lucky and celebrate that we are alive now, in this precious and grand moment in time. Yet in the end it is up to the individual: are you willing to change so as to ride this wave of universal awakening all the way to the shore; to create more happiness and joy, and live a life of abundance? Or do you wish to stick to your old mindsets and patterns, resist the upward flow of universal consciousness, and wallow about in the dark as a part of you cries out: "Why has God abandoned me?"

Is there a master key for life that can unlock all of your problems?

Is there such a thing as a magical master key for life? If you owned a key that could somehow fill your life with blessing and contentment, would you be willing to completely overhaul your life? And how would you wield this magical master key that can lift you spiritually and deliver an awakening of the consciousness? Indeed, from ancient times until the present, this magical master key has always existed. What's more, finding it is easy, for it is within you, though you have forgotten. If you have in fact forgotten, all you need do now is use the correct method to awaken the memory within you and return to your original, pristine form. However, if you look for it in the wrong place – if you fail to turn inward and instead seek it externally – a lifetime of tireless searching will be for nothing. To avoid this, experienced spiritual organizations familiar with the spiritual path can guide you along the correct, well-worn parts of the path and teach you how to retrieve this magical master key.

The Satdharma Institute bears the mission and creed of creating "Clean Hearts," of illuminating this spiritual path for those who sincerely wish to know themselves better and genuinely wish to attain self-realization. If you wish to better know your "original self" or Svabhava, to know the essence of your supreme and irreplaceable true self (Svabhava), you will naturally connect with the path heading toward Svabhava, and, as a result, gradually open your internal omniscient eye.

Since ancient times, sages have continually passed along this master key. Yet after being handed down so many times and across so many generations, all that remains is often a well-crafted key chest. The key itself vanished long ago. The only thing left to pass along is an empty key chest, the exterior of which is often gleaming with gold. The fact that there is no key inside gets overlooked. Similarly, because religion seems only able to operate based on old, vestigial conventions, the hollowing out of religion continues to occur. Fortunately, an inheritor and custodian of this master key appears in every age. This person does not think of himself as different to anyone else, because we are all in complete Oneness. Nor is he here to create a new religion, or to become the pope or a bishop. He understands his mission very well, for he knows that every living being already contains the essence of wisdom, or as the Buddha put it: "All people possess the Svabhava." Therefore, he is simply the custodian and deliverer of the master key. It is out of a selfless love which transcends the ego that he shares the secret of the key with humanity.

In the first chapter, we touched on the similarities and differences of religion and spirituality. Religion is a necessary outcome of the development of a society, and encompasses the accrued cultural values of an ethnic group. However, all religions naturally draw out the subconscious of the masses. They are like repositories for subconscious projections. This is because the human subconscious yearns to have its problems solved, to be saved, gain salvation, or discover the source of all power. Religion possesses a deep wisdom, but this wisdom has been built over by artificial concepts and structures. In an attempt to make religion accessible, to have it fit into a replicable system, these once-precious teachings have devolved into little more than garden-variety knowledge that can be gleaned on any old street corner. Religion overlooks the true experiences and practical discoveries of spirituality, and thus creates misconceptions of reality.

Most religions these days involve singing hymns, performing rituals, going to mass, reciting mantras, reading or chanting scriptures, praying, or meditating. They do not require people to face their own shadows, to see their own projections, and this is insufficient. Many so-called "spiritual" experiences in religion are simply projections of the subconscious mind, as the practitioner has not yet integrated the opposing aspects deeply enough within themselves, which can have the contrary effect of inflating the ego. For religions that pride themselves on passing down supreme wisdom, spiritual classes may seem childish, as though lacking depth or diverging from the ultimate goal. But to those taking spiritual classes, religion can feel overly rigid and inflexible. These people wish to pursue growth in a more laid back way and do not want to be hemmed in by religion, religious groups, or religious doctrines.

Spirituality deftly combines the condensation of Eastern wisdom with spiritual growth and spiritual exercises. Sidestepping religion, it guides people to explore their internal realm using language that is easily apprehensible. You could say that spirituality is the bridge that runs between spiritual groups and the religious world; the bridge for the transmission of Eastern wisdom to the general population.

With this as a foundation, Satdharma has developed courses that are unlike "regular courses." Not wholly spiritual or religious in nature, the courses allow you to reclaim your self-consciousness and transform your life by handing you the master key. They draw on a vast pool of Eastern wisdom, and though this wisdom is not only found in religion, its dissemination is extremely important. In fact, religions can utilize spiritual science to enhance the practical and empirical nature of their teachings. To make teachings more practical, the Satdharma Institute uses language the average person can understand, avoiding descriptions that are too esoteric. By offering exercises that are simple and easy to implement, we nurture the ability to become subtly aware and perceive the energy that permeates the Dharmadhatu. This allows you to get closer to people with an indiscriminating love, and to awaken your "mind" so that the truth of reality you wish to transmit will naturally flow from you. Generally speaking, if a spiritual course does not touch upon Svabhava, it is missing that elusive master key. This is not to say that these spiritual courses are bad. I have been to a great number of such courses. Some are filled with positive energy and encouragement, while others enable you to unlock a part of your awareness. (I will discuss in a later section the four phases for spiritual growth, the first three of which inevitably bring some degree of change.) Slowly, as you enter a progressively deeper realm of awareness, you will find that all courses have their own value or purpose for existing, as each helps solve a piece of the puzzle. Yet they are unable to solve the problem on all levels. Imagine for a moment if a tree becomes diseased. To try and heal it, we would apply lotion, enzymes, or nutrients to the roots of the tree, so that it absorbs into the roots. We would not apply it to the tree's leaves. The many facets of life are just like a tree: some spiritual courses solve one of the tree's conditions, while other courses solve another condition. In the end, however, you will find that they are perpetually solving leaf or branch-level problems. So, how about the roots?

You have to find the wisdom that allows you to "untangle the roots." If we want to solve the problem at the root level, it inevitably involves going to the source – Svabhava. Hence, I want to once again emphasize that this course gives you the master key to your "spirit," and is not simply a course on the mind. The mind is just the tip of the iceberg, and does not possess the same depth as the "spirit," though the two are interconnected and mutually entwined. Knowing one's spirit offers a path for holistic growth, and allows you to avoid the pitfalls of getting lost in the mind. For instance, some people who do psychological exercises or have a spiritual cultivation – but do not wish to conform to social norms – are actually unable to live a normal, down-to-earth lifestyle, and fail to gain a true grasp of their own nature; they have just been fortunate enough to never encounter any real difficulties. So, when they come upon a dilemma or setback, they are unable to face it, unable to shoulder responsibility, and are thus misunderstood, censured, and attacked by those around them. However, no one can really judge the actions of another, as the potholes, imprints, and lessons to be learned in the subconscious differ from person to person. The crux of the issue cannot be seen from the surface level. You may look at others and feel that they have easy lessons to learn, and so you give them plenty of advice, telling them to simply "overcome the obstacles." Yet when it comes to your own lessons, you simply cannot "overcome the obstacles" blocking the way. At times like these, keeping the person company in a professional and selfless way is very important. It will influence their ability to move forward in a more expansive, holistic, and self-realized manner. So-called holistic development encompasses seven distinct aspects of life: one's health, family, career, interpersonal relatioships, romantic relationships, intelligence, and spirituality. These seven facets perfectly correspond to the seven chakras.

The first chakra corresponds to survival: Known as the root chakra, it is the source of kinetic energy for all living beings. It relates to the vitality of the body, the strength of the immune system and one's health. Many religious people or those concerned with spirituality place much emphasis on spiritual pursuit and practice but neglect physical health. Both the body and the mind have to be whole. Exploring the wonder of the spirit can be likened to a rocket that is about to launch – it has to have ample kinetic thrust to reach its destination.

The second chakra corresponds to family relationships: One must not embark on a single-minded pursuit of religion or spirituality and abandon familial energy. This is because families provide a deep source of nourishment and support. This chakra relates to the fulfillment of life lessons regarding the family and the energy of self-realization. Of course, many people choose to remain single, which I believe is fine, as long as the lessons surrounding family have already been learned. This is relevant to one's personal karmic bonds for this lifetime.

The third chakra centers on the display of personal power and corresponds to one's career: Studies show that if a problem emerges in one's physical energy (the first chakra) and the family relationship (the second chakra) is strained, then the individual will not do well in their career, or will be unable to make a breakthrough. This means their career energy is insufficient, that they lack the nourishment and support of the family. Another way to put it is like this: due to the pitfalls and "potholes" in their subconscious created by their original family, red flags have now appeared in their health and marriage, and if the roots of the problem are not "untied," these problems will only get worse and the individual will be unable to develop completely.

The fourth chakra has to do with love, starting from loving oneself and then gradually growing in empathy and intuition, and extending one's love on to others so as to bring people together.

The fifth chakra relates to communication and innovation: This chakra is associated with good interpersonal relationships.

The sixth chakra has to do with intelligence: The pineal gland is the wellspring of wisdom. To truly develop wisdom, one must access the Eye of Wisdom so as to view things more directly and really observe an issue in its totality.

The seventh chakra is the crown chakra, which relates to the need for spirituality and is the core of our lives. When this core is activated, all aspects of life begin to take on a different value and meaning. If this core meaning disappears, all you have left are the basic elements for survival, yet you would feel no amusement, would not understand what you are supposed to learn in this lifetime, and would fail to grasp the true value and meaning behind events and incidents in your life.

When you enter deeply into the seven chakras, the seven facets of life all begin to develop simultaneously. This is precisely what is meant by a holistic spiritual education. The wondrous master key of Satdharma preserves the legacy of Eastern wisdom, allowing key holders to open their own treasure chest of wisdom through access to the source, to the mind, and through their own mystical explorations. The key to transforming your life lies within you. It is *you* that has to unlock that power. We are just here to accompany you when necessary, to point you to the source of the power, as you are still unable to see it. It is like a mystery that permeates everything, and you yourself are a mystery, as is life. Yet if you do not open your eyes, how do you hope to see it?

Obstacles to Awakening in an Evolving Age

It is specifically because people lack a true understanding of themselves that we now view the world in a "divisive" manner, whether it be our views towards the world, our problems, external objects, spiritual growth, and even "awakening" itself.

Nowadays, we hear a dizzying number of spiritual slogans, an endless procession of spiritual movements. Yet what does "awakening" actually mean? And what benefits can it bring to us personally and to the world?

These days, new spiritual courses are constantly being launched, with some of them being scams. Many people talk of how they were harmed by some teacher or some group. A lot of people have even witnessed family members take part in a course and then, after making some changes, the family member goes nuts, committing all their energy to serving the group while abandoning their family or falling under the control of the group's leader (some of those being controlled appear to act "voluntarily," yet do so as a result of the markings imprinted on their subconscious minds). One cannot help but be skeptical: Is this really "awakening"? So, people like this who have had a negative experience feel a heightened sense of disdain and antipathy, which in turn prompts even sharper opposition and more distrust.

As for those who have had no such experience yet still spout harsh criticism, they are simply intent on seeing things burn to the ground, so such input bears no weight whatsoever. I truly believe that in this current wave of "spiritual growth" there are indeed imposters (both individuals and groups) that are cynically preying on people to make a buck. However, I also strongly believe there are wonderful groups that genuinely want what is best for people and sincerely want to make the world a better place.

Before discussing exactly what "awakening" means, I will first describe my experience over the last 14 years, as well as the global awakening movement I have witnessed and some of the problems that the public and certain groups have encountered. I provide this description as a kind of self-reflection, on the one hand, but also to give the reader a chance to gain a different perspective.

Problem 1: Have not yet gained a clear understanding of the true meaning of "awakening!"

Problem 2: Mainstream awareness of truly innovative systems of awakening is still very limited.

Problem 3: Too quick to label innovative spiritual exercises for awakening as a type of "cult."

Problem 4: Lack a comprehensive structure for exploring consciousness in a complete and multifaceted way.

Problem 5: Have not applied integrated wisdom to expand globally and make contact with other demographics (markets).

Problem 6: Lack metrics for rigorously measuring and monitoring activity.

Problem 7: Failed to view things from the perspective of the average person.

To follow is a discussion of each of these points.

Problem 1: Have not yet gained a clear understanding of the true meaning of "awakening!"

When your mind is clogged with the typical errands of day-to-day life, "awakening" seems like an entirely distant concept, a far-flung notion unrelated to us and removed from our lives and everything in it.

However, in reality, "awakening" is in fact a new type of lifestyle. Given your current lifestyle, have you ever considered that there are perhaps "new" possibilities for leading your life? Is there a "new" way of living that would allow us to break free of narrow limitations; allow us to step out of the drab lifestyle or drab job we used to have, to break free and make a change? This new lifestyle allows us to start anew with a fresh lease on life, to once again reflect on the value and meaning of our existence, and seek out the things of greatest value to us. It also allows us to once again "see" a new direction, and "see" a new life path. "Awakening" feels as though waking up with a heightened clarity. Through all the incidents we are now encountering, it is as though the current era is beckoning us to "wake up," to "gain clarity," so that we may re-examine our lives and realize what the most significant things are, what truly matters, the real meaning of everything we are doing. We must use our minds to rediscover our wisdom and power, so that even in an age of high risk we can handle affairs with competence, stay calm and collected, remain balanced, and be at peace and healthy; and even in the most dire of circumstances and the deepest of mires, or in any one of a range of predicaments, we can overcome the obstacles with class and elegance. We can also add more beautiful elements to life. When we are awake and see clearly, our life is different.

"Awakening" fills life with an array of possibilities. It allows us to "live our potential and more fully enjoy life's beauty!"

Problem 2: Mainstream awareness of truly innovative systems of awakening is still very limited.

While mainstream consciousness is still seeking out solutions to its various problems and symptoms, numerous innovations have emerged in a range of fields: innovative medicine, innovative class formats, innovative ways of living, innovative economic modes, innovative systems of awakening, and so on. How do people view such innovative systems and ways of thinking? Often, they wait on the sidelines and observe. Some even scoff at innovation. Asia's richest man, Li Ka-shing, once said: "Poor people refuse things in suspicion; rich people try to understand them in suspicion." This corresponds precisely to the mindset described in the book *Rich Dad, Poor Dad.* *234 A poor mindset leads a person to be suspicious, distrustful, and to refuse to believe others. Of course, those who have a rich mindset are still suspicious, but despite their suspicions are willing to learn about the new trend or innovation, to see the value in it, to give it a try, and to improve and update themselves. This not only benefits themselves but also helps society as a whole to move forward.

Mainstream consciousness still requires time to observe and understand objects of "form," not to mention objects that are formless. So, when an innovative form of awakening appears and the formless begins to merge with objects of form, it is understandable that people would find it difficult to comprehend, be suspicious and distrustful. After all, who wants to be used as a guinea pig for "experimenting" with unknown things? If the experiment succeeds, people will say "You have so much foresight, how did you know?" If it fails, though, they will take the chance to kick you while you are down, and say "I told you it wouldn't work. I told you to be careful but you didn't listen."

It is precisely because formless objects are difficult to comprehend that people do not dare to even try to comprehend. Plus, people like to hear gossip, to read about it, and rarely if ever actually verify the truth of it. Rumors spread and multiply, and become ever more exaggerated and sensational. Yet this is what people enjoy. Then there are those who at the drop of a hat label others as "scammers," as "weird," as a "Ponzi scheme", or as being too "commercialized." This muddies the waters and makes it difficult to tell truth from falsehood. New business models require innovation, and so will new societies in the future. Should innovation only be limited to these areas and not to the formless? In fact, the opposite is true, for the formless is the precise source of innovation. Or do we have to wait until overseas spiritual groups are already well along the path of innovation before we believe, and then proceed to follow in their footsteps, unable to walk a spiritual path that belongs to us, to Taiwan and ethnic Chinese people?

If we do not innovate, I do not know how we will progress, especially in the current age of innovation. If businesses do not innovate, they hit a dead end. If religions do not innovate, they flounder about in a pool of stagnant water. If society does not innovate, the smell of inertia permeates the air. If people lack the energy to innovate, lack the spirit of innovation, then does Taiwan really have a future? If we are confined to this island state of Taiwan, too afraid to even dream or believe in ourselves, too afraid to innovate or "revolutionize" our lives, then do we really have a future?

Spirituality and awakening must both move along the path of innovation. Just like the grandpa in the book *Fruits of Faith* (written by Takuji Ishikawa), whose efforts allowed people to "see" the apple, we can only "see" the spiritual fruits after a person has changed. This is an arduous yet heroic journey. But isn't it a little like the onerous journey toward innovation?

In every age there are pioneers who do things that make others shake their head, things others do not think possible. If the grandpa from the book had not persisted, how would he have been able to endure those seven or eight years of hardship? If today, eight years later, he still had not succeeded, I am certain he would persist until he had succeeded in creating a truly healthy apple. Innovation requires courage, persistence, and resolve, and requires others to join in and help.

It is through the process of being misunderstood, being the subject of rumors, and being scolded that we become more steadfast and persistent. After all, it is only through experiencing life's countless trials and tribulations that we become stronger and shine, like a radiant flower that has endured the freezing winds of winter.

Problem 3: Too quick to brand innovative spiritual exercises for awakening as a type of "cult."

As people tend to be on guard when it comes to unknown elements, and because society consists of all different types of people, there are those who, under the guise of "kindness," "spiritual growth," and "awakening," seek to fulfil their own personal desires, or engage in deceit or corruption. Dr. Zohar once wrote: "There are no evil people as such, but any of us might be capable of evil." This potential is buried deep in man's subconscious; it is the "potential" for the extreme loss of one's core and one's spiritual intelligence.

In the dialog of a movie I once saw dealing with exorcism, one of the characters states that in Italy alone there are over 800 anti-Christ organizations, and that these organizations are rapidly growing.

Of course, we cannot possibly verify whether there really are 800 cult-like organizations disseminating their teachings and opposing Christianity. What I would like to express here, however, is that the term "cult" has been severely misused. During Christian times, any group that did not believe in Christianity was branded a "cult." In the middle ages, the persecution of witches - chronicled in the book the Hammer of Witches - has left an indelible imprint on the collective conscious of humanity, and this abiding imprint is waiting to be understood and loved.

At the time, anyone who had the ability to heal, any kind of ability to foretell the future, and even those who had caused some perceived slight or been misunderstood, were labelled witches and sent to the gallows, where they met a brutal end. Schemers seized the chance to eliminate their "adversaries" in an attempt to fulfil their own ambitions. Who knows how many kind and innocent girls were put to death in that period? Till today, this tragedy has not been properly addressed.

If the term "cult" has connotations of being disreputable or self-interested, of having a dark ulterior motive hidden under a wholesome veil, then should unscrupulous businesses also be considered evil "cults?" Are hate-filled youths who slaughter their relatives and loved ones also possessed by a "cult-like" sense of evil? When society blithely labels spiritual groups it does not understand as "cults" simply because it cannot comprehend or understand the unknown, I believe this to be a little extreme.

The existence of evil individuals and groups does not justify the smearing of good businessmen or people suffering from mental illness or individuals and groups that simply want to do good in the world. Is this not akin to a modern day witch hunt, rooted in the evil notion that it's better to kill 100 innocent men then let a bad man walk away scot free?

Everyone makes mistakes and should be given the chance to start over. This is especially the case for so-called "cults" that have never cheated anyone, never hurt anyone, and only want to help others and help the broader society. All we can do is urge people to raise their spiritual intelligence so they may see with more clarity and give such groups a chance to prove themselves. If a spiritual group is the genuine article, it will stand the test of times.

Problem 4: Lack a comprehensive structure for exploring consciousness in a complete and multifaceted way.

Before explaining this problem, I must share with you the four levels of spiritual growth so that you have a better, more complete understanding of this process. In spirit science research, spiritual growth is separated into four main facets:

The four stages of spiritual growth (Figure 8)

① Personal growth
② Psychic training
③ Spiritual cultivation
④ Spirit workout

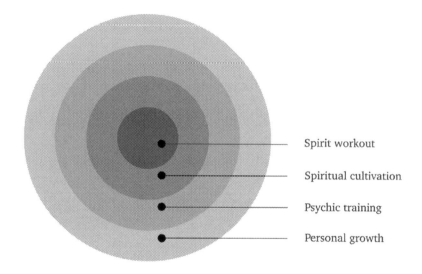

Spirit workout

Spiritual cultivation

Psychic training

Personal growth

① Personal Growth

The majority of personal growth courses fall into this category and such courses are now very popular. Course content ranges from self-development, motivation, informative lectures, to religious principles and basic introspection, and can even include some spiritual exercises. Why is this so popular? It's because it is straightforward and topical, and touches on subjects such as wealth, relationships, communication, health, and so on. It does not require a great amount of thinking, so it is not a great burden. By just listening and taking part, participants can gain a little insight and do not have to face their true selves, their core selves, nor do they have to face their shadows or core obstacles.

In this phase, participants already start to discuss "love," beginner level meditation, as well as concepts such as joy, comfort, letting go, and the practice of changing or reframing one's thoughts. This is a happy learning experience with no stress.

② Psychic Training

When you have been working at personal growth for a while and want to go deeper or are curious about other levels; or if you are interested in the deeper potential, wisdom, or essence of the human body, then it is time to progress to this level. This level involves training to acquire spiritual powers such as ESP, psychokinesis, out of body experiences, hypnotism, intuition, sorcery, a range of healing treatments, energy courses, deep-level Qigong, exploration of structures of consciousness and the subconscious, quieting the mind, mysticism, and so on. At this level, your spiritual depth is gradually enhanced and the dimension of consciousness is elevated, which allows you to embark on even deeper explorations of your consciousness, experience deeper levels of joy, slowly "meet" the unknown self, enter on a tranquil path in your subconscious, and more intimately understand your own strength. A renewed understanding of the power of the "mind" is gained here, and the wisdom of "love" manifests more clearly.

③ Spiritual cultivation

As one goes deeper and deeper, they will start to enter the spirit realm. This brings one to a deeper spiritual essence – Svabhava, the essence of all things. This realm is for people who wish to see and understand more deeply, to more thoroughly explore the wisdom of "binary" opposition, and to enter a deeper level of one's subconscious shadow. Through integration one can "see" their deeper selves and "see" the gifts that live below the surface forms. Such programs include more advanced courses for quieting the mind, yoga courses, more advanced courses for exploring consciousness and the essence of life, and sometimes even courses on enlightenment and awakening. In this stage, some of the courses will incorporate elements of religion, while others enter the realm of religion entirely, but not all courses in this stage involve religion. Conversely, some religions actually offer spirit training courses, yet the depth of the material and how deeply the subconscious shadow is integrated depends on the teachings of each particular religion. In reality, however, most religions virtually ignore the existence of the subconscious shadow, and only offer training in their own teachings. There are also a great number of people who, having joined many spiritual groups or taken many courses and seen the way things are run "behind the scenes," or who find the doctrines of an organization too restrictive, decide in this stage to engage in "self-cultivation."

Peak experiences, quiet meditation, "numinous" experiences (as Jung puts it), and mystical experiences are important experiences of consciousness in this stage. Many suddenly "enter" this sublime "peak experience" of consciousness without going through religion, and it changes their lives forever; or they begin to believe that a larger and greater power exists, and so enter the world of the spirit. They come to know their mission and are thus able to help themselves, help others, and help the world.

④ Spirit Workout

The spirit workout is an entire series of scientific courses for expanding one's consciousness that was developed based on the core element of life – Svabhava. The workout incorporates a comprehensive spectrogram for raising consciousness. The self is already "perfect", but if we do not integrate and transform our consciousness and deeper subconscious, we may fall into the trap of reciting empty concepts without really experiencing it ourselves. Through a mix of psychology, existentialism, Jungian psychology, and systems of ancient Oriental wisdom, this series of courses brings one to the core of all life and the perfect prototype of life, the Svabhava. This stage of learning encompasses all of the previous three stages and allows the learner to truly know themselves, and therefore move toward a state of true liberation.

Visually, the structure of these four stages could be likened to expanding concentric circles, for we cannot distinguish which one goes above or below the other, or which one is the best. They are simply the four stages one passes through in the process of "spiritual growth." If you do not have a complete understanding of spirituality or of your spirit, there is the risk of feeling self-satisfied or overly happy with oneself without actually having achieved real growth.

If a spiritual growth organization does not have a well-charted map of consciousness or genuine experience in spiritual cultivation, has not completely integrated the shadow of binary opposites, or has not had a tangible experience with Svabhava, it will not be able to guide people in the direction of holistic growth. Nor will it be able to provide or give rise to personal consciousness, or produce a deeper transformation. In fact, it may even become unmoored and get lost in the vast expanse of consciousness, leading to any number of unfortunate outcomes or misunderstandings, which would be a great pity.

Problem 5: Have not applied integrated wisdom to expand globally and make contact with other demographics (markets).

There are two aspects to discuss here: one is our mindset, and the other is the world. For many who go deeper and deeper into the spiritual mindset, a chasm emerges between them and the world, and they gradually separate and keep a distance from the world. Some even take a stance of opposition to the world, and ignore or justify this by pointing to how "low" other people's level of consciousness is, saying that such people do not even understand what realm they are in, or some other such justification. Thus, they cannot calmly enter the world and in fact come across as self-righteous. Of course, this prevents others from understanding the value of the message they are trying to disseminate.

Conversely, there are those who, in an attempt to approach the masses and spread their message to even more people, lose sight of their original mission and values, and desperately adjust their approach to accommodate others and allow more people to join. In the end, their message is so diluted that is has no substance and no pull. Then there are those who base their approach on market trends, and set out with the market in mind. Indeed, such people often attract many learners, but if there is no comprehensive blueprint or structure, this will also lead to a dilemma whereby they did successfully enter into the marketplace, but were unable to truly elevate the consciousness of the learners and guide them to see their real selves.

The Buddha taught us that "The realm of all living beings is the Dharmadhatu, and the Dharmadhatu is the realm of all living beings." If we leave the realm of all living beings, we cannot come to know Svabhava, nor can we know the ultimate realm of the Buddha nature. These two polarities of consciousness are like the *Yin* and the *Yang*. They need to be verified by going deep within and integrating the two polarities of the mind, which in turn gives rise to "integrated" wisdom. Having perfected their technique, when they enter among the people, they are able to truly raise the consciousness of others and generate real change. In addition, this world is the best cultivation ground for you to increase personal wisdom, to realize the inseparability of substance and function, which exist side-by-side and complement one another. This is the true path to enlightenment in this era.

Problem 6: Lack metrics for rigorously measuring and monitoring activity.

As the world is moving increasingly toward values of fairness and justice, and as consumer awareness continues to grow, we can no longer think only in terms of the "formless" (with too much emphasis on spirit one overlooks the logical). An optimal blend must be achieved between the formless and form objects. Moreover, organizations should operate on principles of justice, fairness, and openness, while their finances and administration must be transparent. They cannot operate like they did in the past, believing that left-brain thinking is irrelevant, or use the excuse that the spiritual realm transcends all else and fail to set a path for organizational development or measure the effectiveness of their participation in public welfare initiatives. In this era, if you want to develop in a long-term, sustainable way, we have to keep updating the way we think and allow even more professionals or outstanding groups to join us. We must apply whole-brain thinking, integrate logic and intuition, and find a method for increasing the efficacy of the group. We must apply our own wisdom to guide more people onto this path, encourage them to work together for the better good, operate more effectively, and play a part in the evolution of our world. We should also provide people with metrics that can be monitored and collectively monitor the efficacy of a group's development. This way, we can offer practical and useful suggestions for improvement and establish greater trust by implementing a transparent social monitoring mechanism. On the other hand, an organization should not move away from its inherent value and meaning. It must hold the human spirit as its ultimate guiding principle, as a yardstick with which to measure organizational development, and avoid falling victim to Problem No. 5, where the organization shakes from side to side, unable to find stable ground.

The mindset applied in "social enterprises" *235 these days will without doubt become more and more mainstream. It will improve corporate practices and make the world a better place. Moreover, it will prevent the increase of social costs by prompting companies to become more self-sufficient. When a surplus emerges, the additional funds can be used to bring even more benefit to society, thus creating a positive and virtuous cycle.

Problem 7: Failed to view things from the perspective of the average person.

Laozi wrote the following in the 49th chapter of the *Tao Te Ching*:

The sage has no invariable mind of his own; he makes the mind of the people his mind. He is good to those who are good, and he is also good to those who are not good. There is thus goodness. He trusts in those who are trustworthy, and he also trusts in those who are not trustworthy. There is thus trust. The sage in this world has an appearance of indecision, and keeps his mind in a state of indifference to all. People fix their eyes and ears on him, and he treats them as though his children.

Having no "invariable mind" is a type of realm, a realm in which the essence of the "Tao" has already been entered. In this state, things are simultaneously empty and have substance, and the sage's mind is the essence of Svabhava. He views the entire world from a realm that transcends the "Tao." Because he has no invariable mind of his own, he makes the mind of the people his mind when dealing with all things. He accommodates the people, provides them with all they need, and loves all beings and all things with an undiscriminating wisdom.

This kind of selfless, higher realm perceives common people as the essence of "Tao," as the Ultimate, as the Higher Self. This essence is encapsulated by the following logic: When meeting a kind person, I am kind to them. When meeting an unkind person, I am also kind to them. Only by doing this can we bring a satisfactory end to an interaction based on "kindness." Only by doing this can we turn an unkind person into a kind one. If I meet a person with integrity, I treat them with integrity. If I meet a person with no integrity, I also treat them with integrity. Only by doing this can we bring a satisfactory end to an interaction based on integrity. Only by doing this can we turn a person lacking integrity into someone with integrity. When a sage or wise king interacts with the people, he is self-possessed and humble. When governing the state's affairs or organizations, he applies wisdom. This kind of undiscriminating wisdom is akin to the innocence of a child, and it prompts the common person to focus on the example sages set through their actions, and not just their words. It is this kind of innocent and undiscriminating child-like spirit that sages apply to educating the people. They do not just teach, but educate; they do not just educate, but nurture character.

This is the level of magnanimity that spiritual organizations should show. After all, there are very few people that show such magnanimity. In the past when I treated unkind people with kindness, treated untrustworthy people with trust, I received a lot of criticism. Others asked me why I put my trust in and treated kindly people who "shouldn't be treated with kindness." So, we can see that if we don't have a deep understanding of love and don't understand the "Tao," our world view becomes myopic.

Furthermore, the way some organizations operate is to view their learners or disciples as "property." They do not let them learn with any other groups, nor do they let them leave the organization. Some groups even threaten, slander, and attack those who leave, labelling them as "traitors" and preventing other members from having contact with them.

Another example is when individuals or groups selfishly try to gain benefits only for themselves. This prevents even more people - who do not understand "awakening" or are afraid of getting burnt again - from building a mutual relationship based on trust. Instead, they are left outside in the rain, never again coming in contact with awakening. Isn't this a great shame?

If organizations can really put themselves in the shoes of the common person, they can create a win-win, "triple win", or "quadruple win" situation. They should do their best to avoid generating additional social problems, and in fact help to solve society's problems, reduce the risks that exist in society, enhance social cohesion, and join the forces for stability, thus helping to make society even better. Any surplus made should be optimally allocated so as to generate even more public good, both for society and the world.

Bring forth the higher wisdom of all people with the undiscriminating love of Svabhava; strive for the sustainable development of the planet, so as to collectively create more well-being for all humankind.

The seven main problems listed above can help us better understand "awakening" and the challenges that spiritual organizations face. This is not a matter of right or wrong, but about how we can truly address our weaknesses, collectively transcend our egos, and trigger a mass wave of awakening around the world.

In the last 14 years, I have met a number of "spiritual people," including both spiritual teachers and spiritual groups. In the past I remember stumbling along in fits and starts, a process of innovation but also exploration and development. I sincerely hope that all individuals or groups that wish to develop can collectively elevate themselves and grow. Yet this inevitably involves a period of painful and self-reflective reform. Below I have listed some of the mistakes I made along the path. After facing these mistakes, I then transcended them, and I list them here as a way of encouraging others.

Common fallacies of spiritual groups:

1. Many groups that classify themselves as "spiritual" are reluctant to adopt a business approach to their operation, thus limiting their perspectives and effectiveness (the fear of being labelled a "commercial" organization leaves them fettered.)

2. By rationalizing their interpretation, they try to reinforce the superiority of their system, or believe that the standard of the average person's awareness is insufficient, or view everything from a position of self-superiority. This approach backs them into a corner, as their message is only heeded by a small few, and they are thus unable to achieve their ideals.

3. Fail to use normal, mainstream language or terminology, and instead use weird and contradictory spiritual jargon, thereby creating a large psychological chasm between the organization and the rest of society, which finds it off-putting. This constrains

the organization from ever expanding and sharing their message with even more people.

4. Become attached to the spiritual system they created (or conceptualized) and so fall prey to the illusion that they are "already perfect," or are the Ultimate. As a consequence, they may become severely stuck in their ways (stubborn and unyielding), and be incapable of self-reflection, learning, and improvement.

5. Citing the need to be content with the present moment, lead an unbalanced life that is neither secular nor spiritual (content and happy to amuse themselves), but find it tough to face the trials and tribulations of reality.

6. Are too idealistic or propose ideas for innovation that are too extreme, and then lack follow-through or lack the steps or strategies to assess the effectiveness of these ideas. These ideas thus remain empty pipe dreams, hollow ideals that never get implemented.

7. Are too theoretical and subjective, and therefore treat concepts such as spirituality, empirical experiences, the different realms, and wisdom as mere slogans. They believe that all known things have been proven. They have too much knowledge, but too little practice. The resulting imbalance this causes in the mind is relatively trivial. The real tragedy is that it prevents large numbers of people from ever knowing their original nature (they miss the chance to know themselves). Such groups must realize that "knowledge" and "empirical experience" are two totally different things!

8. As the consciousness of the two binary opposites has not been completely integrated, the organization places too much emphasis on "doctrine," which leads it to brush over the dark aspects and only promote kindness, a situation which gets progressively worse with time. Consequently, the organization develops a "kind" and "positive" façade, while the opposing elements that it "doesn't want" (such as mistakes, divorce, failure, bad energy or contradictory tenets) all get brushed under the rug. Such groups must know that their so-called "kindness" actually helps nurture "evil." The binary opposition or discrepancy between spiritual and worldly, good and evil, grows larger by the day. They do not realize that their actions

only reinforce their stubbornness, creating a more acute division or chasm between them and the world.

9. Too absorbed in their own internal world, which can lead to the illusion that others are lower than oneself, and thus cause the individual or group to stay in their own spiritual ivory tower, unwilling to hear other viewpoints or collaborate with others.

10. They forget their initial aspiration, why they started learning about spirituality and truth, and why they wanted to see the reality of the world.

11. This heroic journey toward awakening is a long path. If you see some truths along the way, don't stop and don't be under the illusion that you have achieved awakening. You must know that even if you see the reality and gain the Ultimate Wisdom, its essence is unobtainable. To make the world a better place, restore it to its original order, help all living beings move away from pain and toward joy and rediscover their initial state of Svabhava, remember to keep meditating and practicing.

12. For some people, the longer they spend in spiritual circles, the more they suffer from "big head syndrome." If we do not experience for ourselves the divine realm of emptiness that transcends all things, the cup of knowledge we have accrued fills up and we are unwilling to let it go. When the cup is full, the space left for learning is far smaller than that of a beginner.

These are the lessons I have learned from reflecting on my experiences. Over the years, I have tirelessly shared these experiences with like-minded friends. I hope that those of us in this field can galvanize a movement toward spirituality, and that the public can assess spiritual organizations with increased clarity and insight. Only when we have the correct perspective can we see with clarity and have an experience rooted in truth. Spiritual groups, on the other hand, should move with the times and evolve their thinking. They should reflect on everything so that they can grow in maturity, take part in mutual collaboration, and jointly create a world of Great Unity.

Spiritual Growth - Different Types of Spirit Workout Courses

With the continual improvement of technology, our minds have become fragmented. While we enjoy the convenience brought by technology, we also pay a substantial price, much of which is not immediately evident. Thanks to the advanced state of telecommunications, the world has gotten smaller, as messages become ever faster to send. However, without even noticing it, this has caused our stress levels to increase. We sit for longer in front of our computer screens, which not only keeps us isolated, but also leaves our body and mind feeling tight and tense.

Stress has made us less and less healthy. And in order to survive in such a competitive society, we have moved farther and farther away from our own hearts.

Living in what the Buddhist texts call the sad-dharma-vipralopa, our minds really are ill. Many factors that cause impermanence weigh on us and make it difficult to breath. Although medicine and technology are highly advanced, more accidents occur now, and there are more unknown illnesses (and symptoms) than ever. And because of the constant stimuli of technology, we have even more material desires and so our wallet can never keep up! Many people are plagued by suffering from not getting what they want. The wealthy, for example, might suffer from not having any children, or feel lonely due to a lack of real romantic love. Someone with many career achievements might feel vexed if they cannot find an apprentice to take their place. We are beset by all kinds of unfulfilled desires and hopes, yet we don't know how to tell anyone! There is also the "suffering of being around people one despises" caused by an increase in competition, as well as the "suffering due to separation from loved ones" brought about by various unexpected elements of impermanence. We can never know when we will have to part with family or friends, to separate from everything we love. But it will one day happen. Due to a wide array of factors, our attachment and clinging, anxiety and fear, have grown more severe, and led to the "five aggregates of suffering." *236 The rate of impermanence has sped up and amplified our insecurities. This in turn strengthens our attachments and our tendency to cling, and so we become disappointed, and slide into a bottomless abyss of suffering and helplessness from which we are unable to get out. Various types of suffering and division have caused our minds to become ill, and it is getting worse and worse. Now our whole society has fallen ill and we see a multitude of strange phenomena occurring. These types of illnesses cannot necessarily be treated by modern medicine, so numerous spiritual growth courses and alternative medicine treatments have emerged to fill the gap. They provide us with a path to salvation (a path on which to rescue ourselves).

Nowadays there is such a dizzying array of spiritual courses that it is hard to decide which one to take, which one will lead you to the path of self-salvation. We may not be able to change the impermanent rhythm of this world, but we can always choose the path that will change our life. Yet what is this path? What spiritual course suits us the best?

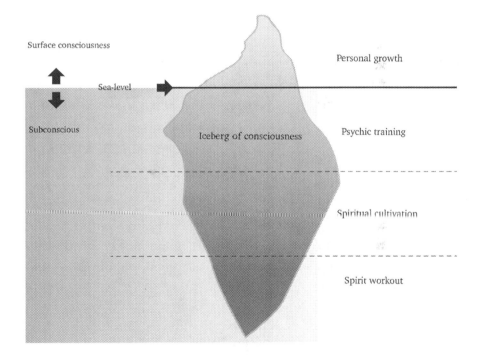

Most spiritual courses fall into the following categories:

1. Courses for unlocking one's potential (content includes self-growth, motivation, intuition, and developing one's ESP abilities.)
2. Courses for releasing emotions
3. Intellectual knowledge course
4. Courses on clairvoyance

5. Healing energy courses
6. Courses for people of high awareness
7. Courses on Zen meditation
8. Yoga and well-being courses
9. Courses that complement religious doctrines.
10. Courses that promote spirituality as a support tool.
11. Hybrid courses
12. Holistic elevation courses.

Each of these 12 courses has its own strengths, while the height, depth and breadth of each course differs. Moreover, the abilities of the instructors also vary based on the amount of spiritual training they have undertaken. So, how do we choose the best one for ourselves?

I once heard a story about something that happened in Tibet: There was once an elderly lady in her seventies whose partner had died 20 years earlier. On the same day 20 years later her son, too, passed away. The tragedy of an elderly lady burying her own son led her to suffer from the most common 21st century affliction – depression. Trapped in an abyss of pain and not knowing how to carry on, she sincerely knelt at the gates of the Jokhang Temple, Lhasa, and prayed that the Gods would illuminate the way forward. At that very moment, a flyer for yoga lessons blew toward her, and she instantly responded: "Bodhisattva, is this what you want to tell me? Is this a sign you have sent to show me the path forward?" She immediately dialed the number on the leaflet and made a hugely positive change to her life. Indeed, nothing in this universe is simply an accident. Synchronicities from the entire divine source field are constantly helping those who require it. Sometimes we really need to trust the message placed before us, as this message does not manifest for no reason. Trust your own intuition because this intuition comes from your heart, and the heart always guides us to the most suitable path. Sometimes, when planning to take some kind of course after receiving a message, we hear from others about the repercussions of taking such a course. At times like this, it is far better to try it for oneself than to listen to conjecture. Otherwise, we will never really know the truth – all we can do is say, "I heard…" and this is a real shame.

This is not just an observation but also my personal experience. Ten plus years ago, someone kept on recommending a certain spiritual course. At the time I didn't really feel I needed to take that particular course. I knew I wanted to take a course, but I wasn't ready yet and didn't know which course to take. Yet by "chance," I later received a flyer for a different course on consciousness and I knew right away that it was what I had been looking for. And I did indeed gain a lot from that course. So, trusting your own intuition is important, because He knows what it is that we need the most.

After going to spiritual courses in so many countries (sometimes as a student and sometimes as a teacher), I have found that, in some ways, Taiwanese are adorable, while in other ways they are somewhat close-minded. Taiwanese are generally not so open to new information, but like to indulge in gossip, bandying about rumors and speculation that swell into an ever-growing cloud of misinformation. This deprives us of the ability to judge objectively, as we are swept up in a vast cloud of false rumors and gossip. Nowadays, fewer and fewer people care about facts. Given their reluctance to verify the truth of a claim, and a mindset best portrayed by the motto "the less trouble the better," without the proper guidance, they become more and more "spiritually closed" and increasingly distrustful of the world.

How to Choose a Genuine "Spirit Workout" Course

In terms of both local and overseas courses, course fees can range greatly, from a few hundred NT dollars or a few thousand dollars, to tens of thousands of dollars, and even millions of dollars. Many Taiwanese people take spiritual courses for two or three hours in the evenings. On the one hand, they can grow and improve; while on the other hand, such courses are very cheap. For people in the beginning phase of spiritual growth, this is an excellent option.

After being on this path for many years, I have realized that it is a little like learning to cycle. At first, you invariably start from the entry-level bikes, which cost a few thousand NT. As you gain more and more experience, you begin to challenge yourself on longer, more "demanding" stretches of road. For this you need a more high-end, lighter, and professional bike; and you may even need different types of bikes for different types of terrain. Those who enter cycling marathons sometimes pay up to hundreds of thousands or even millions of NT dollars for a bicycle, which is already enough to buy a car, and yet there is a high demand for such bikes as different people have different needs.

So, regardless of which phase along the path you currently inhabit, let me first take this chance to congratulate you. After all, you have already taken the first step on the path of truly knowing yourself.

Over the past 24 years, as I myself have moved along this path, I have come to see that there really is no such thing as a free lunch. Being blessed and happy comes at a price. Sometimes you really do get exactly what you paid for. At the age of just 25, I already knew that I had to invest in myself in order to grow. I knew it would be quicker and more effective to learn from a qualified teacher than to try and figure things out by myself. After all, they have been in this field for so many years that sometimes all it takes is for them to make one comment, or share one trick (a technique, a method, or a skill) for us to improve in leaps and bounds. We can gain far more this way than we would just learning from a book. We may even have an actual experience and only then realize the true meaning of what is written in these books. I have also found that when someone is ready to invest in themselves, they are happier, more willing to learn, and more committed, and the "return" that they receive for it far outweighs their initial investment.

Education is not just some kind of cheap commodity. This is the case for regular education, not to mention spiritual education and training. Think of it as if we are travelling and exploring uncharted territories. In such a situation, what we really need is a qualified and experienced tour guide to lead us into the deeper parts of our subconscious, our unconscious, and even our supra-conscious minds. The more we integrate the disparate facets of ourselves, the greater our transformation will be. This is what happens when we use our professional skills to change the subconscious mind buried under the iceberg. For example, do you still remember the so-called "black forest" mentioned in Chapter 4? The deeper we encroach into the "black forest" of the subconscious mind (20% encroachment, 30%, 40%, 60%, and so on), the deeper one can sense the source of the binary, the division, and the shadow that has not yet been healed or integrated. When we courageously face these aspects of ourselves and apply the correct method to integrate them, we receive the best and the deepest healing, and are able to easily transcend our egos, enter into supra-consciousness, and "see" our real essence. This is how we "transform" our lives with ease. Nevertheless, having professional teachers is still an important requirement, as life-altering changes cannot be made in a short, three-day course.

The accompaniment of teachers strengthens learners' resolve. Nowadays, however, practically all spiritual courses operate on a "collect on delivery" method of payment, whereby a course is held and the learner pays for it, and then the two go their separate ways. I like this method, but I've discovered that it is not very feasible due to the need for "post-sale service." Can spiritual courses actually offer post-sale service? This level of customer care is very rare, especially when a foreign guest speaker delivers a lecture and then leaves right away, either heading to their next speaking engagement or to tend to the next item on their agenda. This phenomenon has spawned countless spiritual course "orphans," people who have taken spiritual courses but have no spiritual teachers, and so find comfort by hanging around with other such "orphans" or forming "spiritual groups" and attending courses together. When they are not "chasing the stars" (following after renowned spiritual teachers), they are rushing to the next spiritual course, terrified of not learning enough or of "regressing."

The path that leads from personal growth to the spirit workout is a long one. The content taught in the course must be slowly assimilated into the lives of the students, and this requires the ongoing assistance of teachers as well as a platform, and for both student and teacher to share their experiences integrating knowledge into their lives. This is why we have a support system consisting of senior and junior learners, and a mechanism for life-long learning and assistance provided by the Clean Life Foundation. So, when choosing courses, you have to know what it is you want to achieve!

On the other hand, there are also many people who have never been to any spiritual courses and who have entered the spiritual space almost "randomly" to learn and grow after becoming vexed by their current situation or life conditions. I do not believe that this is a random "coincidence," but is instead part of the Ultimate arrangement. Perhaps in a previous life you already experienced spiritual growth, so in this life you can progress directly to the Spirit Workout. I have seen many people, many families, that have totally transformed after coming in contact with spirituality, and who have found a world of new possibilities.

Another option is to use prayer. Regardless of your religion, and even if you have no religious beliefs, the universe will respond to your prayers. As for professional spiritual courses and teachers, finding the right one is not always easy. And Taiwanese people often have a bias in favor of Western things, as though the grass is always greener on the other side. Yet in many courses touted as "Western" or featuring Western teachers, the methods of raising of one's love or spiritual level are indeed off-putting. After taking so many courses, I have realized that the ones on a higher spiritual level, with more profound content and more undiscriminating love tend to have a broader inclusivity and tolerance and have a consistent public and private face (not the ones that show a loving façade but then treat different people with different standards, and criticize students behinds their backs.) Another interesting observation is what I call the "birds of a feather" phenomenon. A correlation tends to occur between the types of courses offered and the types of people that attend them. This is the universe's law of attraction. Yet because students tend to have a similar mentality, it creates blind spots, which prevent humanity from continuing to expand and progress.

Therefore, I personally recommend taking an all-round enhancement course with a spiritual element. Regular spiritual courses, on the other hand, might be too constraining, as they do not allow the individual to see the full picture. If the course has its foundations in spirit science, not only will it allow you to explore your inner self, but it will also keep you on the right path and prevent you from getting "lost." It is just like the remarks made by the famous Guru Padmasambhava: "Insight comes from top down; cultivation develops from bottom up." If the knowledge taught in the course is comprehensive, if it is the "Ultimate insight," then you will gain a clear view of the blueprint of consciousness. It is as though you have a well-delineated map and know exactly where you are going, and thus will not lose your way. Courses without Ultimate insight can be likened to trying to complete a puzzle without first seeing the finished picture. If the puzzle only contains a few dozen pieces, then it's not a big deal. But if it has thousands of pieces, it takes great effort to get every piece in the right place, and you will most certainly step into a thick patch of mist and get lost along the way. Spending more money is often worth it in the end, as courses that are not comprehensive often do more harm than good.

An "all-round elevation" of our spiritual level gives us insight into all of life's mysteries and the most personal, private issues in our own lives. Not only does it allow us to develop our potential, it can also continuously lift our level of compassion and wisdom, lead us to understand the reality of how the universe operates, and be calm and at peace no matter where we go or what we encounter. Moreover, it enables us to make important life decisions with added wisdom and continually accrue positive energy (blessings and wisdom) for ourselves, others, and the planet. This is analogous to accruing invisible assets in a "spiritual bank book." As we continuously collect this positive energy, we continuously attract positive people, events, and objects into our lives, and can work with them to benefit ourselves and others.

The benefits from lifting our spiritual level are too numerous to count. Suffice it to say that any course that provides a spirit workout and a comprehensive elevation of one's spiritual level is a blessing that comes from self-cultivation in a previous life. It is just like the Zen proverb stated by Daoyuan Shi in the *Record of the Transmission of the Lamp*: "The person who drinks it knows best whether the water is hot or cold." (In other words, one must personally experience something to know what it is like). Perhaps in the past you have had a bad experience with a spiritual course. This is unavoidable. Yet perhaps you consequently faced a karmic remnant from a past life and gleaned the life lesson you were supposed to learn this lifetime.

Either way, the chance to take such a course and improve oneself is a massive blessing. Living in such busy and tense times, how many of us can afford to simply let go of what we have and move closer to and understand our true selves? If you are currently in a state of what I refer to in this book as "suffering," do not hesitate. Quickly seek the help of a professional or a course. If, on the other hand, you have a clean bill of health and ample blessings in your life, there is even more reason to start cultivating oneself. The key in this situation is "prevention" – sowing the seeds of all-round health and well-being of the body, mind, and soul in the future. Is that not an even greater blessing? Like myself, you will find a joy-filled path of your own, and your life will become fuller and happier.

A Comparison of Satdharma Courses with Other Courses

Many spiritual courses feature similar activities and content, such as experiential learning activities, music, breathing, and meditation. The chart below displays the differences and unique characteristics of Satdharma courses compared to other courses (Activities / comparative purposes and primary differences / types of courses). There are no good or bad courses here, just ones that suit certain phases of spiritual growth or certain people.

If we only look at the surface level activity, we are unable to glimpse the internal substance. Yet as we gradually cultivate stillness and expand our awareness, we unlock our inner eye of wisdom – the all-knowing eye – and are able to see with ease. When this occurs, even when participating in activities or exercises that seem the same, the depth of such activities and their capacity to change one's consciousness, or their "after-effect," is entirely different.

The creed and objective of the Satdharma Institute is to utilize easy and systematic exercises – methods that seem simple yet contain great depth – and spiritual workouts based on spirit science to allow learners to feel at ease and become reacquainted with the Ultimate Svabhava essence, their innate wisdom, power, and love; and to use their power to make breakthroughs, overcome, and even create the lifestyle they truly wish to have in this lifetime.

Things that are mysterious possess a kind of hidden existence that cannot be expressed in words. Ancient religious texts, whether it be the Bible or Buddhist scriptures, all point to an Ultimate essence that is omnipresent. God is there in every single moment and in every single life, and yet He remains mysteriously hidden from sight. Indeed, if your inner eye of wisdom has not yet been unlocked, this inner Divine order will remain elusive and you will not be able to manifest Him externally in the form of love, power, and wisdom.

Due to the current social climate, we concern ourselves with items that are extremely superficial and place most of our attention on aspects that relate to our egos. Thus, we are unable to use our senses to feel, perceive, or become aware of this hidden wisdom. As a result, we miss many opportunities to prevent or diminish the amount of risk in our lives.

With the advent of a high-risk society, the Satdharma Institute hopes to serve as a stabilizing force. In a society plagued by unrest and widespread unease, we provide an environment that is safe, comfortable, professional, and full of love. We guide learners to look inward, discover the mysterious master key hidden inside, and unlock the divine font of power that resides within. Thus, you must learn how to use your mind to first untie the various fetters that keep you trapped. We then show you how to connect deeply to the energy of the Dharmadhatu using a spirit science method passed down for countless generations. During this process, divine healing can occur in an instant. All miracles occur when you first heal your mind and become one with the source of Dharmadhatu. One after another, all difficulties start to be transformed and overcome, and miracles begin to organically occur in every moment.

The Satdharma Institute hopes that everyone can have an all-powerful master key and find their inherent wisdom, power, courage, love, and healing power. Key in hand, we can untie the dead knots in our lives, solve all of our difficulties, and uncover all the mysteries we hope to explore. When we can reconstruct our minds, in the instant that we merge with the source of the Dharmadhatu, we manifest the power of heaven on Earth. So-called heaven or "Western Paradise" is most certainly not somewhere we only go after we die. In every single moment we should be living in paradise, for all living beings are blessed by the power of the source of Dharmadhatu. It's just that we do not have that all-powerful master key and so do not know how to once again unlock the vast power that lies within.

Once you use the all-powerful master key to gain this power and realize that you already live in paradise, and have a fulfilling life with a well-rounded body, mind, and soul, an incredibly deep love will rise within your heart and you will feel continuous joy and contentment. When you sense the perfection of the essence of wisdom, you no longer need to seek externally, because all of this already exists in the deep recesses of our hearts. We can then apply this power to perfect every aspect of our lives — first our own family, then other families, and then society as a whole. When this happens, we will jointly build a paradise made of love.

How to Truly See New Opportunities

In a Buddhist scripture known as the Vimalakirti Sutra, a monastic asked of the Buddha: "The worlds of the Buddhas are dignified and majestic. As you have become the Buddha, why is the Pure Land of this world so imperfect and filthy?"

The Buddha responded: "If a blind man does not see the radiance of the sun and the moon, is that the fault of the blind man or the sun and the moon?"

The monastic replied: Of course that's the blind man's fault!"

The Buddha used this as a teaching opportunity, explaining that: "The people of this world are just like that blind man. They do not see the radiant brilliance of the Saha world and certainly do not see the grand wisdom of the various Buddhas." *237

"Seeing" can be very simple; yet it can also be very profound! It can be superficial; yet it can also be the deeper reality. Viewing the world from a fixed perspective is "seeing;" yet viewing the world from different reference points is also "seeing." Peeking out at a small patch of sky is seeing; yet merging with the universe is also seeing! Viewing the world from the perspective of the ego is "seeing;" yet viewing the world from the Higher Self or the Essence is also "seeing!"

So, what is it that we are actually seeing?

"Seeing" can heal your body, mind, and soul, and allow you to become one with the Essence. Or, seeing can cause illness and countless problems. So, how do we "see" the Ultimate reality? What are the different effects of "seeing" in 3D and "seeing" with the omniscient eye? Is the world imperfect? Or is it that our vision of the world is imperfect, so we are unable to see the whole reality?

When walking along the path of spiritual healing, understanding oneself is an extremely important first step, and "seeing" is a great awakening. Simply by seeing, we can change the nature and state of the object being seen, because seeing injects light (consciousness) into the seen (all types of symptoms or shadows), and the darkness or the symptoms automatically disappear.

Often, when we encounter a situation that differs from what we expected, our first reaction is to try and change it. Yet if the situation does not progress as we had hoped, we suffer or struggle. We may even may blame ourselves and descend into a deep abyss from which we cannot get out. In such situations, all we need is the right method of viewing the situation (contemplation or a deeper observation) and the ability to restructure it. In reality, one of the primary goals for human spirituality is to be able to see deeply into every situation or object, and understand that every situation or object has its value, and consists of the same perfect essence as the higher self. This is true self-understanding. Therefore, if there is anything that is troubling you and that you want to try to "change," it means you do not yet have true self-understanding (in other words, do not simply try to change the external appearance or exterior. Instead, try to change it from the roots up, from the heart.)

True seeing is a deep and complete seeing.

True "seeing" is a state of being, a state in which you can view all things in the world with pure stillness. It is a deeper way of thinking based on a deeper and more complete view, which comes of stilling one's mind and allowing insights from one's intuition to rise up. It occurs when one is firmly rooted in stillness and can look within to see their various conditions, such as illnesses, symptoms, and problems, as well as the essence behind these conditions. If one's mind is sufficiently stable and at peace, then when they use this pristine state to view a situation, from its birth to its completion, it helps to expand the wisdom of their self-understanding. Some things do not need to be experienced to be understood. Before the Buddha became an ascetic, he lived in the royal palace and led a life of leisure. He had never thought of leaving home to explore life.

Sāriputra replied: Not so, Blessed One; it is the fault of those born blind, it is not the fault of the sun and the moon. Similarly Sāriputra, if beings cannot see the virtues of the Buddhakṣetra of the Tathāgata, the fault is in their ignorance; the fault is not the Tathāgata's.

One day, after seeing the way people pass through birth, aging, sickness, and death, he began to contemplate why all human beings experience such a cycle, and how they could escape this cycle and avoid all the pain and suffering. To seek answers to these questions, he left the comfort zone of his former life. And though he had been tutored by various teachers, he was still unable to find the Ultimate answers. Then, one day, as he sat under a Bodhi tree thinking and meditating, he "saw" the answer and became aware of reincarnation. This kind of "seeing" is a deeper and thus more comprehensive view of reality, and it allowed him to fully awaken.

Are we really "seeing?" Most of our mental patterns are simply reflex reactions, and the vast majority of thoughts only show us what we want to see. The regular kind of "seeing" is a self-oriented view of life that has not yet been integrated. When viewing the world with a binary outlook, we remain attached to the perspective of the ego and thus produce all kinds of value judgements. When we make such value judgments, we become more deeply constrained by this imperfect material world, which strengthens attachment and spawns even more value judgements. This, in turn, makes it difficult to identify a resolution and thus see the essence of all things.

From a young age we are conditioned by a wide array of factors. Growing up surrounded by our family, we develop a view of ourselves that is shaped by the real-life experiences of older family members and others, as well as various forms of interaction: poor communication, arguments, advice, and instances of persuasion (all of which leave an indelible imprint). Unfortunately, such imprints and perspectives stick with us for the rest of our lives (and even several lives). If we had a chance to inspect such imprints and perspectives, we would see that they are usually superficial and limiting. Society tells us that we should love our family and love our parents for who they are. Yet this can sometimes lead people to blindly honor the "conventions" of their family, to believe the dogmas and doctrines espoused by one's parents, and to respect and obey family legacies without applying any form of introspection or reflection. Even if the child is able to disobey, resist, or extract themselves from their family situation, they will still feel a great sense of fear or guilt. We are therefore heavily influenced by the myriad concepts imparted by our families, even if such concepts are negative or outdated.

To conform to society's expectations, gain public approval, or receive the support of our peers, we often have to concede and compromise, so that we, too, can become part of the group. And the various conditions required to "follow the masses" lead to mediocrity and uniformity. From a young age, we all have a plethora of different experiences: good experiences filled with success; bad experiences rife with failure. Due to the social tendency to view successful people as heroes, mistakes and failure can cause us to lose our momentum and feel embarrassed. Conversely, because of the negative label attached to failure, when we fail we feel isolated and without help, which has a large impact on our spirit. If "perfection" was demanded in one's early years, the impact of failure can be particularly severe. If our parents, siblings, or teachers, or bosses from our first few jobs, overemphasize the severity of mistakes, it has an extremely limiting effect on our ability to develop and grow, as we are reluctant to try anything new in the future.

If we are terrified of change or filled with fear at the thought of making a mistake, we will be unable to excel in the face of the unknown. This leads us to analyze everything in terms of advantages or disadvantages or pros and cons, and to naturally choose the safest possible path, thereby constraining the growth of our body, mind, and soul, and passing this same pattern on to posterity.

Our fear of failure gives rise to a separation of body and mind, and prevents us from being at peace. Fear always attracts fear, pushing us toward and then trapping us in negative energy. It begets cravenness, timidity, and an inability to shoulder responsibility, and greatly magnifies the reasons for failure. We become hesitant of attempting to change, reject all challenges, and are unwilling to take on the risk of making further mistakes or of once again failing.

This state corresponds precisely to the seven major modes of karma: arrogance (pride), addiction (laziness and a wide variety of addictive behaviors), prejudice (suspicion), hate (jealousy), violence (persecution), fear, and shame. These modes are very common in the world. A lot of thoughts and behaviors revolve around these seven major types of karmic modes and affect the karmic lessons we need to learn.

These factors disturb our peace of mind. They prevent us from realizing that the reason we are unable to truly "see" is that our vision is "imperfect." If we cannot truly see, then we are unable to know ourselves in every moment and every situation of our lives.

To resolve any situation, we have to address the root of the problem and "untie the roots." We must once again breathe light (consciousness) into the tree's roots and gradually attain a deep state of stillness through a process that involves peeling off, cleaning up, facing it, integration, and transcendence. Only by entering deeply into our own heart can we truly feel a sense of tranquility and stillness. When we practice our ability to "see" in this focused state of stillness, our hearts transcend layer upon layer of obstacles, and are reborn.

Limiting conditions such as our beliefs, behaviors, and attitudes can all be reversed and re-shaped as a result of our will. Our body, mind, and soul require our intuition (direct awareness) as well as nourishment in order to grow and develop. When we embark on the path of internal healing, we have unlimited potential to change, transform, and transcend. Most importantly, we possess a unique opportunity to integrate and heal the binary division of awareness in our minds. This transforms us into a completely different person; no longer someone who passively reacts to his or her environment, a mere appendage to the group.

To maintain the clarity of our consciousness requires awareness and perseverance, and the inspection of our myriad beliefs to ensure that we are no longer trapped by the limiting conditions that stifle our growth. This is an extremely trying feat. Yet if we succumb to these limiting conditions or shun them and refuse to face reality, then what we lose (in other words, our diminished capacity to really live our lives) will manifest in the form of physical symptoms. After all, physical symptoms do not lie!

Many people who are healing themselves or developing their spiritual healing powers get "stuck" between two separate worlds. One is the old world we need to let go of (the perspectives, concepts, habits and objects that no longer support our growth). The other is the new (intuitive) world that has the potential to transform us. We want our awareness to become limpid and bright, but in our hearts we feel a sense of unease and fear. After all, if our awareness is totally clear, it implies that we must take responsibility for everything in our lives: our health, career, family, and even our physical symptoms. As soon as we are willing to shoulder responsibility, we can no longer use "groupthink" as an excuse, and can no longer refuse to utilize the power of the spirit and thereby remain trapped in the conditioning of binary consciousness and external limiting conditions, cowering in fear and hesitancy forever.

The question of how to master both worlds is a spiritual growth issue. We must learn to calm our minds, learn how to "see" and where to look. This will allow us to have a brand new perspective and brand new insights in each moment.

The Power of Stillness — Utilize the "Unseen" Power to "See" Again

The key to health for your body, mind and soul in the new era: Meditation.

Meditation / through stillness gain calmness → calmness breeds wisdom → wisdom manifests all things.

In recent years, meditation, yoga, and breathing techniques have become popular in the West. The ancient culture of eastern spirituality, which dates back thousands of years, has been ascribed growing importance, and meditation is now a daily habit for many renowned leaders. Examples include former United States vice president, Al Gore, famous Hollywood actor and director, Clint Eastwood, international megastar Madonna, Nicole Kidman, and Richard Gere. Other well-known figures that had a daily meditation routine include the now deceased Founder of Panasonic, Konosuke Matsushita, and the former CEO of Apple, Steve Jobs. Meditation is also a widely-embraced "lifestyle exercise" for many Japanese office workers. Each day we should spend at least 20 minutes of alone time meditating. This ancient practice has also grown in popularity and gained prevalence in America's Silicon Valley, where the power of silence has brought technological change. Meditation can lead to a reduction of stress, a calming of the body and mind, and greater levels of concentration. It can inspire the power within us, enhance workplace efficiency, help us to think with clarity, and make the correct judgements and decisions.

The nerves in our brains are malleable and can be influenced by our experiences. We can also influence and adjust these nerves ourselves, through the practice of meditation. Our brains' response to certain events or incidents is a type of habit, an imprint that was etched into our brain from past experience. When we change a habit, we activate a new neural pathway and create a new response, and no longer repeat the old, fixed mental loop of the past.

In her book 'Mapping the Mind,' Rita Carter applies experiments to prove that "positive thoughts can retrain your mental habits. The brain is malleable and nerve connections can be changed. Positive thoughts can generate new mental loops... Those who practice meditation will rewire their thoughts and feelings, decrease right prefrontal cortex activity, reduce the appearance of negative emotions, enhance the resilience of the left prefrontal cortex, and lead to an increase in happiness." *238

Meditation can increase our ability to concentrate, and with high-level concentration we can better control our emotional responses and level of attention. When encountering problems, we recover and return to our regular lives more quickly. Our level of self-awareness also increases, as does our sensitivity to our bodies.

Chinese Confucianism also emphasizes the importance of spiritual practice to enhance concentration and still the mind. As noted in The Great Learning: "When you know where to stop, you have stability. When you have stability, you can be still. When you are still, you can be at ease. When you are at ease, you can deliberate. When you can deliberate, you can attain your aims."

Being still can help us activate our wisdom. Buddhism talks of the dual practice of 'Zhi' and 'Guan.' Here, *Zhi* refers to concentrated or focused practice: using some form of meditation technique to quiet the mental noise and gradually enter a state of "stability." *Guan* implies "seeing;" an open, relaxed attitude of just seeing that gradually allows the individual to gain direct access to wisdom. It is the same as the dual practice of "stability and wisdom" in Zen Buddhism. In the Zhaode Xinbian, Chao Jiong offers a similar concept: "When the water is still the image is bright; when one's mind is still wisdom arises.

Not only does meditation afford us a wonderful experience and positively influence our life and physical and mental health, it can also calm our noisy minds and bring us to a tranquil inner state. It allows us to taste stillness and a greater awareness. We are so used to all our feelings, emotions, and thoughts that we mistakenly think the sum of these parts is who we are. Yet with awareness we can witness at a higher level and give rise to internal wisdom. The primary purpose of meditation, however, is to reach the Ultimate state and truly awaken to our original nature, which is the same nature as that of the Buddha, or of God, and to realize that the Holy of Holies is in fact inside us.

We can find signs of meditation as a spiritual practice in almost every religious tradition for the past several thousand years. And today, more and more scientists are discovering the benefits of meditation, and have begun to "popularize" it. Meditation is no longer confined to the narrow space of religion; it has led many people to enjoy a positive, stable, and clear body, mind, and soul, and is even recognized as a spiritual practice that can assist in the sustainable development of life.

Scientists have found that meditation can change the long-term functional circuitry of the brain, boost one's sense of inner enrichment, and effectively raise one's overall happiness.

The "heart," or "consciousness," is an incredible entity that is filled with endless possibilities. These endless possibilities would regularly be extremely difficult to fathom, but now we can use meditation techniques to enter a super-conscious state with infinite possibilities. It is just like in the movie "Lucy," where the main character's brain is unlocked, which gives rise to limitless potential.

Through meditation, as our ability to observe internal changes and not be affected by them grows, we find that we are better able to "transcend" and not be easily affected by the various unpleasant issues or events in our lives, such as handling the stresses of life and work, irate or upset co-workers, unruly children, a less than ideal financial situation, or a relationship on the rocks. As a result, our sense of happiness grows by the day.

America's Wisconsin University carried out research on the "comfort state" of expert meditators and found that the "comfort state" helps practitioners still their minds and maintain a high state of awareness without the need to focus on any single object. It broadens their minds, so that they are neither excited nor drowsy but can instead openly observe all that occurs internally from a neutral vantage point, without trying to change, interpret, deny, or ignore any painful feelings. They simply observe. Researchers found that although the degree of pain itself does not reduce, when compared to the control group, long-term practitioners are less affected and disturbed by the pain.

Before the pain stimulus occurs, activity in parts of the brain that trigger anxiety – such as the insula and amygdala – is lower among experienced practitioners than novices, and after the pain stimulus is administered, experienced practitioners tend to recover far quicker.

A vast swath of research has discovered that positive thought meditation helps to alleviate symptoms of anxiety and depression and can even improve one's sleep. *239

In 2000, a clinical psychologist at England's Cambridge University, John Teasdale, and Dr. Zindel Segal from the University of Toronto conducted research on patients who had suffered at least three bouts of depression. After practicing positive thought meditation and cognitive behavioral therapy for six months, the chances of illness recurring within a year of the previous bout dropped by 40%. Segal also recently found that meditation is more effective than the placebo effect, and more effective than traditional maintenance treatments in preventing the recurrence of depression. *240

The purpose of ancient meditation techniques for exploring compassion and love is to cultivate an attitude of compassion and love toward others and to all things. The way to practice this is to become aware of what others need and desire, whether it be family members, friends, strangers, or enemies, and then to help them with an attitude of sincere compassion so that they may avoid the devastation brought about by their self-destructive behavior, and perhaps even be free of suffering. Meditation practitioners must be willing to embrace a selfless attitude and help people who are in a state of suffering. Through compassionate empathy, we must give rise to love by putting ourselves in the shoes of others. This is different to regular empathy, as regular empathy and sympathy is an attempt to understand someone else's feelings and does not always lead to compassion and love.

This exercise has already been verified as being helpful to medical and health staff, as well as teachers and any others who have to deal with people in painful predicaments on a daily basis (such as healers, counselors, volunteers, and so on). It allows such people to avoid extreme reactions of empathy which can in turn lead to emotional outbursts or depletion of one's energy.

Dr. Clifford Saron of UC Davis researched the way in which meditation can affect the molecules responsible for regulating the longevity of cells. This kind of molecule is an enzyme known as a telomere. Meditation can extend the DNA at each end of a chromosome (i.e. the telomere), ensuring the stability of the remaining cells upon cell division. Each time a cell divides, the telomere grows shorter. When the telomere cannot get any shorter, cell division ceases to occur and senescence ensues. Incredibly, the study found that when it came to long-time meditation practitioners, those with the least pressure had the most active telomeres. In other words, a regular meditation routine can reduce the process of cellular aging and the rate at which senescence occurs.*241 It is no wonder, then, that those who have a regular habit of meditation tend to look younger and younger over time.

It is for the above-mentioned reasons that we constantly teach meditation. To spread awareness of the benefits of meditation we have set up and actively promote meditation classes in areas around Taiwan. And this year we will be holding a number of three-day meditation retreats. We genuinely hope that, through meditation, the local population can achieve the goal of holistic health for the body, mind and soul by way of preventative and integrated medicine.

The Pineal Gland – the Gateway to Divinity

Since ancient times, numerous religions and age-old civilizations viewed the pineal gland as an organ imbued with spiritual significance; as the one and only path that connects humans with God.

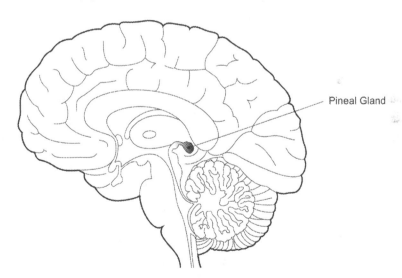

Pineal Gland

The pineal gland is a small, reddish-brown bean-like gland located in the geometric center of the brain where the two halves of the thalamus join. It has a hollow structure and is filled with watery fluid. It is oval-shaped with a length of around 5-8mm and a width of 3-5mm. It weighs around

120-200g. In terms of blood flow through the organs, it is second only to the liver. The pineal gland secretes melatonin. From birth to age six, such secretion is especially abundant, but then declines with age. Melatonin can inhibit the excitability of the sympathetic nervous system, lower one's blood pressure, slow one's heart rate, and reduce the burden on one's heart. It can also alleviate mental stress, enhance the quality of sleep, regulate one's biological clock, relieve the effects of jet lag, bolster the immune system, fight bacterial viruses, and prevent a number of illnesses, such as dementia, cancer, and so on.

The pineal gland is known as the Brow Chakra or the sixth chakra. As most people never utilize the pineal gland, it eventually withers and atrophies. Scientists have found that the structure and function of the pineal gland is similar to the eyes, and that it possesses retina cells identical to those found in human eyes. Thus, through methods such as meditation, we can stimulate activity in the pineal gland and can see light that is inaccessible to the naked eye without the need for neurotransmission. In the book "Taoism, Esoteric Buddhism, and Eastern Mysticism," *242 Master Nan Huai-Chin states the following: "When it [the pineal gland] is unlocked, even with our eyes closed we can see the outside world and faraway worlds with no obstruction." From this we can see that the brow chakra is the gateway that connects the material with the spiritual, the individual with the vast, expansive universe.

It is here that insight, intuition, innovation, and enhanced sensory perception are developed. The correct development and use of this gland is the key to unlocking all wisdom and power. The sacred power of the sixth chakra allows us to remain in a state of transcendence and clarity, and to avoid being disrupted by the illusion of duality. Therefore, it has been traditionally referred to as the "third eye" or the eye of wisdom. Unlocking the sixth chakra is transcending the "ego" of the planet and the "soul-self" of the astral body. It is a higher expression of awareness and the vortex for entering supra-consciousness. Thus, it is also referred to as the "Home of Divinity."

If you want to see your inner God, to know and integrate your true self, and understand your soul's mission in this lifetime, then you must unlock and activate your third eye, awaken the power of your sixth chakra. The core power of the third eye derives from the pineal gland, as this is the gateway that connects to the Divine. It can enhance your intuition, insight, your ability to objectively see things for what they are, and to achieve harmony and balance between reason and emotion. (Chapter 3 contains a detailed description of the sixth chakra, so we will only touch on it briefly here.)

Because the pineal gland is not protected by the blood-brain barrier (BBB), it accrues more and more mineral deposits, called "brain sand." And as this brain sand has similar optical and chemical properties to tooth enamel, if we take an X-ray or MRI scans, we see what appears to be a calcified object, like a bone. Neurologists use this tough white matter to look for signs of tumors in patients. In the scan results, if the white dots have moved to one side of the brain, it means the tumor has already changed the overall shape of the brain.

The more we know about the pineal gland, the more we realize how crucial it is to our health. Scientists have now discovered that the pineal gland converts tryptophan into serotonin, and then into melatonin. For every gram of pineal gland structure, up to 3140 micrograms of serotonin are secreted, which allows us to produce feelings of happiness and joy.

Because the pineal gland also accumulates fluoride deposits, the highest concentration of fluoride in the body is kept is stored here. Studies show that fluoride accretion influences and inhibits the production of melatonin and serotonin and thus can seriously affect one's health, causing conditions such as early maturity, as well as degenerative diseases such as multiple sclerosis, Tardive dyskinesia, and Parkinson's disease. Even epileptic fits are affected by the pineal gland.

When the pineal gland becomes severely calcified, it loses its functionality and causes conditions such as depression, anxiety, eating disorders, schizophrenia, and other psychological illnesses. *244

A Healthy Diet – The Key to Eliminating Calcification in the Body and the Pineal Gland

Drinking a large volume of healthy, life-supporting water *245 can help the liver and kidneys expel toxins. Try to consume seasonal produce and avoid processed foods. Cater your diet to the natural farming methods in each season. In addition, a special kind of meditation can also reduce the chances of calcification.

In *The Source Field Investigations: The Hidden Science and Lost*

Civilizations Behind the 2012 Prophecies, David Wilcock describes how an American doctor named Weston Prince found a compound known as Activator X or Vitamin K2 in traditional food. This is a key element of traditional food that keeps people healthy.

If you are a vegetarian, you can obtain Activator X from foods such as organic butter and nattokinase. In the book titled Nutrition and Physical Degeneration, Dr. Prince shows that Activator X consumption can help heal cavities, cause tooth enamel to grow back, and even clear up arteriosclerosis – one of the basic causes of heart disease and stroke. Suffice it to say that a healthy diet is beneficial to our health and the health of our pineal gland, and can prevent severe calcification. We can also activate the pineal gland through meditation to unlock the power of our body, mind, and soul, and maintain our youth and health. *247

Meditation really offers a multitude of benefits to our body, mind, and soul.

Last year, Prof. Dingyi Yang released a bestselling book entitled *The Science and Medicine of Meditation and a Journey of the Spirit: The Most Practical Guide to Transforming Your Body and Mind in the 21st Century*. In his book, he states: "The correct meditation practice allows one to expand their spirit to the remarkable infinite. The spirit cultivated from this practice has no barriers, nor is it inhibited by rigid rules. It represents the heart of a sage. This kind of spirit can lead humans to evolve and move towards wisdom, or so-called "Prajna," and elevate their spirit." *248

"The highest form of psychic ability is wisdom itself. Wisdom encompasses all things and can solve all problems. When we are at peace and living in a state of wisdom, we no longer feel the urge to discuss psychic matters or try to change our psychological state. Such phenomena are trivial when compared with the endless, unbounded nature of the spirit; a mere ripple in a tranquil ocean." *249

Meditation is the process of recognizing yourself and reclaiming your power. It is a tool to transport us along the path and not the destination.

"We do not actually gain anything new from meditation, as all we needed was already there waiting for us to discover it for ourselves. From this perspective, meditation is simply a process of cleaning away the surface layer mess that was obstructing the spirit. It is a technique for quieting the mind and enhancing one's attention, enabling our spirit to delve down under the turbulent surface layer and place its attention on something deeper." *250

At the Satdharma Institute, we use the term "meditating on Ultimate Truth" to include the oft-mentioned practice known as "meditation." This means observing everything while dwelling peacefully in the essence, in original enlightenment, the original self. Regular meditation is simply the foundation for this. It calms the mind and allows us to maintain a depth of concentration and tranquility. Only by doing this can we enter the ultimate realm and observe the entirety. These two elements – meditation and the ultimate realm – have a mutual karmic relationship. Another foundation for "meditating on Ultimate Truth" is incorporating the five basic elements of the universe: earth, water, fire, wind, and spirit; and resonating with the source field of Divinity, love and compassion. When our heart and consciousness have been entirely dissolved and integrated, the foundation of our stillness will be stable.

While meditating on the Ultimate Truth our heart is calm, which is why many people find that their thoughts are particularly active, and find it hard to still their minds. This is normal. We are used to thoughts racing around our minds, like a restless monkey that cannot sit still. Yet we usually lack the awareness to notice it. Because of this many people give up, which is a real pity, as this is a process of change and awakening.

Our subconscious mind contains countless seeds. Each day, we produce around 60,000 thoughts. Thought waves are a type of energy, so as we incessantly shift our thoughts and attention our energy is being pulled this way and that, and constantly being depleted. Through meditation, we focus our attention internally. In other words, we bring our attention back on to ourselves, and nurture ourselves. Thus, meditation is another tangible way of showing ourselves love.

Meditation helps modulate our brain waves, taking us from beta waves associated with stressful work to more relaxed alpha waves and the theta waves of sleep states, as well as the delta waves achieved during deeper rest. When the brain enters the theta state, its neurotransmitters begin to secrete endorphins, dopamine, and serotonin. Endorphins provide rapid relief for anxiety; dopamine brings momentum and energy, and serotonin gives you an unprecedented sense of satisfaction, joy, and happiness. This is the high-quality state that can be reached through meditation. If we master

Ultimate Truth meditation so that we are brimming with happiness and blessings, then based on the law of attraction, we begin to attract people, events, and objects that bring more happiness. If our sense of internal happiness or contentment is insufficient, everything we attract to ourselves will test us, as if to show us the parts of ourselves that are still not whole. For people who have not dealt with issues on the level of consciousness, once they reach a certain stage in their meditation practice, the seeds they sowed in previous lives appear and they feel the urge to wail or scream during Ultimate Truth meditation, as though releasing all their pent up stress. If this situation occurs, just go with it and let it happen!

When your capacity to achieve stillness gets deeper and deeper and becomes increasingly stable, your ability to observe and your intuition naturally grow. Moreover, your internal wisdom and compassion continually expand until you "revert" to your original Svabhava state. This state is the Ultimate Truth. When you are able to observe everything from the perspective of your essence, your true, original nature and your innate self, this, too, is the Ultimate Truth.

Deep and Comprehensive Insight Born of Neutral Tranquility

Are you awake? Or are you asleep?

Our "perspective" is the angle from which we view an issue. It affects the lens we apply to look at a problem – our level of nuance, depth, breadth, and how comprehensively we see it. On the other hand, our view might be entirely blurry.

Deep and comprehensive insight is a wonderful thing. The unlocking of the brow chakra gives rise to a deep awareness, and when our mind is in a state of tranquility and we have dissolved or transformed our emotional or mental energy blocks, our awareness naturally grows and it becomes increasingly easier for us to see the essence of all things.

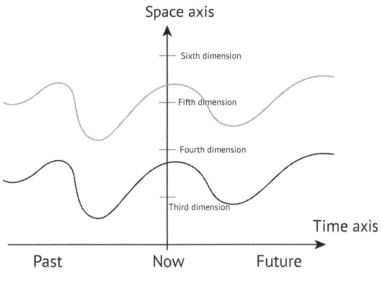

Deep and comprehensive insight

Life is actually very simple. It is us who complicated it because of our duality of consciousness. The universe is made up of time and space. And in each moment, the combination of time and space merge to create our outward appearance in that instant. If we treat the present moment as the focal point of our lives, the ripples produced by our consciousness will continuously extend outward.

With the horizontal axis representing time, it appears to only include the period since our birth until the present. In actual fact, the time axis encompasses an extremely long period of time. When you continuously expand your consciousness horizontally, you will be able to easily see your previous lives; and because consciousness expands very quickly, as long as you are willing, you will see your previous lives and meet the previous incarnations of yourself. The vertical axis (space axis) symbolizes our nine major chakras, which correspond to the seven bodies:

The first level is the physical body.
The second level is the etheric body.
The third level is the mental body.
The fourth level is the astral body.
The fifth level corresponds to the fifth body, which is the cosmic body,

or universal consciousness. It is what transpersonal psychology refers to as the "higher self." "Universal consciousness" is the state of consciousness and tranquility that extends from the first four bodies to the universe.

The sixth body is an extra-cosmic body that corresponds to the brow chakra. This body is reached when our consciousness expands outside the boundaries of the universe. It is characterized by tranquility and neutrality. When we continue to move up horizontally and expand outward, we arrive at the omnipresent sea of infinite light (the infinite sea of protons). This is the most remote place in the three worlds spoken of by the Buddha. If we continue to expand upward we come to Svabhava, which is the seventh body.

In the changes to which the space and time axes correspond, the past, present, and future unfold simultaneously. So, if your brow chakra has been unlocked and your awareness is tranquil and lucid, you will simultaneously see the state of the first three bodies of a person, along with his past and many other layers and aspects. You will even see the brightness of his Divinity. Yet if you only look from the angle of the first three bodies, you will not grasp the deep mysteries held beyond the fourth level.

Many of us think that our current limitations derive from the imprint left in previous lives. However, consciousness possesses huge potential. Unlocking "wisdom" is the result of "deep looking" at one's various layers and finding commonality, relevance, meaning, and integrity. When deep looking, as consciousness passes through the singularity, it transcends time and space and you see something wondrous and incomprehensible – all that cannot be seen with the naked eye.

So, when we understand ourselves from the prism of the seven quadrants of life, as well as the time axis and the seven bodies, we begin to view ourselves differently in the present moment. When you want to look deeply at the wonder contained in a life lesson or a chakra, all you have to do is place your attention on the corresponding body or chakra. This was elaborated on in Chapter 3.

After the sixth chakra, leading to the gateway of Divinity, has been opened, the innate psychic abilities of our third eye are unlocked. Everyone's internal view differs and we each have our own way of "seeing." Some use their noses to "see," while others use their ears; still others use their feelings to "see." Thus, visual learners will achieve wisdom through pictures, images, and visual symbols. Auditory learners receive internal messages through sounds. Others perceive the world through smell or taste; while others still come to know themselves or the entire world through touch or intuition.

The wondrous key used for deep looking is located on your person, and allows you to see a different version of yourself. When we merge the time and space axes, we see from a more holistic, deeper perspective – we gain a comprehensive insight. When learning about or practicing spiritual growth, many people emphasize horizontal development and overlook vertical development. In terms of horizontal development, once we penetrate time and space we unlock the divine eye, as well as psychic knowledge of past lives, and intuition. Thus, we are able to see our past lives. Yet this does not elevate our spiritual level, nor does it heal our root-level problems, symptoms, or illnesses. Real improvement comes from "simultaneously" developing our horizontal time axis and our vertical consciousness-space axis. This allows our awareness to observe things from different states of consciousness, which evokes different feelings so that we are no longer constrained to "seeing" from the smaller self of the first three bodies.

When our behavior is produced by our thoughts, we act based on our interpretation of the world, and not the true state of the world. In the three dimensional realm, we are constrained by the dualistic mode of thinking and its implicit attachments, subconscious imprints, and values. In this situation, a perspective becomes a kind of "framework." Deep looking and comprehensive looking changes the vantage point from which we view things, and therefore imbues us with unprecedented levels of spiritual intelligence and wisdom.

Genuine "seeing" essentially involves changing the position from which you view things and using "expansion of consciousness" and meditation techniques to escape the bounds of the first three levels. It implies viewing things from a different level, and thus changing the way you see them. The height and depth generated from this shift naturally gives you a fresh perspective. It is just like something I shared many years ago: when viewing the world from the first floor, the 10th floor, and the 100th, the things being observed on each floor have their own intelligence, source, commonality, relevance, meaning, and integrity. They will all be observed clearly by you, and whether viewed up close or from afar, they are wondrous.

In the first three levels outlined above, we are affected by a range of self-illusions which block our growth, such as self-approval, defensiveness, and the shadow; while we are also affected by an array of emotions such as fear, worry, and shame. Many people think that their physical body, emotions, and thoughts are who they really are. If we do not change the position from which we view things, we will be controlled by these feelings and will never be able to see the relevance, integrity and meaning of our problems or symptoms. When you start to see the meaning behind these things, to see the gift that lies beyond the surface, your life will begin to transform. We have to experience viewing the world from a higher place, experience changing the position from which we view things. Only then can you truly master deep looking and comprehensive looking, and understand that every symptom, illness, or problem is only there push us and make us more whole. You will thus start to treasure, accept, transform, and transcend yourself.

From what position do you view things?

Is it from a self-oriented perspective? Can you expand your perspective farther?

Can you attempt to add the time axis?

Can you observe things from different levels of consciousness?

Our viewpoint is actually just a product of our attachments and habits. As long as you are willing to change the way you view things, your perspective will naturally change. We are used to viewing things from a fixed point of view. We are used to interpreting matters with our mind and not comprehending them with our spirit. Thus, we are unable to see the commonality, relevance, integrity, and meaning of these matters. The scary part is not the attachment itself. What's scary is when you do not quickly become aware of this attachment. When you decide to change the position from which you view things and no longer stubbornly cling to your personal point of view, you are already starting to heal and to integrate the various aspects of yourself, and your "future" is beginning to change.

Do you believe that you can see the future?

Do you believe that you can see the universe?

If you trust in yourself, you will in fact see! When you are willing to shift the position from which you view things, your view of life changes, and, at any given moment, nervousness, fear, anxiety, and rigid opinions dissolve as a result. The energy field surrounding you will also become more lucid, which means you are healing. When your mind changes, an immediate shift occurs in your perspective, state of consciousness, and energy field. You are no longer looking at problems or symptoms from a three-dimensional state, but instead see them from a multi-faceted perspective, which includes viewing things from the time axis and the consciousness of the various aforementioned levels. This, in turn, allows you to view your own state, your habitual patterns, and your framework, and then identify the core of the problem and transform it.

Three-dimensional love involves experiencing and receiving; it is a balancing act in a reciprocal relationship. So, when viewing oneself from a three-dimensional perspective, there is a lot of criticism, guilt, lack of forgiveness, dislike of oneself or another, or feelings that we or another are not good enough. When observing ourselves from a higher level of consciousness, however, we find that we have been shackled by toxic beliefs; "ripped apart" and knocked off balance by divisive, dualistic consciousness. We are therefore unable to give full play to the potential of our spirit. "Seeing" helps to unify and merge our dualistic consciousness, and unlock the love and wisdom and the incredible spiritual healing power that already resided in the depths of our hearts.

When you continually expand your consciousness from the astral body, the solar system, the Milky Way, and the universe until you see the reality of life in its wholeness; here, you will witness true love. From that day onwards, you will love your internal self, the self that is the universe. This is because the self at the fourth, fifth, sixth, and seventh level of consciousness is entirely different to the self you are familiar with in everyday life.

When you view your symptoms from this higher level of consciousness, you will clearly comprehend why it is you are having these experiences; why you are undergoing these life lessons. You will start to support yourself, keep yourself company, and love yourself. Through this love, you have already gained healing and completion. Yet this is a continuous process of exploring oneself. While diligently pursuing this process, we come to discover the treasure trove of wisdom and potential that was originally hiding in our minds.

In my many years of observation, the higher the overall life energy of a person, the easier it is for them to change the position from which they view things, and the greater the power of their healing.

The more flexible one's thinking is, the easier it is for them to reframe their thoughts, and thus the easier it becomes for them to train themselves to try new things. If you are at one with the higher consciousness inside you, then when you encounter any manner of setback or frustration, you will be able to view it from various perspectives and gain more wisdom, and thus view the mistake or failure as a road sign that helps to guide you and adjust your direction. Thus, mistakes and failures not only serve to strengthen one's life force, but also act as an important and valuable life guide.

As your ability for deep and comprehensive looking grows stronger, you become more at one internally, and more able to help yourself. You must first become your own instructor. When you are very used to serving as your own instructor, you will easily become an instructor that can guide others. It all starts from first helping oneself.

True "healing" is not an external but an internal process. In the distorted "conventional" view, however, we are always seeking wisdom and healing from a so-called "master" or successful healer, and we forget that the wisdom these healers possess also exists in our very own minds. When you maintain your focus on the Ultimate Truth, continue to make inner progress, and realize the intense momentum that comes from the treasure hidden in your mind, you will begin to focus more on the true contentment inside you, feel as though life has started to have meaning, and find that contributing to the greater good is meaningful beyond imagination. During this process of internal seeking, the mind becomes liberated and one's horizons expand. We come to understand that unlocking wisdom and true success does not involve having more money or success than others. On the contrary, the meaning of wisdom lies is whether we are able to transcend ourselves, mend the divisions in our mind and consciousness, and integrate the duality of our thoughts.

Effective and aware development of healing power and wisdom provides a form of internal strength. It can give you an infinite amount of drive and determination, and help you to realize your ambition of achieving perfect wisdom in this lifetime. In *Zero Limits: The Secret Hawaiian System for Wealth, Health, Peace, and More*, the author explains that: "When you are willing to take responsibility for everything that is in your life, including your thoughts, language, actions, and everything that happens in your life, you have already begun to change your life." It is only in this phase that you can become the person you most want to be and lead the life you most want to lead. "Integrating oneself" is a process of healing oneself. In the teaching material entitled "Transcending the Self (Part 3)," which we developed for the Satdharma Institute, I wrote:

Spiritual healing gives rise to a power that can be characterized as complete confidence. It allows your wisdom to flow forth, bestows clarity of thought that allows you to see the deeper meaning of your symptoms in great detail; and, because of the subsequent feeling of love, enables you to overcome dualism and become One. Complete healing is a result of the expansion and maturity of consciousness. It frees us from a materialistic (physical) existence so that we can achieve true fulfillment (wholeness) and oneness (fully healed).

The definition of "healing" is no longer merely the healing of physical ailments. "Healing" is a combination of physical healing, self-healing, education, and edification. It is an acceptance of duality that causes one's symptoms (here, the term "symptoms" does not only refer to medical symptoms, but to the various forms of discomfort or suffering in one's life) to be transformed, leading to oneness. Thus, it is a method for restoring one's body, mind, and spirit to a state of balance and fulfillment. In the book *The Healing Power of Illness: the Meaning of Symptoms and How to Interpret Them*, the author states: "The reason we get ill is because we lack oneness." And "sickness" can refer to any type of symptoms in one's life. So, we could rephrase the above sentence to say: "All symptoms that appear in our lives derive from a lack of oneness." Complete healing is a state in which duality is transcended. In the universe, there is only one force that transcends duality, and that is "love." Love is the impetus for integration, and not to duality or division. Love possesses the power to transform and elevate. After all, "It is through loving evil that redemption occurs."

"Healing" is not simply the curing of disease, but is something deeper and broader in scope. It is an all-round "self-healing" that spreads outward to the healing of all things and leads to the overall elevation of life. From here, our perspective expands and we gain a brand new understanding of our own vast and remarkable internal healing power.

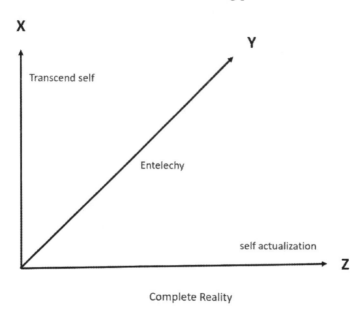

Complete Reality

When observing every object that exists and every event that occurs, we should not be so quick to either approve of it or try to change it. We must learn to view things in an entirely "neutral" and "peaceful" light, to contemplate the illusory façade of all forms and shapes. This is the perfect state that Dajian Huineng referred to when he said "Think of neither good nor evil." Even a slight thought of good or evil (good or bad) can pull our spirit into a chaotic tug-of-war struggle and exacerbate situations of "opposition," from which we might find it hard to escape. Every "view," every value judgement, is our interpretation of the world, an internal projection we cast onto the world. Dualistic thoughts of good or evil, good or bad, right or wrong lead only to "attachment," which in turn gives rise to suffering. Attachment generates more opposition, and opposition generates more division and unease!

So, as long as we stubbornly cling to this kind of attachment, we will continually remain in a state of division, incompleteness, or sickness, unable to escape from all the symptoms. Thus, if we do not start to change internally, we will always be craving a brighter future or perpetually trying to change the world, until eventually we become exhausted or feel thoroughly disillusioned or helpless. In this situation, those whose thoughts are more extreme might start to find fault in others or in the world itself. They do not realize that we are like the blind: If our vision is impaired, we are unable to see the brilliance of the moon. It is only by seeing and knowing ourselves in every single object and event that we can have true tranquility.

"Tranquillity" is the quality of directly connecting and becoming one with internal Divinity. It allows us to find a balance in the constantly interlocking and clashing duality, and to even become One; and from this place of balance, to observe completely the dual nature of opposition.

A neutral, tranquil state allows us to observe phenomena with a mature attitude that is free of judgement. It does not lead to emotional responses, is neither positive nor negative, and does not seek self-approval from any aspect of duality. We are used to imposing value judgements on all the things that happen to us in our everyday lives, and this gives rise to criticism, clashes, division, and imbalance. Yet when we begin to practice spiritual healing and meditate on Ultimate Truth every day, we turn our attention inward and become one with Divinity, which helps to develop the quality of our love, and leaves us deeply interested in elevating our own consciousness. And because of this love we make an oath and build up enough courage to explore our own internal conflicts.

Most people do not like to get embroiled in conflicts. They believe they can get all they want by repressing their desires or avoiding conflict. Real healers, however, understand that conflict is a product of duality and division, and is also our essence. When we begin to expand our Divine love, we are no longer scared and consciously start to face and accept the binary opposition in our minds. Only by "seeing" the opposition and the conflicts can you become One. By being brave enough to face it and to integrate the opposition that exists in our heart, we see everything from a view that has already transcended opposition. This also gives us the courage to face external conflicts and opposition, which brings this external opposition into alignment, causing it to become One. This is the true path of healing.

Real "seeing" inherently brings with it the remarkable and Divine "healing."

The Compassion, Wisdom, Strength, and Beauty of Divinity; the Divine Wonder of Prayer

...and knew now what prayer really is: to return from the solitude of individuation into the consciousness of unity with all that is, to kneel down as one that passes away, and to rise up as one imperishable. Earth, heaven, and sea resounded as in one vast world-encircling harmony. It was as if the chorus of all the great who had ever lived were about me.

Malwida von Meysenbug *251

I am sure that many people have had experience with prayer throughout their lives. Of course, there are many others who are unfamiliar with prayer, and even have a stereotypical impression of prayer, believing that it's just something Christians do before eating or going to sleep.

In the ancient wisdom passed down by peoples living in the Himalayas, prayer is the key to entering the "sacred realm" and having a glorious experience involving ultra-consciousness. Prayer and meditation have a similar function and in fact are complementary. Correct prayer has five transcendent effects, as follows:

① Effects:

    a. Takes one's spirit from external awareness and brings it inside, focusing one's heart and consciousness on the internal experience.

    b. Allows body and mind to enter the sacred realm through stillness.

    c. Gives one the feeling of being one with the eternal splendor of the Divine and of love.

② Offers a mystical experience: Allows us to connect with a spiritual state we have never connected with before.

③ Systematically enter the domain of ultra-consciousness: Systemically elevate the spirit to the domain of God.

④ Elicit deep insights: the insights produced after elevating one's clarity of consciousness are deeper and more essential than all extant knowledge. It is a direct, first-hand experience.

⑤ Application and practice: The amazing energy one gains from mystical experiences, as though being "reborn," flows over into one's life and allows even more people to wake up, so that the world naturally becomes one.

In the wondrous manuscript that is life, prayer is the realm or effect produced by the power of Svabhava. Svabhava is the source and origin of all things in life; it is the wellspring of all power. With Svabhava, everything is already enough, already complete, and nothing external is required. The power of Svabhava extends through prayer into the material world. I'm sure everyone has heard the story of the ancient sorcerer who prayed for rain. Suffering from a water shortage, the people begged the sorcerer for help, and he began to perform rituals praying for rain. Three days later, the rain came pouring down.

Someone asked the sorcerer how he did it. His reply: "I prayed to the rain." This is a critical point: He didn't "pray for rain." Instead, he "prayed to the rain." From a place of abundance, he used his body, mind, and spirit in focused meditation. Through the power of the spirit in "active imagination," the power of Svabhava flows through and manifests in real life.

Prayer can be divided into "essence" and "function;" its essence is two sides of the same coin, like two sides of the same hand. Though the two sides differ, they are both essentially the hand.

By practicing emptiness and being entirely focused, or in Buddhist terminology "anenjya-samskara" and "anabhoga," the essence of prayer allows you to have a mystical experience in a state of "wuwei" (inaction) and produce a thorough connection with Divinity and the Buddha-nature.

It is just like in the book The Varieties of Religious Experience, wherein the author William James talks of one of the highest experiences Mother Teresa had, a mystical experiences that arose due to oneness prayer:

"In oneness prayer, the soul entirely awakened to all things related to God. Yet worldly things and things related to the self were stagnant. In the short period in which oneness persisted, she appeared to have lost all sense of feeling, and even if she wanted to, she couldn't think of anything...... In short, she lived within God. *252

Moreover, "During prayer one day, God in an instant made me sense how all things in the universe exist within Him and how He views all things. I did not perceive these objects in their appropriate form. Instead, in my eyes they were extremely distinct and left behind a lucid impression. This is one of the special graces that the Lord bestowed upon me......this scene is so fine and nuanced, and not something that can be grasped by reason." *253

Canadian psychiatrist R.M. Bucke uses the concept of "Cosmic Consciousness" to describe the remarkable nature of this phenomenon: "The primary characteristic of Cosmic Consciousness is, as the name implies, a consciousness of the cosmos, that is, of the life and order of the universe. Along with the consciousness of the cosmos there occurs an intellectual enlightenment or illumination which alone would place the individual on a new plane of existence - would make him almost a member of a new species. To this is added a state of moral exaltation, an indescribable feeling of elevation, elation, and joyousness, and a quickening of the moral sense, which is fully as striking and more important both to the individual and to the race than is the enhanced intellectual power. With these come what may be called a sense of immortality, a consciousness of eternal life, not a conviction that he shall have this, but the consciousness that he has it already." *254

After deepening his awareness of the state of Samadhi, he experienced "the ability to directly see the truth that his instincts or rationing mind were unaware of." He states:

"That the mind itself has a higher state of existence, beyond reason, a superconscious state, and that when the mind gets to that higher state, then this knowledge beyond reasoning comes...... All the different steps in yoga are intended to bring us scientifically to the superconscious state or Samadhi.... Just as unconscious work is beneath consciousness, so there is another work which is above consciousness, and which, also, is not accompanied with the feeling of egoism.... There is no feeling of I, and yet the mind works, desireless, free from restlessness, objectless, bodiless. Then the Truth shines in its full effulgence, and we know ourselves- for Samadhi lies potential in us all- for what we truly are, free, immortal, omnipotent, loosed from the finite, and its contrasts of good and evil altogether, and identical with the Atman or Universal Soul." *255

I myself also had many mystical experiences in 2007 at the thousand-year-old holy site of Gangotri, India. What I found most remarkable was one time, during a deep stillness, where I gained direct insight into the darkness of Avidyā that remained internally. If I could quantify it, I would say it was approximately 0.3% of my entire consciousness. It goes without saying that I directly moved into that final and deepest part of Avidyā.

This final bit of Avidyā was also in fact the darkest bit. And as darkness breeds darkness, it seemed as though my entire consciousness had descended into a boundless, infernal field of consciousness, and all of my negative emotions and thoughts dramatically erupted like a volcano, with the fire of darkness everywhere. Surprisingly, this fire of darkness rose up from the deepest recesses of Avidyā, of ignorance. During this whole terrifying incident, Svabhava is always present in the background, as though observing self-consciousness being burned up from the darkest recesses. Yet I knew that after experiencing this, the seed of dark "karma" would naturally have been plucked out; and in doing so, all the gifts that come with these deep insights would merge as one with this darkness, and the karma would return completely to a state of neutral tranquillity; to the essence of karma, which is love.

From here, the effect of karma would transform into a more "subtle" dimension, and may even turn into "love." Yet this process is unimaginably painful. All the illusions spring forth and all the fear, distrust, anxiety, greed, and fury rise up. In this situation, if the śūnyatā of dualism and one's experience with undiscriminating wisdom and love is not deep enough, the body, mind, and spirit will most certainly be swept up in this, and the time it takes to experience and surpass this will be proportionate to the size of the karma.

After going through this for one day and one night, the "self" had been well and truly ground away. I was used to going outside twice a day to get some sunlight, but when I went out this time, I had to drag my exhausted body and mind along until I found a patch of open space on which to sit down. Suddenly, I felt a huge wave of love that seemed to completely envelop me. An incredible stillness accompanied a massive wave of nada vibrations, which felt like it resounded through the entire dharma realm. In an instant, I realized my heart had already been completely one with Svabhava, with God. This insight was deeper, more comprehensive and complete than previous experiences of oneness, as though past experiences of oneness were all in 5D, whereas this experience was in 8D, 9D, or even 10D. My consciousness lifted to a completely unimaginable state. In this state there was an immense energy that does not have a name, but which I refer to as "love." This vast love dissolved everything: all karma, all heartache; all that exists within everything.

This energy was more than my body could take, and all I could do was cry tears of gratitude; and as my tears flowed without cease, the internal sound of silence (nada) grew stronger and stronger until it felt like the entire dharma realm was playing a sacred tune that had never before been heard. The entire thing sounded 20 octaves higher than usual, as though played by a vast, 20-strong orchestra.

In an attempt to capture this wonderful moment and record this sound, I brought the frequency down to a high-pitch human frequency, and suddenly a thought flashed through my mind: Why not make it into a song?

In an instant the lyrics were flowing effortlessly, one by one, from my pen onto the page; it all simply appeared with ease, even for someone like me, who had never written music or lyrics before. It was then that I realized that all the master musicians of the past must certainly have done a similar thing: recreated for humanity the frequency that they heard within.

I would now like to share with everyone this "Song of Sacred Love," which has an extremely high level of energy to it:

Love…is too grand for my heart to bear,
Let me wholeheartedly salute the entirety (of all things) and wish you joy;
Whether winter or summer, day or night, how are we so mischievous?
You eternally open your loving arms and lead me to the light;
Whether happy or sad, hateful or selfish, how are we so ignorant?
You eternally transform the spirit with love, and teach me how to be great.
Love…is too grand for my heart to bear,

We are eternally surrounded by love, from which flows grace;

Intoxicate me with your embrace, and my heart will be full, with no requests.

Love…is just so grand, let my heart lie eternally within Yours;

Let me wholeheartedly salute Your all (everything in the Dharma realm);

I pray that all the glory of love belongs to you (a heart free of desire);

I have given my all, and my heart will always be with yours;

I have given my all, and my heart will always…be with yours.

This song was first published in 2009. It's a song that we all really love, and so we hope to share this "Song of God" with you and the rest of the world, and to bring comfort to the depths of countless souls.

Prayer allows us to effortlessly move toward "the sacred" without the need for any religious ceremonies. Of course, if you already believe in a faith, then prayer in the context of that faith is also wonderful. Either way, connecting with "the sacred" - in other words Svabhava or the power of Divinity - allows one to enter into the internal sacred realm. From there, they can experience Svabhava - the magnificent experience of love. This is the most direct method.

How do you partake in correct prayer? Manuscripts of practitioners from the Himalayas and the legacy of masters and sages all point to the following:

① Concentrate and allow the mind to become empty.

② Master the art of connecting Svabhava to the infinite power of love in Divinity so as to enter the "sacred realm."

③ Feel the internal state of fulfillment that comes from abundance.

④ While in this state, use your entire heart, mind, and soul to send out the feeling of what it would be like to have already completed it (already accomplished it).

⑤ Give blessings and be thankful for all that transpires and for everything.

These five processes all contain a deep meaning and state of being. If you can "know yourself" more deeply prior to prayer, so that the energy of some of the deep, internal heartache has been released, whether it be to do with romantic relationships, family, or any other heartache you have experienced in the past, and if you can heal and forgive and love that part of yourself, then prayer will become much more effective. The process of prayer does not necessarily require speaking, but speaking does not hurt. The most important thing is that, through this process, you connect with "the sacred" and the source of all things - Svabhava. By doing so, you are already in a different state to the rest of the world: you are in the sacred realm experiencing your intrinsic completeness. When you have a strong feeling of already "having" enough, the universe instantly senses this and responds in kind to the energy you emit, giving you experiences of plentifulness. This is the universe's law of karmic causality. It is only by doing this that we can see perfection in this imperfect world and imperfect life; and thus give yourself and the thing you are praying for a whole-hearted blessing, filled with love. You will find that by doing this, God, the Universe, Tao, or whatever you like to call It, will immediately respond to your prayer in the most authentic way possible, allowing you to experience "plentifulness" and abundance once again in the material world.

Saint Francis of Assisi once said: "The result of prayer is life." Prayer brings life, as it irrigates the land and the spirit.

As we come to know our true selves better and better, become more and more acquainted with our true state, and are immersed in this state of abundance increasingly often, prayer will effortlessly bring abundance to your life. To follow are two miraculous, real-life stories that occurred at the Satdharma Institute.

Miraculous Story No. 1

One time, there was a mother with a pair of adorable twins. The twins had a good energy about them, yet didn't like going to school or studying, which caused their mother a lot of headache. The mother came to the Satdharma Institute to study because she felt she was unable to improve the family situation. As she came to know herself better, she became more aware of how to keep her children company, how to interact with them deeply on an internal level. Incredibly, as the mother grew and matured, her children also suddenly "grew up" and became more thoughtful. Their behavior began to automatically adjust, and the mother didn't need to worry any longer.

One day, while her second eldest child was in the first year of junior high, the mother noticed a tumor growing on the child's neck. She took her child to see a Chinese doctor, who said "Don't worry about it. Simply adjust your diet and you'll be fine." She then went to a Western medicine doctor, who also told her not to worry about it, which left her feeling relieved.

A year later, however, the tumor had grown, and the grandmother was very worried. At the time, a Taiwanese doctor just happened to be holding a medical clinic on the remote, offshore island on which they lived. After seeing the doctor and conducting a biopsy, they found that the tumor was benign. Nevertheless, the doctor recommended that they have it removed, but explained that this still involved some risk, as the tumor may get stuck during surgery and so removing it could harm the nerves on the right-hand side, and could even leave the child's right hand crippled. 'If the child's right hand becomes crippled,' thought the mother, 'how would they cope with the rest of their life?'

On hearing this, the child was very scared and even thought of ending his own life, not wanting to live any longer (he didn't tell his parents, but instead kept it all inside and simply gave up on life). Soon after, the doctor returned to Taiwan and scheduled the operation. At the time the mother was working in Taichung, and upon hearing the news, she thought she would completely fall apart or become depressed to the point of being unable to continue working. To her surprise, though, she noticed how much she had grown over the years, and how much she had learned.

The mother prayed daily and encouraged her child over the phone, telling him to read the "Flow of Light" prayer and saying the following four things to the tumor: "I'm sorry; please forgive me; thank you; and I love you." Two weeks later, the operation was held at the Chang Gung Memorial Hospital.

The mother said: "My husband and I accompanied my child until the moment he entered the operating room, and then led him in a final prayer."

Who would have thought that a miracle would really occur? After the tumor had been removed, the doctor held it up and showed us. Amazingly, it had shrunk and been flattened and was the size of a soya bean. The doctor found it unbelievable, and the operation was a success.

It was only then that the child expressed his true feelings, explaining that, when first hearing the news, he had really wanted to die (to give up on life). During a phone call with his mother, he angrily said: "I didn't do anything wrong. Why should I apologize to the tumor?" Yet he still did as he was told. During this process, he felt the energy in that region "flowing," so in order to survive, he did as his mother had instructed. The occurrence of this miracle filled the mother with an infinite amount of gratitude, and so she often encourages other people, telling them that they absolutely must believe in the power of prayer.

Miraculous Story No.2

One of our learners once shared the following:

"My husband is a hardworking and responsible repairman. Too busy at work with all his responsibilities, he neglected to look after his liver, the organ that gives off the fewest warning signs. After being examined by the doctor, my husband began taking medicine to treat his liver, and thanks to implementing a more regular routine over several years, he gradually started to recover. Yet for some reason he then began to experience rectal bleeding. After continued urging by his mother, he finally arranged to have a colonoscopy at the Veteran's Hospital. Initially, he insisted that he go for the checkup himself, but as his wife I felt that I was obligated to be there with him, no matter how busy I was. So I accompanied him to the hospital despite his objections.

"As my husband went in for examination, I sat outside the examination room for ages with the feeling that something was 'not quite right.' I began to pray – praying for Guru Satdharma's loving assistance.

"Soon after, the nurse came out and shouted: 'Can the family of patient number XX please enter?!' Her voice confirmed my feelings of unease and I entered the examination room with apprehension. After I had entered, the doctor said: 'You are really lucky. Your husband was just spared from going under the knife (referring to having an operation). This whole time I couldn't find the point from where the blood was exiting. I was about to give up searching when I suddenly spotted a giant polyp, so I can remove it right away and take a biopsy sample. If I hadn't discovered the problem, we would have had to schedule a time to operate, which, I mean if you forget about all the time and money involved; what's really painful is the physical ordeal you'd have to go through.'"

"As the wife of the patient, I kept on thanking the doctor. Thanking him for his love, his patience, and his medical skills. As I stepped out of the examination room, I broke down with tears of gratitude; gratitude for this vast love; for the teachings of guru Satdharma; and for having chosen the right path on which to progress. For me, this was a further affirmation of the miracle that is love and the genuine power of prayer, which had saved my husband from having to bear the pain of an operation. In that moment I vowed to do better, to try even harder to improve and move forward. Because of my belief and because of love, I can help even more people move away from suffering and toward joy."

Jesus once said that to return to god, you must go through the body. This is why we are here: to change the collective consciousness of the planet. Yet before we do this, we must first learn how to change ourselves. A "revolution" is a personal reformation, not an external battle. If you look externally, you will never find the answers. You must look inside and work together with the Divine and Buddha-nature. It is only through the lifting and metamorphosis of the consciousness that you can recognize your true self.

"Avidyā," or "ignorance," is the source of life's suffering. "Avidyā" refers to not understanding or knowing one's true self, not knowing that our essence is the Buddha, is Jesus. When we realize this and see our intrinsic nature from the inside, we are instantly freed from the various states of "Avidyā." The Sixth Patriarch said: "Bodhi is no tree. / Nor a bright mirror a stand, / Nothing is really there, / Where can any dust land?" All troubles in one's life, along with the shadows of one's subconscious, are illusions created by oneself that prevent us from seeing the bright light of our own Svabhava. Of course, human nature also consists of a dark side. When there is light there is certain to be a dark shadow. Yet this dark side is there so that we may get to know our true selves and realize love.

Prayer opens a direct pathway to the "sacred realm," allowing us to effortlessly experience our self-nature, love, and achieve a state of love.

The courses we have designed at Satdharma take you on an invaluable superconscious journey to the internal universe. When our consciousness expands and rises up above the cosmos, and our view has been opened and our consciousness awakened, all internal wonders, forces, and wisdom open up. From time immemorial, this heroic journey inside has required seekers to experience awakening themselves. When you arrive at supreme consciousness and truly become the Divine, you will know that The Lord is not inside or outside, and yet is both inside and outside. Regardless, you will find that He was already there in the deep recesses of our souls waiting for us to once again discover this incredible "endless treasure."

Through this process of elevating consciousness and developing wisdom, you are already bringing benefit to your entire family, because our DNAs are all connected and our energy networks linked. When one person in the family decides to raise their consciousness and energy, and thus decides to change (this requires a lot of courage!), thanks to the principle of energy "resonance," the rest of the family will be elevated and begin to change.

When we bless everyone we know and everyone we don't know through prayer, as well as all animate and inanimate objects, this invisible energy – "the infinite net" – entwines all life and elevates and transforms it. You are your own savior. The Buddha says to "follow the teachings, not the teacher; rely on wisdom, not on knowledge." Although life is impermanent and the teachings are impermanent, the path to the Supreme is always there. When walking along this path of awakened consciousness, the deeper you go, the more equanimity you feel. The deeper you go, the more you understand that you are one with the earth, water, fire, wind, and space, and with all things; everything naturally operates with love, because love is our intrinsic nature, the real essence of who we are internally and of all things. Thus, in this state, everything you encounter will naturally take on its most perfect and complete form.

Are you still waiting for a guru or a certain person? Are you still hoping to put your faith in someone else, hoping that they may save you?

As long as you are willing, you can always re-open your Eye of Wisdom, re-open your omniscient eye, and see once again. With this, you can see the limitless potential of all life and re-write your own script, for you are the master, the architect of your own life! You have the power to change your own destiny. Out of love, you must bear one hundred percent responsibility for your own life!

The Age of Aquarius is an age in which people reclaim their own power; an age in which people save themselves. There is no need for you to wait – you can create a miracle and create your own destiny. All of life's wonders lie within! Save yourself. You can only help others if you first help yourself! When you truly experience "love," truly experience the incredible power of prayer, and at the same time gain deep and complete insights into all aspects of life, you will find that life itself is like a monastery. Your daily life is a monastery, and so is your job, your company, your family, and so on. In fact, there is nothing that is not a monastery. Where you are now is a sacred temple, a mandala. This is because you already truly realize that your true self is the Buddha, or Jesus.

When you return to your true self, you truly are an "awakened" Buddha, an "awakened" God. When this happens, you will know how to utilize this power to live in the world. You will know and understand completely why you met your family on this planet and why you met us here. You are not here for Satdharma or some spiritual or religious group; nor are you here for your guru or anyone else. You are here for yourself, for the promise you made to all beings. You are on this planet for the promise you made to yourself deep in your heart. That is why we came to Earth, to experience pain and love; and in the process of experiencing all this, to fix everything in all the lives we have lived throughout time. We are here to fix the potholes, fix our shadows, heal the world's sorrows and transform its consciousness. We are here to disseminate the Wu wei love distilled in the lines "Nothing is really there, / Where can any dust land?" We are here to make humanity a loving paradise once more.

PART IV

CULTIVATION

Chapter 7 Searching for the Universal Value of the True Self

Chapter 8 A Global Initiative for the Spiritual Industry — From a Global View to a Super Cosmic View

Chapter 7

Searching for the Universal Value of the True Self

"Only after experiencing the existence of another world can we wake up in that world."
— Albert Soesman

"There is only one truth, which is referred to variously by sages."
— Ancient Indian classical text (*The Vedas*)

Look around you. Really, I'm not kidding! Look around you at your family, at the society and this world. What is happening at this moment? Every day there are endless incidents happening in real life that show the impermanence of life. On January 15, 2015, a mother who was getting on in years suddenly felt discomfort around her heart. She was immediately rushed to the hospital and housed in the regular hospital ward. She was treated with a vasodilator and scheduled to undergo heart stent implantation on the morning of the 21st. Initially, her family was not too worried about this commonplace procedure, but during the surgery the doctor was unable to implant the stent because three of the arteries were over 90% blocked, while one artery had already been dissected, and the remaining arteries were all too thin. All the doctor could do was implant the stent in one of these arteries. In the end, the procedure lasted almost 12 hours. And although the coronary artery bypass surgery was successful, the pre-existing conditions she suffered, such as arterial clogging, caused her heart to swell up, and after the completion of the procedure and the suturing of the wound, her blood pressure was still abnormal.

After the operation, she had still not regained consciousness, and the doctor said that if her condition did not improve in the next 24 hours, her family would have to start preparing for the worst. On the morning of the 21st, her family received a notification of critical illness informing them to quickly make their way to the hospital...

In another situation, there was a mother whose child had suffered from severe obsessive-compulsive disorder for many years. The mother had spent countless days and nights keeping the child company, but saw no improvement to his condition and grew exhausted. This courageous mother then entered our integrated body, mind, and soul system in a last ditch attempt to help her child. Yet the rate of improvement the child experienced in six short months left her physician feeling astonished. He asked the mother what it was she had done. The mother told him the truth, saying that they had come to the Satdharma Institute for study. The doctor told her: "Out of all the patients I've worked with, there are very few who show such rapid signs of improvement." Of all the severe patients he had treated, only this child had recovered at an almost unbelievable rate. All the doctor could say was: "You've found your path forward!" He even told the child not to forget to do the exercises from the course. When the mother embraced me, her emotions and her gratitude flowed forth, and that was when she shared this story with me.

One day, a patient at the hospital was waiting for the doctor to explain the results of the follow-up examination report. The patient had originally been diagnosed with second stage ovarian cancer, yet had gotten better thanks to early treatment, and only had to undergo a regular annual checkup.

Yet this time the expression on the doctor's face made her feel as though something was wrong. Indeed, the doctor told her: "Your cancer cells have recurred and there are signs that they have spread." She was left speechless, but then composed herself, as though she had already known this would happen. What was she to do now?

The owner of a biotechnology company once took classes at the Satdharma Institute. At the end of class, he hugged me in excitement and said "What type of 'miracle course' is this?" Apart from being filled with love, he also sensed our sincere desire to pass this teaching on to others. "As long as we're willing to learn," he stated, "the teacher is willing to selflessly teach us all the wonders of the Tao. What they offer here is not the performing of blessings or initiation rituals, but the path to truly knowing oneself, truly completing oneself. The teacher wants us to be as good as he is. He wants to make the world a better place! How can one's love be so selfless?"

I was very grateful for his foresight and commended him on his courage. I told him that at the end of class, people are often excited and feel that they have gained a lot, and may even observe a change in themselves or their family members. However, other people, such as associates and partners, may in fact think that you have gone crazy. Your employees may start saying things like: "I don't what type of strange course he took, but ever since he came back he's been acting all weird! It's hard to describe." It's because they do not yet understand how the course benefits and helps you. So, just take it slowly. This is a treasure that needs to be explored over a lifetime, to be internalized while simultaneously sharing it. Sometimes change really cannot be rushed.

Every day, we experience many situations. Some are sad and unexpected, while others are urgent, joyous, boring, startling, happy, or touching.

Some people right now are worried about how they will eat the following day, and have no money to see the doctor or pay the rent. They are worried about the vast pit of debt underneath them that is expanding every day, about their children, whose body and mind have been weakened due to malnutrition, or about family members suffering due to illness. These people do not need to wait for an Armageddon to occur; their Armageddon is already here!

Yet does our current predicament include only the emergencies that lie right in front of our eyes? On Jan 23, 2015, a major news article featured the following headline: "Have Humans Gone Too Far? Four Out of Nine Planetary Boundaries Have Already Been Crossed!"

The international research team cited in the article pointed out that, out of the nine systems that help maintain the planet's regular function, four such systems had already been destroyed by human activity, and that the planetary boundaries had already been crossed. On the 16th, 18 scientists published a study in the academic journal 'Science' entitled *Planetary Boundaries: Guiding Human Development on a Changing Planet.* The study noted that the system that regulates the planet's resilience is undergoing change and that this could affect human society in either the present or the future.

Either way, the threshold figure of a two degree rise in temperature is not something that can be negotiated. If we exceed this figure, our planet is destroyed. Moreover, chemical fertilizers such as nitrogen-phosphorus fertilizers have severely damaged Earth's ecosystem, while the nitrogen-phosphorus cycle plays an essential role in the question of whether we are able to obtain clean food and sources of water. When fertilizers used on land eventually flow into the lakes, it causes the volume of algae in surrounding areas to increase and produces matter that is toxic for humans and other animals. This in turn leads to the death and decline of other creatures.

Prof. Elena Bennett from McGill's School of the Environment described how: "About half a million residents of the city of Toledo found out that their tap water had been contaminated with a toxin called microcystin last summer. And in 2007 the Quebec government declared that more than 75 lakes were affected by toxins produced by blue-green algae. This kind of problem is likely to become much more common. We will see more lakes closed, will have to pay more to clean our water, and we will face temporary situations where our water is not cleanable or drinkable more and more frequently. That's what it means to have crossed this planetary boundary."

The concept of planetary boundaries was first propounded in a 2009 study, in which scientists proposed nine major planetary boundaries that have been affected by human activity:

① Climate change
② Complete transformation of the biosphere, loss of creature diversity, extinction of species
③ Destruction of the ozone
④ Ocean acidification
⑤ Change in the biochemical cycle
⑥ Change in the soil systems
⑦ Use of clean sources of water
⑧ The concentration of aerosols in the atmosphere; atmospheric particles that affect the climate and the ecosystem.
⑨ The introduction of new materials, such as organic pollutants, radioactive materials, nanomaterials, and plastic particles. *256

Thus, it seems as though there are both internal and external difficulties to overcome. It is not only humans that are faced with challenges. Regardless of which way you look at it, the global crisis we face today is extremely urgent. In the book *Paths Beyond Ego: the Transpersonal Vision*, the authors state that "[the severity of the crisis] is not simply due to its scope, complexity, or urgency, but also because this is the first time in human history that such crises are all man-made." *257 In these seemingly urgent and severe internal and external (life and the environment) phenomena, what is it exactly that "life" is trying to teach us?

The internal and the external cannot be neatly separated. Internal and external work should be integrated and wise action taken in order to collectively change one's spirit and the world.

In the United Nations Nobel Peace Prize award ceremony, the Dalai Lama presented *The Nobel Peace Prize Lecture: A Call for Universal Responsibility*. In his speech he emphasized that the world is increasingly linked by a mutual connection and dependency. This is because everyone will be affected by the environmental crisis. The authors of *Paths Beyond Ego: the Transpersonal Vision* described the Dalai Lama's perspective:

"Our sense of responsibility and compassion must extend to the entire planet and all its people. He argues that the current crisis can only be solved through the simultaneous development of external science on the one hand, and internal psychological power on the other. The two most important types of internal states are transpersonal emotions, such as love and compassion."

The various life or human crises we currently face all seem to be pointing towards integration of the internal and external. That is to say, on the one hand pursuing the true self internally through transpersonal psychology and a distillation of Eastern wisdom; externally, on the other hand, any important scientific work can bring new solutions, whether it be research in the field of deep ecology, clinical psychiatry, sociology, anthropology, economics, or even philosophy, art, culture, religion, spiritual practices and lifestyle methods. Yet the crux of this change still boils down to a remark made by Eric Damon: "If we can't change ourselves, then we won't change anything." *259

In Chapter 2, we already discussed how human beings have reached an extremely important turning point. People these days exist in an abnormal state having lost the connection to their cultural roots. Prof. Mark says that if we want to overcome these challenges, we have to return to the core of the problem: "Modern life lacks spirituality." People in modern times lack a certain type of "intuition" (I believe that this is direct insight), a certain type of spiritual awareness. This kind of awareness allows people to clearly perceive that all human beings are one, and gradually expands to include an emphasis on the entire planet and its ecology, a need to once again obtain a balance between people, nature, all things in this world, and the universe.

Because we have lost our connection to our roots, we have also lost our connection to the true core of life – the true self (Svabhava). As a result, we are unable to think "as one," which creates an even larger number of severe internal and external lessons to learn. Jung often noted in his books that "The psychological rule says that when an inner situation is not made conscious, it happens outside, as fate. That is to say, when the individual remains undivided and does not become conscious of his inner contradictions, the world must perforce act out the conflict and be torn into opposite halves." *260

Right now the world is "acting out" the internal situation of all people. The impermanence we presently encounter is life trying to tell us that there may be some things of which we were not consciously aware. Perhaps an inner contradiction had existed for a long time, yet we lacked the spiritual awareness to notice it. If we are not aware of it, then we cannot change it. Thus, life is forced to "act it out" so that we may discover the conflict and address it, and then move in the direction that our soul desires for us.

As soon as it is acted out and materialized in the external world, we are immediately "torn" into opposite halves, and the most common emotion that arises from this is fear.

Emerson once expressed his view of fear: "Fear is an instructor of great sagacity...... One thing he teaches, that there is rottenness where he appears. He is a carrion crow, and though you see not well what he hovers for, there is death somewhere. Our property is timid, our laws are timid, our cultivated classes are timid. Fear for ages has boded and mowed and gibbered over government and property. That obscene bird is not there for nothing. He indicates great wrongs which must be revised." *261

Do not be scared of fear, for it is an angel that allows us to be reborn, a metric that points to the issues, people, or things that create fear in us. These are areas that need to be faced, "cleared" and integrated, and then transformed.

If we are too timid to face it, to enter into it and clear it, then it will become our "demon" and prevent us at all times from being at peace.

There is a saying that goes as follows: "Confusion drains all energy from a clear spirit." This is very true. Fear only begets more fear, while confusion begets more confusion, and this continues until all strength has been lost and the individual completely hits a wall, exhausted, and eventually loses all hope. However, life is our most valuable instructor. We are always looking outside for solutions to our problems, yet have forgotten how to raise our own level of consciousness and spiritual awareness so that we may once again receive the wisdom and opportunities that life wants to tell us and send us.

If "everything external is a projection of our internal state," then it seems we have undervalued the power of this statement, and that we are lost and confused, and cannot find the "root" of our existence, and are thus unable to calm our minds and focus on that power within. The "source" of all things, the true self, seems to possess some sort of massive power which we do not yet understand. Yet it is this massive power that allows us to be reborn and instills in us the wisdom to solve all problems. It is also the force that will guide us to advance and develop in the future. It takes us from our initial perspective of torn opposition to a brand new spiritual dimension.

The book *Paths Beyond Ego: the Transpersonal Vision* mentions an article written by Christina and Stanislav Grof by the title Transpersonal Experiences and Global Crises. The article points out that some people who have explored the depths of their inner selves and who have had many transpersonal experiences have found their own value system automatically shift toward service of others and a greater respect for all living beings. *262 In summary, the main challenge we are facing in this age is in nurturing a brand new understanding of life and coming to know "the source," so as to overcome personal crises as well as massive global crises. To do this, we also have to integrate our internal and external worlds and react in an appropriate, flexible, and sagacious manner.

And this can no longer wait, as mentioned in *Paths Beyond Ego: the Transpersonal Vision*: "Clearly, we are currently in a race between [the raising of] consciousness and disaster. The most pressing task for everyone, I'm afraid, will be to utilize transpersonal consciousness to maintain the planet and nature. The objective is to clearly identify the destructive psychological and social forces that have brought us to this turning point in history, and transform them into constructive forces in an attempt to seek survival, well-being, and awakening for all." *263

I believe this to be the correct path for change.

The Power of Identifying with the True Self and 16 Types of Universal Values

A universal problem that afflicts society today is that people know too much, yet understand too little.
– Stephen Arroyo, astrologer

We do not understand our own spiritual power. Nor do we understand the wondrous function of the universe and the Divine source field. Thus, we lose direction in life due to the vast range of false self-identities we assume. There are several erroneous self-identities that are commonly adopted and serve to diminish our connection with the source. They not only prevent us from gaining more wisdom, but also stop us from truly transcending the ego self and reaching the core of the problem, thereby trapping us in our own "cocoon" as it were. Below is a list of "false self-identities:" *264

① Identifying with any of the various roles that one plays.
② Identifying with first or second-order personality traits.
③ Identifying with self-concepts.
④ Identifying with any of one's various states.

It is precisely because we identify with a false self and, by extension, the various states of this false self, that we are restricted to experiencing only certain "quantum states." The universe then responds directly to these restricted states. I shared this same message as early as 14 years ago:

Outlook and View

When you have a certain outlook on life, you will see the world from that outlook. When you see the world from that outlook, you will possess that outlook on life. There are different levels of the self and the spirit, and the view at each level differs. Viewing the world from a new perspective is enough to shift one's entire life.

Raising one's outlook on life is akin to a hero receiving the call from the depths of his or her soul and bravely stepping onto the path that leads to the true self. When we stride along the path laid down by spiritual science and move toward the "Divine inner core," we discover that the view at each point is constantly changing. It is as Proust says: life's vista has not changed. You have simply swapped a new pair of eyes.

① A more correct self-identity

When we learn to see through the murky confusion in our minds to truly understand who we are, and gradually rid ourselves of the tearing, divisive effect brought of erroneous self-identity, we can slowly come to meditate on the Ultimate Truth, and gain a deep grasp on, and even experience, the true self. André Lefebvre in *"Transpersonal Psychology"* wrote that: All things impermanent could not possibly be the self. Nor could the true self exist in anything I own; it is within the owner. The true self could not possibly exist as the object of my observation; it is within the observer." *266

This significant passage (above) conveys the essence of "transcending" the self.

② More stable emotionally

As a result of being more "centered," one's emotions do not contain as much destructive power, which itself brings positive energy. The individual can therefore move in a direction that corresponds to the true self. "If I can identify with the 'center' then I can sample a taste of the eternal, the unchanging, and from a place centered in stillness observe the flow of my thoughts and feelings, stable as a lighthouse; and yet keep a distance from these thoughts and feelings, allowing me to remain objective, tranquil, calm, and strong." *267

The practice of "centering" in the Ultimate Truth is the best way to return to one's self-nature or Svabhava, stabilize one's emotions, and free oneself from suffering.

③ Unconditional self-acceptance and self-love

In the three-part course "Transcending the Self," we guide students to deeply explore their various personality and second-order personality traits, and to experience the effect of the shadow, the potholes, and imprints in the subconscious. This includes self-beliefs such as "I'm a failure," "I'm an alcoholic," "I'm a liar," "I'm a cowardly, weak person," "I don't love myself," "I can't forgive others," and so on. We also deal with misconceptions borne of false self-identities, such as construing the perceiver as the perceived, the observer as the observed, and "I am" as "I have." This causes a number of negative effects, such as the severe belittling of the self, negativity, and the inability to forgive. An example is the false self-identity created when someone's marriage, romantic relationship, or business fails. Instead of thinking that they failed in this one relationship or situation, they generalize it and believe that "I am a failure." This deepens their self-notion that they will fail in every such situation. This self-belief manifests into reality and becomes a self-fulfilling prophecy, and they become trapped in a self-made vicious cycle based on the negative imprint in their subconscious mind.

Only by bravely delving into the negative imprint, experiencing it completely and accepting it entirely can we be liberated from the myriad false self-identities and "see" the gift hidden behind such identities. The true self does not lie in these false self-identities, nor in one's shortcomings, weaknesses, bad habits, disabilities, detestable qualities, or failures. These are like waves, outward extensions of the true self. Yet the stillness at the depth of the ocean has never been moved. It is only by doing this that we can feel an expansive love, a selfless love, and thus love all of our defects and every aspect of ourselves. When you refocus your attention onto the true self, the energy of compassion and self-love grows by the day, and these shortcomings and defects gradually lose their power to affect you, and are eventually healed and even transcended.

④ A unified and integrated center

Due to the fact that society has lost its cultural and educational roots, a multiplicity of false self-identities lead people to overlook the oneness of themselves and their true core – their true selves. This results in a fractured consciousness that can be likened to a plate of scattered sand granules – you cannot see a clear oneness of energy or a driver of this energy. Through the practice of spiritual training, however, we return to the true self and the various fragments of consciousness fit back into the right place, forming an energy with the true self at the center. The power generated from each fragment being in the right place automatically brings order to one's life, a Divine order as prescribed by the universe. This power allows one to live in balance, and to discover and see clearly each part of the first and second-order personality traits in one's consciousness. It allows one to possess wisdom and power which is coordinated, unified, and integrated centrally. *268

⑤ The value-affirming power of being

Our ego leads us to believe that everything we have is who we in fact are. This may include our physical body, emotions, feelings, reason, our loved ones, family, career, and so on. However, I am not that which I own. I am much "more" than what I own, much more expansive and more complete. When you return to the center of your "true self," you are able to effortlessly feel the present awareness of "being" (or "existing," as sometimes translated) and easily perceive and understand the difference between being and having.

As soon as one gains this insight, the consciousness can be separated and even freed from all of the ego's belongings. Being separated and freed does not imply that we no longer love them, but that we now have more space in which to admire our mutual existence. Thus, we understand how to truly love them and possess the value and power of being. In Transpersonal Psychology, André Lefebvre quotes a passage from Erich Fromm's book "*To Have or To Be?*" as follows: "If I am what I have and if I lose what I have, who then am I? Nobody but a defeated, deflated, pathetic testimony to a wrong way of living. Because I can lose what I have, I am necessarily constantly worried that I shall lose what I have......If I am who I am and not what I have, nobody can deprive me of or threaten my security and my sense of identity. My center is within myself." *269

⑥ A deeper and truer freedom

Freedom has always evoked a multitude of projections and misunderstandings. If I asked you "What is freedom?" I am sure that many people would respond "The ability to do what I want to do;" or perhaps quote a line from this classic advertisement: "As long as I like it, why can't I do it?" However, the level of freedom in one's consciousness is vastly deeper than these aforementioned responses. Generally speaking, we create false self-identities by identifying with the first three bodies of our self, or with second-order personality traits. Thus, we are trapped within the "ego self." In fact, we may have been abducted by the self and not even know it.

Dane Rudhyar, a famous astrologer, once said: "Man's ultimate freedom is in choosing the attitude with which to address the situation before him."

In the book *Astrology, Psychology & the Four Elements: An Energy Approach to Astrology & Its Use in the Counseling Arts*, Stephen Arroyo cites a description used by psychologist Carl Rogers:

"It is this inner, subjective, existential freedom which I have observed. It is the burden of being responsible for the self one chooses to be. It is the recognition, by the person, that he is an emerging process, not a static end-product......The second point in defining this experience of freedom is that it exists, not as a contradiction to the picture of the psychological universe as a sequence of cause and effect, but as a complement to such a universe.

"Freedom, rightly understood, is a fulfillment by the person, of the ordered sequence of his life. As Martin Buber puts it, 'The free man believes in destiny and believes that it stands in need of him.' He moves out voluntarily, freely, responsibly; to play his significant part in a world whose determined events move through him and through his spontaneous choice and will. Let me again quote from Buber: 'A man who can forget about cause and effect and make a decision from a deep place within......that is a free man. In this situation, the destiny that he meets is the corresponding product of this freedom. Destiny is no longer a boundary for him, but instead an opportunity for him to manifest.'

The freedom mentioned here exists as the subject of the person. Through such freedom, the individual chooses to perfect himself by playing a spontaneous and responsible role within a destined incident. This recognition of freedom is the most meaningful direction of development for my clients, as it can help them become complete during the process of interpersonal interaction." *270

When we are centered in our true self, the core of our self, we can recognize the real value of freedom. Freedom allows us to choose the sacred core – our true selves, oneness. It allows us to choose Him as the true master and transcend our own personal destiny, to become aware that we are playing an assertive and responsible role; to become a hero to ourselves and bring about completion for this lifetime.

⑦ Expansion of consciousness

Through the numerous expansion drills in spirit training, we gradually come to know the vast breadth of consciousness, adjust our identity to align with our larger selves, and elevate our perspective. "I am that awareness," the omnipresent awareness of Svabhava: pure, existing, being, and boundless awareness. The deep-seated recognition and deep-level awareness of this must be nurtured through meditation on the Ultimate Truth again and again until it becomes a fixed understanding (a fixed and deep understanding). However, our consciousness may once again get "trapped" in identification with any of a number of "objects," such as one's physical body, emotions, personality, second-order personality traits, thoughts, concepts, objects floating in our mind, our shadow, and so on. Therefore, awareness once again drops to the level of perceived objects and items, and is no longer vested in the true self. "This is analogous to the sky incorrectly identifying as clouds, birds, and planes" wrote Lefebvre. Awareness is the key to once again breaking free. Maintaining a perception and awareness of the true self helps you to perceive the vast breadth of your awareness while simultaneously maintaining a balance with all objects. This sets your heart free so that you are the "master of both worlds."

Many of the courses offered at the Satdharma Institute provide a wealth of practice that helps you break free from identification with objects. "Going from consciousness that is restrictive and inhibiting, and returning to pure consciousness. The expansion of this kind of consciousness often gives people an extremely deep sense of liberation." *271

⑧ The value of knowing oneself

When you get to know yourself deeply, the veil of ignorance that blocks the true self begins to peel away, one layer at a time. "Many people are afraid to enter their own heart, as they might find things there that harm their self-image, and thus find any excuse to avoid any chance of introspection. They are not truly willing to know themselves, and so naturally find it hard to progress. There is another type of person, however, who yearns to know himself, yet unfortunately does not have the proper outlook, and becomes perverted and dangerous." *272

The true self does not hide its bright luster for any of the "objective selves" or the objects they identify with or possess. Emerson once said: "I am like a hidden gem, exposed by my glare." The true value of recognizing your real self is that it gives you the power and courage to transcend the ego and to operate in the world with transcendent wisdom without being sullied by worldly matters. Viewing the world through the awareness of the true self, the individual naturally has a transcendent and practical outlook, and is no longer restricted by a divisive and distorted dualistic view of oneself.

⑨ Holistic and balanced development

After bypassing the wonders of the seven bodies and the complete spectrum of consciousness, and being centered in wisdom, the individual's body, mind, and spirit will undergo a balanced development. The infinite shine of the "true self" will illuminate the spiritual traits of the astral body and you will deeply grasp the value of and your mission for this lifetime. You will then be able to more holistically stride toward your purpose for this life and achieve true completion. Thus, you will no longer blindly identify with just one part of your personality or second-order personality traits, and invest all of your energy into rationality, logic, faith, and mainstream consciousness values, neglect your crucial psychological and spiritual needs, and therefore restrict or harm the power of your wisdom. When we expand our awareness so that we experience the being of the true self, we exist in a state of neutrality and tranquillity. From this beneficial and transcendent vantage point, we can "see" the intrinsic nature and perfection of ourselves and the world, and no longer deviate from the proper course, unable to develop holistically.

⑩ A deeper responsibility for the development of one's own personality

When we discover our true selves and come ever closer to it, we will know who – or, more accurately, what "state" – is our true self among the various aspects of our personality. The more we experience the awareness of the "true self," the more we realize that the egoic self is simply a faithful servant to the true self, and begin to take one hundred percent responsibility for our own life and for all the aspects of personality we wish to develop.

Not identifying with a certain aspect of our personality or the phenomena or states that derive from our personality does not imply that you are severing off or ignoring these aspects. On the contrary, from the point of view of the true self, we can be certain that these aspects of our personality are in fact parts of ourselves. Thus, we have a responsibility to integrate these aspects or transform them. At the same time, we have the wisdom to know that, in order to realize completion, we have the responsibility to freely choose which personality traits to develop. Through the love and wisdom of the true self, we fully develop the power of the chosen personality traits, and even traits of the spirit, so as to thoroughly induce a transformation in ourselves and society as a whole. And while thoroughly developing several aspects of our personality, we also see the essence of the true self, which has never changed. Only by truly knowing ourselves can we shift our incorrect attitudes, which include a refusal to summon our true selves, a denial of our own the power, or repression; or indifference toward life, or finding life meaningless or worthless.

⑪ A relatively objective and correct observational ability

It is very easy for our minds to fall into a narrow and subjective point of view. This is especially so when we have already drifted into a subjective and habitual lack of awareness. Often, such people actually think that they are very objective!

Lefebvre once wrote the following: "When I blindly equate myself with a certain role, second-order personality, self-concept or any other self-identity, I become trapped in the object with which I identify, and can only assess my internal and external situation from that perspective. My vision is thus naturally limited, skewed, like a frog trapped at the bottom of a well." *273

The Consciousness-only School of Buddhism has dissected mind-consciousness in depth, as follows: When we identify with something due to a bad habit or karmic seed ("identification" implies that you enter that state), and therefore assume a certain personality trait, role, thought, perspective, or concept, we are actually entering a "creation" generated by consciousness, from which we have a very narrow perspective.

If you identify with pride or arrogance from your occupation, you create the misconception that all others are inferior to you, and are unable to trust or take on other people's suggestions. If you identify with a sickly personality or state, you will feel that you are always sick in life and become depressed and fall into utter despair. If you identify with a negative or diffident self-concept, you will feel as though there is little to be happy about in this world and believe that you have "no momentum;" you will not trust yourself or feel that others are always attacking you. You may even feel as though other people, and in fact the entire world, underestimate you. When you feel shackled by second-order personality traits, such as pessimism or passivity (implying that if you are completely identified with this, you are being thoroughly controlled), you will feel pessimistic about your current predicament, lifestyle, and world events, and will find it hard to be in a good mood. You will also feel gloomy about your future prospects. If you are under the control of a second-order personality addiction, such as alcoholism, sexual addiction, drugs, or gambling, then it will seem as though everything else in your surrounds are "irrelevant," and you will only be interested in the vice you are addicted to, viewing your reality only through that lens.

When, through training, your ability to stay centered improves, you will be able to extricate yourself from any "creation" of consciousness, and observe and view everything from a state of transcendent neutrality, silence, and depth. As a result, you will no longer create distortions, projections, and misunderstandings due to erroneous identification.

⑫ Full of vitality

All creations of consciousness require attention (energy) to maintain their operation. Life exists at the point of your attention; energy exists at the point of your attention.

When our energy is scattered across various creations, such as our personality, second-order personality traits, self-concepts, and emotions, we have to expend a huge amount of energy, and so our energy reserves are spread thin. This makes it difficult to concentrate, saps up all of our energy, and robs us of inspiration. When this happens, we simply have to practice the exercises and meditations learned in class, which allows us to expand and remove ourselves from all types of "creations" and become naturally centered. After doing this, we feel tranquil, balanced, and full of energy and vitality; at one with the source, the true self.

The true self is like an enormous power station, supplying the self with a never-ending source of energy. At times it is restored, while at other times it is still charging, helping the self to possess massive potential and meet each day with vitality.

⑬ An alarm system for consciousness

When you realize that you are attached to some kind of identity, and you cannot expand and detach from it and return to a state of neutral tranquillity, this is a kind of warning. It means that you are finding it hard to let go of some form of identification or that you may have already entered a severe state of identification and be "imprisoned" by the concepts, values and feelings produced by your self-identity. You will feel some form of suffocation, that you are no longer free, and be entirely controlled by this feeling.

This is an excellent opportunity for awareness training. The alarm has sounded precisely to let you know that you are in a precarious state, to remind you to respond in the correct way, the wise way. In this situation, there is no need to add an additional layer of judgment about the fact that you are unable to detach from identification. All that is needed is to look and observe completely this state of being "unable to detach." Simply watching is enough to transform it. Alternatively, you could use the "procedures for handling energy flows" (*274) to treat this "inability to detach" as just another creation. In this case, you can process it and allow it to return to a neutral state, and then enter second-phase processing, wherein you peel it away one at a time until your energy gradually expands, your mind slowly calms, and you are once again centered. From the perspective of the true self, we never actually separated.

⑭ The experience of awakening

The book *Transpersonal Psychology* contains the following passage: "The experience of discovering your 'true self' is much like suddenly waking up.

It is an absolutely integral breakthrough in their lives, a watershed moment, a new birth. It gives people a brand new self-understanding: 'I'm not what I thought I was.'"

Knock on the door and the door will open for you. Your life is already transformed when you simply send out the thought 'I want to be at one with my true self; I want to know my true self.' Training in spiritual science allows us to sequentially return to our true selves and eventually taste what it is like to experience complete oneness with the true self. This is true awakening. After this happens, the individual has a completely different view of the world, and sees an entirely different life situation and world.

⑮ Improvement in interpersonal relationships

When we truly integrate our shadow from a brand new and complete understanding of ourselves, extracting ourselves from the various erroneous self-identities, we are able to view people from a more neutral, a deeper, and more compassionate perspective. This not only leads to the development of a new attitude, but also produces a wise perspective that diverges from the past. We see the "true self" hidden deep within each person.

Looking from the "correct" perspective of the "true self," when we see people's personality deficiencies, as well as the mistakes they have made, their small-minded viewpoints, the roles they play, their temper, stubbornness, illnesses, and physical disabilities, we have a deep understanding that those are not their "true selves." We therefore treat one another with more compassion and wisdom, which is more in line with the core values of such interactions. It produces lasting value through mutual honor, support, and trust. Even when the "true self" is hidden under the ugly façade of human nature, we are still able to maintain a balance and neutral state, and recognize the wonder of the "true self" below without reacting in a divisive, dualistic way and generating even more problems.

⑯ The ultimate value of transcending the ego

It is only by first knowing that hidden deep within us is the "true self" that we can rouse the desire to comprehensively develop, grow, and understand our true spiritual potential. As you progress, you will gain a complete map of consciousness for your true essence – your "true self" (i.e. Svabhava). You will know how to expand your consciousness and transcend the boundaries of consciousness one step at a time. You will also learn how to develop the power of self-wisdom.

André Lefebvre once wrote: "It continues rising and transcends the physical self, the emotional self, and the rational self; it transcends 'what I have' and moves toward 'what I am.' It transcends the objects of consciousness and sublimates into pure consciousness itself, transcending my personality and second-order personality traits and moving toward the center and driver of the personality. It transcends the false self and moves toward the true self. The ultimate objective is not just to 'become myself' but to 'become a better version of me,' and subsequently become 'the best version of myself."

I believe that this is the most valuable thing in life, and the most important universal value. When everyone becomes more and more aware of the real existence of their "true selves," then, through practice, they will naturally and gradually restore the intrinsic splendor of life. By gradually transcending various "creations" of consciousness and coming to know oneself, we come in touch with the "source of power that created all things" and receive an endless supply of kinetic life energy. This allows us to bravely embark on our own heroic journey and, one by one, overcome and transcend all obstacles that lie on the path, generate an endless supply of innovation and therefore enrich the scenery of our life. The ultimate destination on this path is to transcend the consciousness of dualistic opposition, recognize that the source essence of dualism is the "true self," and shine this "true self" light of ultimate wisdom onto the world so as to restore its original, sacred order and, together, create a paradise suffused with love.

The Path to Transforming the Individual and Society

"The journey of awakening occurs because the self-nature wants to connect with us."
—— Jung

At the beginning of this chapter and in the previous chapter, I explained that true transformation only occurs when the inner and the outer, the horizontal and vertical axes of consciousness, are simultaneously developed. This is critically important to whether the individual and society will be able to transform and get through this transition period, as the status quo tends to bring development to a stagnating halt. The force of stagnation itself is formed as a result of the operation of subjective consciousness by the individual and society at large, and this is something for which the individual and society will pay a huge price.

Duane Elgin is a scholar of future studies, and the author of the book *Voluntary Simplicity*. *276 He states that when people have an open and broad awareness, it is reflected in the quality of their lifestyle. They seek harmony between the internal, the external, and nature, and do not seek to control nature. Such people undoubtedly have a close connection with the larger whole and shoulder responsibility for it. *277 In the article *The Path of Individual and Social Transformation*, Elgin mentioned the following:

• Restoring Balance (I): the Path to Personal Transformation

Simone de Beauvoir once wrote: "Life is filled with processes that make it enduring and splendid. If we simply live life for the sake of living, then it would be nothing more than a slow march toward death." *278 Life itself is a wonder. Through the awakening process of understanding our true selves, our awareness and sense of responsibility expands to encompass the entire society, ecosystem, and the greater whole. Despite this, we are still currently poised in an evolutionary crisis.

Elgin has said: "There are two basic reasons for the emergence of this kind of evolutionary crisis: one reason is that, during the evolution of the external and material, an equivalent 'internal' evolution is lacking. The second reason: the inability to recognize 'internal' growth is the core of the process of human evolution." *279

Today's mainstream consciousness has not identified the true "universal value" of human existence. If people can only strive for self-actualization, the situation that Maslow warned of will come about: self-actualization will lead to self-limitation and selfishness, and a concentration of superficial values will emerge in the self-consciousness. It will not bring about a larger, more comprehensive achievement of completion.

It is only by experiencing the "true self" that we can expand people's power to move others through love and compassion; and this can transcend ethnicity, nation, culture, and can extend across the entire globe and universe. Our responsibility is to help others to elevate their awareness and their sense of responsibility to partake in the cultivation of the universe and of all humans. Moreover, if individuals can live with greater resolve and determination, this will certainly align with the higher self of the universe and create incredible inspiration that will benefit all of humanity.

• Restoring Balance (II): the Path to Social Transformation

Elgin once wrote the following:

"We face an extremely complex dilemma in our social, political, and economic system. Our technological ability is sufficient to create robust super systems, and yet we cannot convert this into a commensurate ability to understand what we have created. In the end, we rely increasingly on these super systems, but do not understand them. The purpose of building technological societies was to make technology serve us. Yet in the end we have become slaves to technology.

"We have gone from reasonable material happiness and pushed it to the point of excess material consumption. We are owned by our property and exhausted by consumption.

"Put simply, we have no choice but to re-evaluate the meaning of our lives and where we want to go. We have to distinguish between what is trivial, what is important, what is transient, and what is enduring. We must also identify an alternate possible image for humanity and society so that we may achieve collective creativity and provide a brand new sense of direction as we move forward into the future." *280

I personally very much agree with Dr. Elgin's assertion. Many people who explore humanity from a deeper awareness discover and affirm the follow basic views:

⊙ There is a deep layer of harmony underneath the random, chaotic events that occur on the surface. This layer seems to want to lead us to more balanced and moderate ground.

⊙ The way to move society toward a place of fulfilment and abundance is by leading a balanced life that emphasizes nature and simplicity, and then expanding this out to the greater whole through wisdom.

⊙ The purpose of the current sustainability crisis is to prompt humanity to discover a way of living that balances the inner and outer, so as to bring about a sustainable future. The company Infinitas International was established with this as a backdrop, and has embarked on a mission to bring about more balanced evolutionary development and achieve sustainable living.

We strive to: raise people's spiritual level, taking their lives to new heights, and create new opportunities for global sustainability. Someone once said that this dream was too large; that it was too difficult to achieve. I told them that "The hero's journey is always a difficult one."

Our lifestyle revolves around a 16-word motto:

Compassion and blessings
Coexistence and mutual honor
Clean LOHAS
Sustainability of life

We hope to attract even more heroes who are willing to walk along a different "path of transformation," willing to stride toward a different and brand new vision of sustainability.

It is with this spirit of self-transcendence that we pass the torch of awakening toward a more expansive future. Life is about experiencing the great journey of discovery and self-transcendence, from the initial raising of perception and awakening of consciousness, to the realization of the true self. The complete development of this spiritual power involves a splendid process of making life whole. The pursuit of awakening through the realization of the "true self" brings a wealth of beauty and wonder:

① Activating total-brain intelligence and expanding awareness allows us to gain a more precise grasp of information.
② Viewing the core of all problems produces critical insight.

③ Alarming intuition allows for novel creativity in solving problems.

④ Mastering the critical power of the subconscious and the universe's laws of creation.

⑤ Connecting to big data databases (*281) of the universe's intelligence ontology and possessing comprehensive "global-view" wisdom.

⑥ Opening up all possibilities in life so that the individual can break forth and fully apply his or her abilities in a unique and variegated way.

⑦ Creating a brand new, self-aware civilization so that the world may move toward a more awakened realm.

Do you still remember the meaning of "spirit-self" described in the first chapter?

Spirit-self refers to our spiritual wisdom nature and our true spirit. When we understand Svabhava, or our self-nature (our true self), it causes our body, mind, and spirit, as well as our spirit energy to become one with the universe; it restores all things to their natural place, to operate in alignment with the Tao, to transcend personal consciousness and be infused in all things, and to possess the wisdom and foresight of the Gods.

Stated simply, the spirit is our original nature and essence. Through one's mental state, the spirit-self applies an infinite, endless amount of wisdom and functionality, allowing the individual to transcend the ego and achieve enlightenment, and naturally restoring the order of truth, kindness, and beauty to life.

The critical force for change in this era has been placed in the hands of the individual. Indeed, the question of how to have mystical experiences, spiritual experiences, and peak experiences through spiritual science training, and even how to have "plateau experiences" in consciousness, should be the individual's highest objective in life. At the same time as we expand our experience of consciousness, simultaneous expansion of our awareness of the state of direct observation allows humans to jointly experience the "highest source" of consciousness – true self, or Svabhava. Due to this incredible experience, people are able to effortlessly apply endless wisdom and spiritual intelligence, and adjust the way they handle all challenges and problems related to the individual, society, and the greater whole.

In his essay "Nature" (1836), Emerson wrote the following: "Can we use a pair of fresh eyes to view this world?" I am sure that after reading to this point, you already have a different perspective to before. Emerson continues with the following: "Try to construct your world with this! Using the purest thoughts in your mind, put this into practice in your everyday life!" I hereby invite everyone to jointly create a different tomorrow!

Chapter 8

A Global Initiative for the Spiritual Industry

From a Global View to a Super Cosmic View
Glory lies in the attempt to reach one's goal and not in reaching it……

Satisfaction lies in the effort, not in the attainment, full effort is full victory.
—— Gandhi

If you want to understand the details, you must first see the bigger picture.
—— Goethe

From a Global View to a Super Cosmic View

How do we go from a local view to a global view, and then expand this to a cosmic view, and finally elevate it to a super cosmic view?!

From the perspective of the continually climbing "social risk" value, humans have a "blunted" sense of awareness. The boiling frog metaphor is perfectly apt here: If you threw a frog directly into boiling water, it would immediately jump out. Yet if you place it in cold water and then very slowly heat it up, the frog cannot detect the change in temperature, and by the time it does sense the change, it is already too late.

I previously mentioned Dr. Mark, who talks of five crises of human change:

1. Very little awareness of danger in our surrounds;
2. Overreliance on past knowledge;
3. A fossilized system that precludes reformation;
4. A dearth of comprehensive all-round, cross-disciplinary thinking;
5. A lack of wisdom in improvising to solve crises.

If we do not make breakthroughs in the face of these numerous challenges, we will have essentially sentenced ourselves to death. The University of Chicago magazine, Bulletin of the Atomic Scientists (BAS), was founded by scientists in the research team that researched and created the first atomic bomb under the Manhattan Project. Its main purpose is to oppose nuclear weapons, and in 1947 the team built the doomsday clock, with adjustment of the clock undertaken by the team's famous scientists and Nobel prize recipients. On Jan 22, 2015, the doomsday clock was moved to just three minutes away from a symbolic apocalypse, which is the closest to the apocalypse it has been since the end of the Cold War.

In 2007 BAS for the first time incorporated climate change into the list of factors affecting the doomsday clock. Richard Somerville, a member of BAS's Science and Security Board, emphasized that last year was the hottest year on record so far. Unless we can immediately bring about a considerable reduction in greenhouse gases, their effect will be sufficient to change the planet's climate before the end of the century, threatening countless ecological systems and leading to the extinction of large numbers of species.

Executive Director of BAS, Kennette Benedict, stated that moving the clock forward two minutes did not signify that it is all too late. On the contrary, it is a way of encouraging the world to "take action!" *282

From the beginning of this book, I have been transmitting a crucial concept, which is this: we are currently in a "transition period," an incredibly significant "watershed moment." Spiritual writer Li Hsin-ping previously wrote in a blog post: "If you have not yet seen the future, it means you are not yet standing at a high enough vantage point!"

When the force of epochal evolution grows increasingly stronger, the eventual collision it precipitates affects all global citizens, and it becomes difficult to avoid being dragged in, as the disasters and incidents that occur in each country and region are so striking it feels as though it is happening right next door.

In his book *Chaos Point 2012 and Beyond: Appointment with Destiny*, Ervin Laszlo, two-time Nobel peace prize nominee and Chairman of the global think tank 'the Club of Budapest,' explained: "What is the chaos point? It refers to an important 'tipping point' in the evolution of a system. With regard to this point, the system was applied to current trends and collapsed, unable to be restored to its previous state and mode of conduct. It was also unable to be salvaged or enter a 'new track.' All it could do, apart from collapsing, was move toward a new structure with a new method of operation." *283

Barbara Marx Hubbard, author of the book *Conscious Evolution: Awakening the Power of Our Social Potential*, has said the following: "This is the first time in history that a species is aware that its own actions are causing it to go extinct......This is a great calling for humanity to move toward maturity. We have entered the first phase of self-awareness, which involves moving from unconscious evolution through natural selection to conscious evolution by choice. As a species, we finally understand the entire evolutionary process and jointly take responsibility for guiding all humans on the planet into this process of evolution."

Marx Hubbard has also stated: "What we need right now is a global summons, a call to everyone to come and take part in what could be the greatest series of events in the history of the planet: a global evolution.

This has been collectively manifested from human awareness. This call to humanity comes right at a time when the global voice for conscious evolution is emerging and the entire world can hear it." 284

Human beings will for the first time play a significant role in shifting the future of the planet. If we continue to only place our focus on our own lives, however, or the area, region, or country we live in, we will not see how serious the planet's current predicament truly is. We will also fail to see why these scholars of Future Studies are rallying the public to collectively "wake up," jointly take part and act for change.

The first step in "waking up," I believe, is the willingness to "see," and the desire to change. In Chapter 6 I explained the essential value of "seeing." Simply "seeing" is enough to induce "change." Only when you want to "see" can you truly elevate your outlook and wake up from your deep slumber. And when you reach the state of "complete seeing" you will know how to adjust yourself, how to act, and how to contribute as we collectively stride toward the path of higher level evolution. Laszlo also mentioned that a variety of clues and pieces of evidence signal that the planet is currently moving toward a place of crisis and collapse. There are five major driving factors, or "drivers of chaos" leading society toward destruction, as follows (*285):

No. 1: The current global method of allocating wealth is unsustainable.
No. 2: Affluent consumption is difficult to maintain.
No. 3: Development of the current global financial system is hard to maintain.
No. 4: The unsustainability of the present social structure will cause the pressure on social groups to climb, which will be unmaintainable.
No. 5: The burden humans place on nature has led to the unsustainability of the ecosystem, making it difficult for the planet to cope.

Humans are faced with one new challenge after another. The current population of the planet has already exceeded 7.2 billion, and it is estimated that it will reach 9 billion before 2050. Gandhi perhaps said it best when he remarked: "The world has enough for everyone's need, but not enough for everyone's greed."

Those who are interested in this issue may want to carefully read the book *Chaos Point 2012 and Beyond: Appointment with Destiny*. Laszlo explains in the book that this wave of challenges brought by civilizational transition display two forms of growth: "extensive growth" and "intensive growth." The prevalent mindset in past eras was a vestige of the Age of Pisces. Human's desire for control reached its apex in the industrial revolution, and can be characterized by "extensive growth" of a "competitive mindset." Yet another type of mindset is emerging in the Age of Aquarius: a mindset characterized by "intensive growth" in the context of mutual honor and creativity. Extensive growth produces unsustainable development and generate even more chaos and tumult. Intensive growth, on the other hand, gives rise to sustainable development and takes society in a new direction. It may even bring about a new civilization.

The ultimate objective of extensive growth can be conveyed using the three 'Cs,' as follows:

Conquest
Colonization
Consumption

Laszlo explains that the old form of society employed several measures to attain these goals: the first is utilizing technology for the use and modification of materials; which is to say, manufacturing technology. The second is producing energy to drive technology for the conversion of materials; in other words, energy production technology. The third is technology that whets the appetite, creates artificial demand, and modifies patterns of consumption – that is to say, marketing, public relations, and advertising technology.

Intensive growth can also be represented with three Cs:

Connection
Communication
Consciousness

Laszlo once again debunked a prevalent misconception that has existed since the Industrial Revolution, which is that the distance between each entity is growing and that the individual is nothing more than a self-centered actor pursuing his own economic profit and narrow interests, and that his interests are not linked to the interests of other individuals, as well as the group and the state.

A new direction in which to work for growth, and the second objective, is recognizing the new meaning of communication: deepening the strength and breadth of communication, while at the same time raising our mutual level of consciousness through communication.

Communication in the new era is multifaceted and involves heart to heart communication. Yet before we can do this, we must first communicate with ourselves, get to know ourselves deeply, and understand the true meaning of our existence. After all, it is only by entering our inner world and connecting with our own hearts that we can connect with the hearts of others. Laszlo refers to people who have entered their inner world as "people who connect with themselves," especially those who can see their "true selves." Such people have an attitude that is more stable and balanced, and are better able to truly interact and communicate with others and with the world.

Deep communication precipitates deep mutual understanding and creates a connection, allowing for the expansion and connection of a deeper consciousness built on a new and mutual set of values. Deep communication requires a highly matching level of consciousness, enabling people with similar thoughts, consciousness, and levels of frequency to utilize the myriad forms of technology, along with other elements, to forge a connection between themselves, the environment, and all things. The new consciousness from this connection will create a butterfly effect, elevating people from the old, outmoded, and self-centered level of existence to one characterized by mutual honor; a level that is urgently needed and emphasizes the group, ecology, the planet, and the sustainability of life.

Laszlo wrote: "Evolution with a focus on connection, communication, and consciousness will create a foundational shift in the dominant civilization of the planet. This will orient the next change in a positive direction; from reason to 'Holos.'" *276

However, history teaches us that the factors determining social change are the collective consciousness of humans and the resolve of all global citizens – this decides the direction in which we grow.

This crucial turning point, this power that will assist civilization to evolve in a new direction, will enable us to more consciously choose the future at which we will arrive.

In his book, Laszlo introduces an interesting perspective, postulating how humans will have developed by 2030, the prevalent world view by then, and the possible differences in lifestyle between then and now. He writes:

"The lifestyle will have changed to allow for sustainable ecological development; from a pursuit of external growth in the past, people's focus will shift toward internal growth; from the initial objectives of conquest and consumption, people's objectives will shift to a hope for improved thought and conduct, and groups will achieve growth. As a result, the demand for energy and material goods will have declined, which will improve efficiency of use. People will work in concert to improve their mutually shared lives and work spaces, and communal living will be restored. The spirit will also be reborn. Men and women will rediscover a higher and deeper purpose to their lives and existence." *287

In 2030, we will move toward a more diverse form of social development, and it will seem as though there is a new type of consciousness taking root, as people gravitate towards mutual and meaningful principles, and strive for prosperity. A summary of this is provided as follows: *288

If the lifestyle led by an individual leads to a reduction in the chance for basic welfare and human dignity of another, then this is unethical.

Establish on the planet a relationship of trust between human beings and natural resources and do not deplete such resources for the sake of certain narrow interests or short-term gain.

Nature is not a mechanism that has been designed and developed, but is instead a type of life system that allows us to live within it, nurtures us, and bestows on us the terrifying power to develop or destroy it. We now have to use this power to care for nature.

The correct method for solving problems and conflicts is not to attack, but instead involves mutual understanding and cooperation, and a consideration of everyone's mutual interests.

Universal rights adopted by visionaries in the 20th century – such as free speech, democratic voting, the right to not have one's freedom infringed or restricted, and the right to food, shelter, education, and work – will apply to people all over the world, and will be worthy of respectful consideration over the interests of the individual, the group, and the state.

Thus, life in 2030 could be very different to life at present. The critical question is whether we can make a crucial decision at present. Gandhi once said: Live more simply, so others can simply live.

We must have common universal values, must start from the wisdom in our hearts, and take action that tilts us toward sustainability. Our mode of lifestyle should move from the external to the internal so that we can solve our core problems. By adopting an innovative method that blends the internal and external we will be able to help all other beings achieve a blessed life.

The correct path for humans no longer involves the four cardinal directions (north, south, east, and west), but instead requires moving "up." Moving up implies evolving and raising one's consciousness. American anthropologist Margaret Mead once said: "Never underestimate the power of a small group to change the world. In fact, it is the only thing that ever has."

When you choose to evolve your consciousness, and this one pure thought manifests into action, you have already affected thousands of people in the instant the thought arose. However you want to change the world, first manifest that change in yourself. If you raise your level of consciousness, you already have what it takes to change the world. Laszlo puts forward ten standards for evolving consciousness. He believes that if the individual achieves the following standards, his or her consciousness will evolve. I personally feel that this set of standards is highly worthy of consideration. Let's take a look now:

① You method of living allows others to live a good life, and the process of satisfying your own needs does not impede others from satisfying their own needs.
② Your method of living respects the rights of all people with regards to life, economic, and cultural development, irrespective of where the person lives, their ethnicity, sex, nationality, lifestyle choices, or faith.

③ Your method of living protects your most fundamental rights, while at the same time protecting the environment that supports all life and growth on the planet.

④ Pursuing happiness, freedom, and personal satisfaction in harmonious coexistence with nature, while at the same time bearing in mind comparable pursuits by others.

⑤ Demand that your government recognize other countries and other peoples in the spirit of peace and cooperation, and that it acknowledges the right of the people to pursue a better life and provide a healthy environment in which humans can survive.

⑥ Demand that enterprises take responsibility for their shareholders and for the sustainable development of the local environment in all of their locations. Demand that the products they manufacture and the services they provide meet legal requirements, that they are not destroying nature, and that they do not diminish the opportunities for new, small-scale companies that lack privilege to compete on the market.

⑦ Demand that the mass media continues to provide reliable information on basic trends and critical processes so that you and fellow citizens and consumers can make informed decisions regarding issues that affect your lifestyle and welfare.

⑧ Make some space in your life to help those less fortunate than yourself lead a life of dignity so that they do not have to go through the struggle and humiliation associated with poverty.

⑨ Encourage the youth, and people of all ages with an open mind, to evolve their spirit, and give them the strength to make ethical decisions regarding their future and the future of their children.

⑩ Collaborate with like-minded people to conserve or restore the fundamental balance of the environment, while at the same time paying attention to your local neighborhood, the area in which you live and the entire biosphere.

You will find that this is the existential consciousness we should have as human beings living in the 21st century. Yet we must avoid the possibility of these principles being venerated and turned into a set of external dogma. The best approach is to enter into one's internal "true self" and Divinity, so that you can restore your spirit consciousness. Then, from this place of expanded and lucid awareness, we can truly understand life, nature, the ecosystem, the universe, and even the spiritual realm, and therefore naturally develop our spiritual intelligence quotient (SQ) while being at one with all of life and all things.

External to internal change is the old and conventional method of change. Internal to external change represents a true revolution of consciousness for this century. If this is accompanied by a pursuit of the 16 types of power developed from the "true self," then I believe this flame of evolution will rise up and sweep across the entire world. If a spiritual component is not incorporated, however, regardless of how much value an external solution may seem to hold, in time it will also be made into a false self-identity, and a new shadow created.

In the book *Transpersonal Psychology*, mentioned in the previous chapter, André Lefebvre wrote the following:

"Logotherapist Joseph Fabry provided an incredibly vivid account of the spiritual dimension, as follows: 'Spirituality is just like your physical body or psychology, it is a part of you and not merely a religious tendency. The spiritual dimension...... includes the determination to seek meaning, the orientation of our goals, our creativity, imagination, direct observation, faith, a longing for growth, transcendence of the physical, the psychological ability to love, the ability to not be controlled by the super-ego (the 'moral ego' mentioned by Freud) and to listen to one's conscience, a sense of humor, and exclusively human traits such as these. It also involves the letting go of ego, or taking a step back to observe oneself, transcend the ego, or show concern for those we love or matters relevant to our beliefs. In the realm of spirituality we are not being controlled, but are in fact the decision maker that can control the bigger picture. Whether a religious or a secular person, all people own a healthy and complete 'treasure chest.' Most of the objects hidden in this treasure chest consist of our (higher) subconscious. The mission of a logotherapist is to help people become aware of the existence of this spiritual first aid kit. *291

Carl Rogers is a psychologist and one of the most influential figures in the field of counseling and psychotherapy in the West. In his earlier years, he also habitually underestimated the importance of the spiritual dimension. But later on, after several experiences with the transcendent, the indescribable, the spiritual realm, he and Maslaow both modified their theories to incorporate a spiritual element. He said: "Humans possess a vast intuitive potential, and are indeed much smarter than merely our reasoning minds. The evidence for this is conclusive."

Rogers was not alone in this belief. Psychosynthesis expert, Robert Gerard, also proposed the importance of the "spiritual," stating: "The spiritual......refers to anything which has a value that transcends the mundane. This includes the empathy associated with putting yourself in someone else's shoes, universal love, wisdom and foresight, inspiration for creativity, aesthetic appreciation, sense of responsibility, and dedicated enthusiasm. It also refers to the so-called mystical experiences of oneness with the universe." *293

Thus, we firmly believe in the need for sustainability, and the need to progress toward sustainable well-being for all humans. We also need to develop the spiritual power hidden in the minds of every individual so as to prompt the emergence of "new humans" in this new century.

In July 1932, American clairvoyant Edgar Cayce prophesized that a new form of human being would emerge between 1998 and 2015.

In transpersonal psychology, when we do spiritual exercises or undergo spiritual training, the remarkable internal experience of having our consciousness raised turns us into a truly "spiritual person" (regardless of whether or not we believe in religion), and we automatically develop the spiritual traits exclusive to this "new human." I have taken the traits of a "spiritual person" and added my own experience over the past several years to formulate the traits of this "new human." The traits this new human possesses include the following ten elements: *294

① **The transcendent:** He not only believes in the existence of the inner core; that is, his true self or Svabhava, but has actually experienced the transcendent life consciousness, and gained power from the experience.

② **The meaning and purpose of life:** He believes that there is a deep meaning to life; that his existence and that of others, and even other living creatures, undoubtedly has a purpose and value.

③ **A mission in life:** A "calling," vocation, or mission is the supreme motivation that spurs him into action.

④ **The Divinity of life:** He believes that the source of all life can and should become Divine.

⑤ **A different mindset toward material value:** He knows how to appreciate and enjoy the material world, as well as the beauty of the material world, but he does not view that as the ultimate purpose.

⑥ **Universal love:** He has a strong sense of intuition, integrity, and compassion, revels in serving others, and can easily expand the scope of his love to encompass people, the ecosystem, and all things.

⑦ **Idealism:** He is willing to dedicate himself for the sake of his noble ideals and to change the world, and works diligently to change himself from the inside out.

⑧ **Awareness of pain:** He feels deeply the pain, suffering, and death of humans and creatures. Yet this experience does not diminish the appreciation he has or onus he places on life, and the deep understanding he has for the essence of life – the true self, or Svabhava. On the contrary, from the pain and suffering of humans and other creatures his realization of the self grows deeper, and he is able to give to others undiscriminating love.

⑨ **Spiritual achievement:** The achievements of his spiritual cultivation can be clearly seen in his lifestyle and in his ultimate existential relationships with himself, others, nature, and in everything that he affirms.

⑩ **Holds the wisdom of "ultimate concern" for all life:** He deeply understands the wisdom that all life and even the origin is in fact at one with himself. As a result, he is able to display "ultimate concern," the higher wisdom of life, to others, the ecosystem, the planet, and all life.

You can imagine that if you develop the previously-mentioned ten standards of evolution plus the above ten spiritual elements of "new humans," you can produce a merging of the inner and the outer, which constitutes true power. In the process of evolution, this enables humans to truly advance and progress toward a new civilization.

This is why we have persisted with such determination and hard work over the years, trying continuously to restore the unbelievable power that exists in the depths of everyone's mind. Only by once again coming to know ourselves and pursuing the universal value of the "true self" can we raise our field of vision, and then search for and incorporate wise external solutions. From here, we not only have a global view, but this global view "turns into" a universal view that embodies the entire universal consciousness. We subsequently move toward a super cosmic view, which is a view of complete insight and undiscriminating love within super cosmic consciousness. By attaining this state we can jointly and easily reverse and change the destiny of the planet's future.

A Clean Life – A Practical Blueprint for the 6Cs

"Humanity will not perish in 1999. The hope for the savior of humanity lies in the East. The West only represents the end."
– American psychic and astrologer, Jeane Dixon

As early as Feb 1991, Czech President Václav Havel delivered a speech to both houses of Congress. In an earnest tone, he warned:

"Without a global revolution in the sphere of human consciousness, nothing will change for the better in the sphere of our being as humans, and the catastrophe for which the world is headed – be it ecological, social, demographic, or a general breakdown of civilization – will be unavoidable."

Back in 1991 this visionary leader had already foreseen that, short of a global revolution in the sphere of human consciousness, any remedial solution would fail to bring a noticeable result. I do not believe that this is a pessimistic point of view, because there are many signs that suggest this, and many scholars, including Laszlo, who unanimously believe that the breakdown of civilization is avoidable. Furthermore, our consciousness – including yours – is evolving. We can even combine our energy to help collective consciousness progress farther along the path of evolution.

This is precisely why you and I have met on this planet in this era, and why we are pushing for a "Clean Revolution" that will change the nature of humans' internal consciousness. In this era of high-risk, it is only by combining a major revolution in human consciousness and devising wise, external solutions that we will be able to help each other get past this catastrophe. Infinitas International brings people together in an attempt to reduce the risk to society as a whole, and in the hope of serving as a bridge for human civilization, assisting people to resume the search for meaning in their lives, generate group unity, and connect platforms of wisdom and power everywhere. We therefore propose the Clean Life 6Cs Practical Project. The Project provides people and societies in this transition period with a method of living that allows them to protect and elevate themselves; a method of living that is full of promise. It provides people who have encountered a wide range of changes in this "transition period" with the chance to be "reborn."

Let me now introduce to you the specific content of Clean Life 6Cs:

Clean Heart
Clean Medicine
Clean Education
Clean Community
Clean Economy
Clean Energy

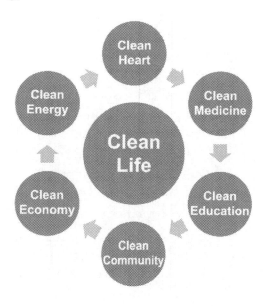

Clean Heart

The mind possesses a power that is not yet understood. Napoleon Hill once said: "*Throughout their lives, people on average only utilize 7.2 percent of their psychological potential. What is the other 92.8 percent of potential doing? The answer: it's in a deep sleep.*"

Experts that research the subconscious believe that your destiny is determined by five percent of your subconscious. Did you know that Einstein and Edison utilized 2.5% of their subconscious minds, Bill Gates and Warren Buffet utilize 2% of their subconscious, and the first African American president of the United States uses 1.8% of his subconscious power?

Imagine if your mind possessed infinite power. What is it exactly that is impeding such power?

A "clean heart" is the belief that the human spirit has infinite potential, a possesses the noble "true self," this infinite wisdom database that stores up all the wisdom – big data. As long as we once again come to know ourselves, reclaim the key to developing the power of spiritual wisdom, and grab hold of the countless obstacles, such as shadows, imprints, and false self-identities that derive from our subconscious and previous lives, and deal with these by first facing them, then clearing, transforming, and transcending them, we will recognize the "clean heart" contained in the following lines: "Nothing is really there, / Where can any dust land?"

A clean heart refers to purity and stillness, just like the realm of tranquillity talked of in the Qingjing Jing. Confusion is born of the heart, yet so too is awakening. When we once again come to know the power of the heart, delve deeply once again into the treasure trove of wisdom, and once again unlock our spiritual intelligence, we will gain a "clean" view of the world, and view with fresh eyes our lives, our surrounds, and everything in nature and the world.

The Satdharma Institute carries the mission of nurturing "Clean Hearts," providing a path for spiritual training and allowing for spiritual growth, spiritual training, spiritual exercises, so that learners eventually gain a blueprint for the complete spectrum of consciousness. This stops us from losing direction in the event that we do not see the "heart" while trying to explore the power of the spirit through research and verification.

We guide learners in a professional and nuanced way to delve deep into their own subconscious and view the different kinds of potholes, imprints, and forces of dualistic opposition, and effectively connect to the wisdom of the "true self" and expand the power of "love," thus dissolving and transforming the oppositional aspects of one's heart. While being guided to expand their consciousness at each level, learners will spontaneously develop intuitive awareness and the ability to observe directly, enabling them to continuously undertake spiritual training through the realizations they come to in their everyday lives as they mature and grow older. Thus, in time we are able to immediately intuit the core reality in any given moment.

When all people – or at least an increasing number of people – gradually come to recognize the essence and power of the "heart," and gradually put into practice inner and outer spiritual training, they will wield in their hands the wisdom to transform their lives and the world. This is one of the pieces of information I hope to transmit through this book. For when you change the angle from which you view things and elevate yourself to have an intrinsically clean and tranquil viewpoint, you can do as we do: jointly witness all the miracles that occur in your life every day and even in every moment. At our Institute, we already have over 10,000 people continuously experience such miracles!

Learners at the Satdharma Institute have in the past tried their best to tell others about the myriad miracles they have experienced, including sharing this with family, friends, co-workers and others. But no matter how hard they try, they can't seem to get the message across, and it only ends up causing misunderstandings. In actual fact, what they really want to say is this: It feels like waking up after many years of deep sleep; being at one again after years of feeling fractured; feeling a wonderful sense of "love" again; a brand new feeling of being "understood," supported, healed; a deep sense of returning "home," as though once again laying down "roots" in the earth of the planet; once again possessing love, power, wisdom, and even the brand new experience of recognizing one's self-nature. We firmly believe that we can only thoroughly change when we change our hearts; that only by healing the "heart" can we heal ourselves, our families, and work to jointly heal the world. We hope to rekindle the light in your heart, so that you may not only light up your own future path, but also for the entire world, illuminating the unknown, evolutionary challenges that lie in the path ahead.

We hope to nurture more and more people who are aware of this light, as well as professional spiritual teachers and instructors. Our goal is to have 1,800 such instructors in Taiwan, and 26,000 around the world, working in concert to drive the infinite power of evolution across the planet so as to help one percent of the world's population awaken, and then connect the infinite power of these "new humans" to form an "infinite power network." In doing so, we will unleash a butterfly effect for the all-powerful force of awakening, and restore the world to its pristine state of "cleanliness." When more and more people change their "hearts" and raise their level of consciousness, it brings up the level of collective consciousness to the point of intrinsic "cleanliness," and increasing numbers of people will "see" that the planet is already a paradise.

We pray that during this chaotic and tumultuous "transition period," each individual is able to gain stability in their heart, kindle the light in their own heart, and wisely protect their own heart, as well as that of their family, the broader society, and the heart of all beings. By displaying the power of their "true selves," they will help turn the planet into a paradise filled with "love."

The Satdharma Institute hopes to become the world's foremost institute in the humanities and the area of spiritual growth. It hopes to nurture exceptional spiritual instructors, thereby allowing the power of awakening to blossom across the world.

The mission of the Institute:

To awaken the intrinsic power of the heart, nurture enlightened individuals who have transcended the ego consciousness and realized their deepest dreams, thereby helping to bring the glory of paradise back to the Earth.

Vision: Build the world's most complete system for spiritual awakening, and create a new era of conscious evolution in the world.

Brand declaration: Become a source of life wisdom that allows people to turn their life around and realize their dreams.

Brand promise: To be able to gracefully transcend one's difficulties, even when one's life is in a state of confusion.

Plan for 2015:

① Promote the popular spiritual growth course "Life Success," as well as the EasyTurn series of courses.

② Promote the Satdharma meditation method. Due to the fact that stress has severely affected the health of people in recent years, the Satdharma Institute offers an ancient Eastern method of meditation. We are set to begin offering meditation classes and large-scale meditation retreats throughout Taiwan, allowing local Taiwanese people to restore their spiritual health. Please search and register online to take part in such events.

③ Enhance the three-part "Transcend the Ego" course, which is designed to completely transform the consciousness of learners and allow them to effortlessly become agents of life wisdom and realize their deepest dreams of fulfillment.

④ Enhance the teacher training program for spiritual instructors, allowing you to become well-rounded spiritual training instructors and offer courses around the world to jointly affect the world and help turn the planet into a sustainable paradise.

⑤ Collaborate with the responsible division at the Fareast Campus of Bircham International University, which allows instructors at the Institute to receive dual certification and an internationally-recognized master's degree. For medium and long-term projects, please feel free to search online. We invite you to clean your heart together with us.

The 6Cs of a Clean Life

Clean Medicine

"Complete health is tantamount to enlightenment" Geshe Yeshe Tobden once said.

Medicine is of primary concern when it comes to matters of life and death. "Cleanliness" implies that we offer a completely new perspective from which to view medicine. If complete health is tantamount to enlightenment, then clean medicine involves helping people to awaken starting from the heart. By cleaning the body and mind from the comprehensive dimension of integrated medicine, people receive holistic and complete health for the body, mind, and soul. In the play Faust, Goethe wrote: "People who research organic entities with a rigid attitude reject the existence of the soul, and so hold a one-sided view of the truth, reflected in their classifications. Yet as a result, they lose their connection to the source of the soul." This line can be applied to everything. Yet when applied to modern day medicine, it underscores the contemporary problem that by only having a firm grasp on one aspect of truth, classification, and specialization, we are unable to view the "complete picture." Diseases and symptoms tell us that there has been a loss of balance in the "whole." "Disease" is a lack of harmony or "ease."

As early as 2500 years ago, the father of Western medicine, Hippocrates *297, said the following: "*The natural healing force within each of us is the greatest force in getting well.*" Another famous quote of Hippocrates: "*Let food be thy medicine and medicine be thy food.*" *298 He believed that the best doctor is sunlight, air, and exercise. An anatomist once went as far as to say: "Our internal healer is the smartest, most complex, and most complete 'entity' in the universe." *299

From the perspective of integrated medicine, a very real doctor exists within us. It is just that modern medicine and education is unable to see this.

"*'The consciousness of the heart' possesses a healing power that medicine is unable to completely understand. To date, medicine has verified that change in a patient's psychological state is critical to the patient's recovery. Whether it be cancer, schizophrenia, or the flu, the source of all diseases points to both the body and mind.*" *300

Dr. Dietrich Klinghardt, an integrated medicine doctor in Seattle, US, has formulated a holistic healing chart for the body, mind, and spirit. The chart perfectly reflects the seven subtle bodies of life outlined in Chapter 3, which operate, coordinate, and collaborate in order to bring about a set of new and unique overall life values, a sense of meaning, and health. Let's now have a look at these five layers of healing (image 14):

① Physical Level:

This relates to the basic anatomy of the human body, as well as mechanics, chemistry, pathology and other related fields. Its methods for testing include: blood tests, biochemical lab tests, MRIs, PET/CT scans, x-rays, iridology tests, and so on. Related medicine includes: all kinds of surgery, wound care, urgent care, emergency treatment, drugs, massage, herbal medicine, nutritional therapy, detoxification, and so on.

② Electrical Control Level (Biochemical Level):

Science related to this level comprises: physics, biochemistry, and functional medicine. Its methods for testing include: EEG, EKG, EMG, monitoring for variations in heart rate, Chinese pulses, aetoscans, AVS, thermogram, Mora, Art (kinesiology), and so on. Related medicine includes: homeopathy, essence therapy, aromatherapy, acupuncture, nerve therapy with short-acting anesthesia, the allergy elimination technique (AET), emotional release, breath therapy, laugh therapy, light meditation, focus training, stress release, detoxification, and light therapy are all related to restoration of health on this level.

③ Mind Level (Mental Level):

Related scientific fields include: psychology, psychosomatic medicine, psychical studies, and transpersonal psychology. Its testing methods include: psychological testing, homeopathic repertorizing, energy equipment testing, and so on. Related areas of medicine include: classical homeopathy, applied psychobiology, psychotherapy, support therapy, faith healing, self-knowing therapy, methods for deep meditation, active imagining, and mental rehearsal. This level already deals with consciousness. This level comprises all placebo effects. That is, a trust and strong belief in the effectiveness of a treatment.

Integrated Diagram for Health and Healing of the Sacred Body / Created by Dr. Dietrich Klinghardt, MD

	Our Experience at this Level	Anatomical and Conceptual - Designation	Related Science	Diagnostic" Method	Related Medical Treatment and Healing Techniques	Satdharma Institute Designations for the Seven Bodies
5th Level Spiritual Body	Bliss, Oneness with God, Satori	God, Spirit, Higher Consciousness	Religion and Spirituality	Knowing and Awareness	Self-Healing, Prayer, True Meditation	Cosmic Body
4th Level Intuitive Body	Dreams, Trance, Meditative States	Unconscious, "No Mind," Family Consciousness	Quantum Physics	Dream Interpretation, Radicsthesia	Systemic Family Constellation, Hypnotherapy, Rituals / Shamanism, Radionics, Past Life Hypnotherapy	Astral Body
3rd Level Mental Body	Beliefs, Attitudes, Thoughts	Mind, Conscious and Subconscious (Logical)	Psychology and Homeopathy	Psychological Testing, Homeopathic Repertorizing	Classical Homeopathy, Applied Psycho-Neurobiology (APN I), Psychotherapy, Self-Control, Deep Meditation	Mental Body
2nd Level Electrical Control Level	Feelings	Nervous System, Meridians, Seventh Chakra	Physiology and Functional Medicine	Automatic Response Testing (ART), Thermogram, Heart Rate Variation, EEG, EKG, EMG, Chinese Pulses, Aetoscan / Dermatron	Neural Therapy (Short-Acting Anesthesia) Acupuncture AET Breath therapy Release of Emotions Laughing Aromatherapy Light Meditation	Emotional Body

238

1st Level Physical Level	Sensations, Action, Movement	Structure Skeleton, organs, cells... Biochemistry	Mechanics, Chemical Pathology / Allopathy	Physical Exam Biochemistry Lab Tests Imaging: MRI CT Scan X-Ray Photography	Natural Medicine Detoxification Health Supplements, Organ Support Herbal Medicine, Nutrients Technique, Treatment Drugs Surgery	Physical Body

Meaning association has a significant connotation in this context. For instance, the meaning of life, and the meaning of diseases and symptoms, can bring about unbelievable power for recovery.

④ Intuitive Level (Celestial Level):

Here we start to come into contact with deeper levels of the unconscious, family consciousness, collective consciousness, and the effect of related consciousness fields and subtle energy fields. Related science includes: quantum physics, Jung's theory of the unconscious, parapsychology, transpersonal psychology, psychical studies, and so on. Related testing includes: dream interpretation, O-rings, and AVS. Related medical treatments include: past life hypnotherapy, consciousness clearing therapy, transpersonal therapy, radionics, therapeutic systems of shamanism, systemic family constellation, source-field constellation, aura therapy, active imagining, qigong, Yana yoga, deep meditation, and so on. This level already involves a connection with a "higher dimension." The power of "order" brought by the bio-photons and the higher "energy field" here can be transmitted from the healer to the patient.

⑤ Spiritual Level (Spirit Level)

This level relates to oneness with the universe, spirituality, religion, and spiritual experiences, and corresponds to the "spiritual" level that Maslow talked of in his later years. The science possessed here relates to traditional religious wisdom, spiritual wisdom, and the wisdom passed down from ancient times. In terms of testing methods, it can only be sensed through intuition, insights, or by medical care personnel whose consciousness has expanded to this level. Treatment methods include precise AVS, related medical methods, higher self healing, prayer, meditation, source field constellation, transpersonal therapy, faith healing, and so on. This level is related to the higher self power of a higher consciousness level. It is also the realm that traditional spiritual seekers from across the world believe hold "Divine power" – the power of universal consciousness is an inseparable power. This level cannot yet be verified by science in a precise manner. Yet well-known spiritual therapists from around the world, regardless of culture, all enjoy a close connection and cooperation with the power at this level.

Each healing level reveals an essential message: Only when we have a complete health and healing blueprint can we grasp the true cause of the illness and avoid the trap of trying to cure the problem at the point where pain is felt. Moreover, the general atmosphere the patient senses at each level of treatment has a significant effect on whether full healing can occur, and this effect cannot be underestimated.

Overseas research on integrated medicine has already found that adopting a single method from the Physical Level, Electrical Control Level, or Intuitive Level will eventually lead to a treatment bottleneck. Only through an integrated treatment approach can we incorporate treatment methods from different levels to attain an optimal healing effect.

Many illnesses have proven to be psychogenic in nature, with the proportion of such cases being relatively high. In the current situation, where the health of the Taiwanese population is growing in severity by the day, if we are able to discover causes of illness at different levels as early as possible, and then address these issues and treat them in a timely manner, I believe that we will reach our desired outcome, which is for prevention to outweigh treatment.

Integrated medicine is a type of holistic, preventative medicine for the body, mind, and spirit. It views the patient as the most important member of the medical team. In an effort to help patients recover the overall health of their body, mind, and spirit to optimal effect, this approach does not confine itself to any single school of medical theory, and instead utilizes all safe and effective techniques available to treat the problem. Integrated medicine consists of the following characteristics:

① It puts the patient first.
② Treatment methods are holistic and consistently integrated.
③ It emphasizes patient responsibility and empowerment.
④ It stresses the importance of diet and nutrition.
⑤ It focuses on the overall recovery of body function and is not limited to the symptoms or treatment of the illness.
⑥ It utilizes the least toxic treatments, or effective treatments that are natural and contain no side effects.
⑦ It emphasizes the innate self-healing abilities of the body.
⑧ It puts an onus on changing one's lifestyle to prevent illness.

The Yana Wholistic Medical Center holds the mission of promoting clean medicine, and collaborates with others to create a truly holistic medical platform for the body, mind, and spirit. Its goal is to nurture professional personnel who truly wish to enter the field of integrated medicine, and treat members of the public who truly wish to restore their overall health. Moreover, it aims to lower the risk of illness in this high-risk society, and help people to regain their basic knowledge of holistic health for the body, mind, and spirit.

The Clinic's plans for 2015:

① Provide effective solutions for total healing of ailments such as insomnia, ADD, sexual dysfunction for married couples, and assisted treatment for cancer; and allow patients to achieve the most marked results in the shortest amount of time.
② The objective of integrated dentistry: public awareness of the facts that "teeth are actually a bodily organ" and "teeth are also a reflex region" is not very widespread. Overseas research has found that almost all causes of illness in the first three bodies are related to one's teeth. In fact, 80% - 90% of illness is the result of problems with one's oral cavity and tonsils, and such knowledge would help to enhance health education and courses regarding the effect of

teeth on overall health. Moreover, the oral cavity is the entrance for the respiratory tract. Healthy development of the oral cavity can help raise the body's oxygen content. By adjusting the oral cavity without pulling teeth, lifting the bite, using a bite plate, and so on, doctors can help patients improve various conditions, including allergies, snoring, sleep apnea, reduce the incidence of pain in the fascia throughout the body, and prevent chronic illnesses from occurring.

③ Regarding the phenomenon of risk factors for health increasing with age, this year we will hold a "Quantum Detox Camp" for the new century which will provide nourishment, detoxification, repair, and reinforcement of the vital essence and strengthening of the 'chi' so as to achieve a state of optimal health and balance for the body, mind, and spirit.

④ Actively expand holistic health education lectures and provide free health instruction on Yana yoga each month to help Taiwanese citizens raise their level of overall health, whether it be body, mind, or spirit, as well as their intellectual capacity.

⑤ We hope to expand the influence of the free medical clinics we hold each year in Cambodia and to cooperate with the local Cambodian government with the hope of achieving an outcome in which prevention exceeds treatment.

Tending to one's health cannot be delayed. Medicine is currently in the process of moving from the old paradigm of treatment to a new paradigm. More and more doctors in the field of integrated medicine have discovered the essential role that "spirituality" plays in the process of total healing. Famous American surgeon Rick Ingrasci once said: "As soon as we undergo a 'spiritual reformation' – that is to say, a change in attitude, values, and beliefs – and recreate a balanced relationship between ourselves and the universe, we will directly produce the outcome of healing as a result of viewing ourselves as the whole." From his many years of interacting with patients, he verified that "As soon as the spiritual pain is removed, the process of healing will automatically commence." *301 A critical mission of clean medicine is figuring out how to expand one's field of vision and how to wield the wisdom crucial to reversing an array of illnesses. Health is a state in which our body and consciousness are able to create new meaning from our "symptoms" and from a variety of "new information" and then change these. If our spirit was more flexible and extendable and could more spaciously adapt to myriad changes in the environment and the effects of risk factors, I am certain that we would regain our power to fully heal. Let's work together to achieve this goal!

Clean Education

Emerson once said: *"A reliable metric for wisdom is the ability to find miracles in the mundane."* The famous playwright George Bernard Shaw once offered the following thought-provoking remark: *"Some men see things as they are and say, why; I dream things that never were and say, why not."* *302

Life is changing at an alarming rate. The world is moving at almost ten times the rate at which the education system is moving, which leads one to ponder: what is the actual essence of education? And what type of graduate are we trying to produce? Moreover, what type of characteristics must "new humans" of future eras possess?

It is not for no reason that we are living in this modern era, an era in which anything can be manifested, an era of limitless possibilities. With this potential for infinite opportunities and in this era of endless innovation, all I know is that everything is going to change. An educational and learning revolution is afoot and proceeding at pace.

American doctor of education, Jeannette Vos, along with Gordon Dryden, wrote a future education book entitled The Learning Revolution. In this book, they talk of a mild yet active educational revolution. This revolution is imminent, and we ourselves will participate in it. Yet it could more aptly be described as a spiritual revolution, a revolution in which we learn how to learn and how to find the optimal answers.

The English term "education" comes from Latin ēducātiō, and comprises connotations of "nurturing" and "eliciting." In other words, education must involve guidance to nurture and elicit or stimulate students' internal gifts and wisdom, and to develop students' life value in a well-rounded manner.

Education pertains to the essence of life. When examining a large array of social problems, I realized that the source of many of these problems is education. Yet just like in the fields of medicine, psychology, and religion, education as a whole is largely unwilling to traverse the "restricted zones" of academia and approach things from a brand new perspective, one that brings students in contact with the true essence – the true self, Svabhava.

Quick question: If an education system does not show students the essence of who they are, what type of person will such a system produce?

When false self-identities and incorrect values have already been "implanted" in us, should we still hope to find a solution through this "fractured" system of education?

Education not only fails to reach its own objectives, but also leads people off the right track. On top of this, a variety of other factors cause people to be "spiritually blocked."

American psychological educator and astrologer, Stephen Arroyo, once said: "When someone constructs a wall around their intelligence, it does not actually affect the world outside the wall. It only blocks the individual from seeing the external really, and may even distort the entire life structure." *303

"If a society continually encourages one-sided perspectives and distorted world views, how can it hope to produce people rich in innovation?" *304

If the values of parents, teachers, and society, as well as the overall education system is skewed toward "blocking spirituality," then there is a thick wall obstructing our view. In this situation, how can we hope to produce exceptional "new humans" of the future? Education determines our position in the universe. It related to how we unlock our potential, and whether we will become a species that transcends the ego and thus creates a new position and new values in the history of humanity. The infinite potential stored up in our intelligence is just waiting to be set free.

I previously mentioned American spiritual revolutionary Marilyn Ferguson. In the book she wrote with Neil Postman and Charles Weingartner, entitled Teaching as a Subversive Activity, several current educational blind spots are mentioned:

"English is not history and history is not science and science is not art and art is not music, and art and music are minor subjects and English, history and science major subjects, and a subject is something you 'take' and, when you have taken it, you have 'had' it, and if you have 'had' it, you are immune and need not take it again."

When learning is broken into small specializations; when all we care about is "taking" a class and not actually the essence of learning, this reflects the disjointedness of our minds. This is because we operate without understanding who we really are and why we need to learn.

In the preceding chapter, I stated that if we do not really know our true selves nor our true value, we will never be able to break free of our mental framework and the rigid values of society.

A long time has passed since Maslow's fifth need of self-actualization affected the values of society and the world. Yet the population has ignored the "spiritual needs" he proposed in his later years. By transcending our own egos, we discover our true wisdom, power, and values, and "achieve self-realization" in our lives. If we want to evolve to a point of "self-realization" in the next generation of humans, "new humans," how should we educate the upcoming generation? What kind of new paradigm will emerge in education and learning? And what effect will this new paradigm have on society and the world? I believe that the question of how to move from a hopeless to a hopeful system of learning will require diligent efforts from all of us. And this is precisely why we proposed our mission of "clean education."

The Age of Aquarius is an age related to technology, concepts, spirituality, and awakening. The approach to education that corresponds to this age is "transpersonal education." Its name was derived from a branch of psychology, as Ferguson notes: "The focus of this school of psychology is on human's ability to transcend. In a more complete form of education, learners receive encouragement for awakening and autonomy, for questioning and exploring all nooks and crannies of consciousness experiences; for pursuing meaning, for exploring external limits, and inspecting one's own alignment and depth." *306

In Chinese, the literal name for transpersonal education is "complete education." In other words, transpersonal education is a "complete education." I call it "fulfillment education."

Today, however, education no longer teaches people how to transcend and overcome (note: 'trans' in Webster's Dictionary), or how to transcend our ordinary consciousness and gain "direct knowing" in the subject we wish to learn. Our personal essence, the true self, can provide us with direction in life so we do not get lost while pursuing our life values and trying to attain perfection.

The world we see requires a various kinds of cross-disciplinary and integrated wisdom, innovation that can solve problems, a supreme value that is humane, and the passing down of civilization and wisdom. Yet if we are still using our past experiences and structures in an attempt to nurture a wise future species, this is just like what Einstein once said: *"As ignorant as wanting to find the correct answer in the wrong place."*

Arroyo once noted: "The more of life's wonders we find, the more we can integrate disparate fields of research and disparate knowledge systems." *307 He also said: *"Creativity is the ability developed from the wholeness of humanity. Thus, we must at least strive diligently toward this wholeness."* This echoes the sentiment expressed by Josef Rudin in his book *Psychotherapy and Religion*: "One cannot escape from his own soul without mutilating his life and also condemning himself to illness in the physical realm and to a perfidious, stereotyped productivity in the intellectual." *308

Today's education will soon shift toward "fulfillment education," and eventually "clean education." Clean education is currently assisting today's system of education to veer toward "fulfillment education." After all, we can only transcend ourselves and transcend this era by first discovering the wonders that lie within.

This is a long road. It requires even more educational reformers to join in as we walk along this path toward educational fulfillment and clean education.

Clean Community

In 1977, Ilya Prigogine received the Nobel prize after discovering a certain theory of change. He stated "We are currently at an exciting moment in history, a turning point." His theory confirmed that pressure and "chaos" will push us toward a higher order, and this applies not only to physics, but also to society.

In actual fact, change, reformation, and evolution are all natural reactions adopted by humans when faced with a crisis. In this critical time of change, what kind of force would we like to have steering us? Steering the direction of society? The chaos brought by these natural forces for change is not in fact the main factor that will cause a loss of control in society as we believe it to be. To the contrary, it is an ally in this time of change, forcing us to face the raft of "abnormalities" and "symptoms" plaguing society. If we try to lead this change using our dualistic and divided consciousness, we will sink into a state of divisiveness, an inability to come together and be as one. However, if we use a universal viewpoint or even a super cosmic viewpoint to examine these "abnormalities" or "symptoms," then such problems will become stepping stones that lead us to new heights of civilizational consciousness.

Ferguson cites the work of philosopher Beatrice Bruteau, who wrote: "We cannot wait for the world to turn, for times to change that we might change with them, for the revolution to come and carry us around in its new course. We are the future. We are the revolution." *309

In actual fact, many reformers have found that when we apply the old structure and the old paradigm to discuss reform, learning, life, and the mind, it elicits even more contradictions and a host of new problems.

A "transcendent" type of society is now gradually emerging, while the traditional forms of "learning organizations" and "learning societies" have already become obsolete. However, although these new transcendent structures appear to be more robust, comprehensive, provide more sustainable insights, and can explain all contradictions, they have been discredited as "heresy" by those of the old paradigm.

This "heresy" has caused panic and resistance from people in the old paradigm, but has also brought with it new principles, new hope, and new "possibilities."

This "transcendent" view easily subsumes the old paradigm, and with a broader view of the world, it reconciles the polarities of contradiction, creating oneness.

Thanks to its deep understanding of ontology, it easily integrates every field of scholarship, and intuitively sees the value of the essence. It also means that methods of problem-solving are no longer one-directional, but diverse.

Yet when a new paradigm emerges, human society is always sceptical, turning its nose up at it, viewing it with cold indifference, or sneering at and mocking it. It is similar to the experience Jack Ma, the Founder of Alibaba, previously had, which led him to believe that most people "Do not understand, do not see, look down on others, and are always a step behind."

A great evolution is presently being born in society, and as it squeezes its way through the birth canal, society is pushed, pressed, can't breathe properly, and feels asphyxiated – an anxiety rooted in essence, and even fear, loss of direction, and an inability to predict the future. Yet within this birth canal of evolution, we can actually provide ourselves with the power of "transcendence," which makes society smoother and more stable, allowing it to endure the "destructive" power of this transition.

Cleanliness is the discovery of the essence and direction of life. A clean society evolves and brings new social value by means of "transcendence."

Starting by cleaning one's own heart, we then progress to having a clean family; ensuring that the smallest unit of society, the family, regains its power and molds society into a stable nexus. Within this transformation, the family will not only help move society from the old paradigm to the new one, but also assists the individual to develop his or her own unique power of "transcendence." A group of "conspirators" will help increasingly to bring about a new (heart-based) consensus which will gradually lead to the formation of a "transcendent" community.

Within this future blueprint, Infinitas International hopes to create a new type of sustainable community that is both international and "transcendent." The details of this planned blueprint are still in the nascent stage and a specific book is needed for further extrapolation. In the meantime, we ask that everyone wait patiently.

On a separate note, a significant question that remains is how to expand our our consciousness to the entire universe and even super cosmos so that we become the "new human" of the "new century," experiencing the splendour of this expanded consciousness and connecting to the big data of the universe, and even effortlessly releasing our power for lasting change. All of this will assist society to undergo a deep-seated change in consciousness. We need ever more pioneers who are willing to help themselves and assist the energy field of the unknown true self, and to integrate, coordinate, and harmoniously connect with the source of all things and the wellspring of all wisdom; to combine internal and external solutions, and move toward a sustainable existence for all.

A clean society is a brand new type of society born of a brand new way of living. As opposed to just staying put, why not get into action? We invite all "pioneers" to jointly create a society consisting of "new humans" who will collectively stride toward a better tomorrow.

Clean Economy

"People who pursue perfection must not only earn a living, but create life" said Marilyn Ferguson, the author of *The Aquarian Conspiracy*.

The economy has gone from a system of bartering in ancient times to today's system of capitalism. Yet contemporary capitalism seems to be veering toward chaos.

In this civilization where we have virtually lost all connection to our roots and society's "immune system" is down, consumerism has caused the public to come down with the most terrifying and virulent disease of the 21 century – affluenza.

The book *Affluenza* emphasizes that this is a society-wide infectious disease. The cause of the disease is excessive want and the constant pursuit of material goods, leading to overload, mounting debt, anxiety, and waste. This ushers in untold pain and suffering, while the inability to quit constitutes an infectious social disease. This invisible and mutating mental virus is currently making its assault on society, on the economy, and on our minds. The author of the book tells a story that aptly describes this disease:

"In his office, a doctor offers his diagnosis to an attractive, expensively dressed female patient. "There's nothing physically wrong with you," he says. His patient is incredulous. "Then why do I feel so awful?" she asks. "So bloated and sluggish. I've got a big new house, a brand-new car, a new wardrobe, and I just got a big raise at work. Why am I so miserable, Doctor? Isn't there some pill you can give me?"

The doctor shakes his head. "I'm afraid not," he replies. "There's no pill for what's wrong with you." "What is it, Doctor?" she asks, alarmed. "Affluenza," he answers gravely. "It's the new epidemic. It's extremely contagious. It can be cured, but not easily." *310

Jeremy Rifkin is a globally-known futures studies expert, economist, and the author of the book *The Zero Marginal Cost Society: The Internet of Things, the Collaborative Commons, and the Eclipse of Capitalism*. A few years ago, Rifkin stated:

"The pace of human manufacturing and consumption vastly exceeds the planet's ability to absorb pollution or replenish resources." *311

Scientists have now shown that if everyone on the planet were to have the same standard of life as Americans, it would require numerous planets to sustain! In many situations in modern society, you will find that all kinds of phenomena and problems that are caused by inner feelings of emptiness, stress, and anxiety.

The same applies to the economic model. The economic model of the past purely focused on market share, while economic actors had no qualms at all about starting a vast range of market wars and using any means necessary to infect consumers and society as a whole with the severe disease known as "affluenza." To date, the backlash from this has been felt by all residents of planet Earth.

The pathogen responsible for all of this appears to lie in our own bodies and minds. Fortunately, though, the market consciousness is currently undergoing certain changes. Ervin Laszlo, author of the book *Chaos Point 2012 and Beyond: Appointment with Destiny*, notes that a type of "subculture" (or alternative culture) is emerging. People in this subculture have noticed that Earth's finite resources are being endlessly wasted and excessively depleted. They crave for sustainability and to lead a simpler life, a healthier, more complete, and an ethical life.

Laszlo notes that the Institute of Noetic Sciences, California, has found that under the excessive expansion of capitalism, society has experienced the following shift in values and behavior:

- A shift from competition to conciliation and collaboration.
- A shift from greed and scarcity to abundance and care.
- A shift from external authority to internal authority – that is, from reliance on external sources of "authority" to relying on internal sources of "cognition."
- A shift from mechanical systems to living systems. That is, going from a world perspective shaped based on mechanical systems to a kind of foresight, method, and principles grounded in explicit domains of life.
- Last but not least, a shift from isolation to completeness. That is, recognizing once again the completeness and interconnectedness of all levels of life and reality.

An even more significant shift has occurred in the behavior of consumers. It seems as though the consciousness of consumers and some enterprises is in the process of awakening.

Laszlo, in his book *Megatrends 2010: The Rise of Conscious Capitalism*, mentioned that a type of capitalism known as conscious capitalism is on the rise. Consciousness-driven (or value-driven) consumption is flourishing. The total value of the US value-driven market at the beginning of this century has reached $230 billion USD.

Conscious consumers are often referred to as LOHAS (which stands for Lifestyles of Health and Sustainability; that is, a lifestyle of healthy and sustainable development) and such consumers are rapidly developing in the following five types of economic domains: *313

① The domain of sustainable development, which includes robust ecological structures, renewable energy technology, and socially responsible investment.

② The domain of healthy living, which comprises the numerous natural and organic food products that have emerged on the market, nutritional supplements, and personal healthcare products.

③ The alternative healthcare domain, which consists of health centers, supplementary or alternative medical services and health protection.

④ The personal development domain, which involves symposiums, advanced learning courses, and sharing of experiences in the areas of body, mind, and spirit.

⑤ The ecological lifestyle and culture domain, which pertains to ecological products, recycled or recyclable products, and ecological tourism.

It seems, then, that this is a new economic model that requires us to collectively awaken so as to create it. Indeed, the economy is deeply rooted in the values of everyone on the planet. So if everyone underwent a change, the economy would naturally follow suit. If we turned inward and listened to our true internal needs, we would no longer need to perpetually spend money treating "affluenza" or use consumption as a kind of anethesia or painkiller for disappointment, frustration, anxiety, and stress. The strongest motivation in the old economic paradigm was to pursue endless capital. Yet the present-day consequences of this have left us reassessing whether the endless expansion, endless depletion of resources, endless production of even more oppositional issues (whether it be between labor and capital, the rich and the poor, social justice, and so on) is actually the right thing to do.

In actual fact, when material abundance reaches a certain level, we begin to focus on other essential needs, such as health, true love, applying our abilities, sustainability, and having meaningful jobs and lives. **So, this nascent economy is not an economy, but a new set of values for human society. The fulcrum of this economic paradigm is no longer material value, but the sustainable value of people and the environment. An economy characterized by inner and outer oneness is soon to be born.**

As early as 42 years ago famous economist E.F. Schumacher proposed "A Study of Economics As If People Mattered." *314 He also posited that the "super-economic" level is a better direction for the development of economics, which encompassed two parts: one part deals with human issues, while the other pertains to environmental issues. Jeremy Rifkin, mentioned previously, has said that a new type of economy, one that rewrites the market economy and overturns industrial operation, is on the rise. This economy is set to rewrite the historical script of humankind. Those who are interested in finding out more can check out his YouTube videos and his new book (*The Zero Marginal Cost Society: The Internet of Things, the Collaborative Commons, and the Eclipse of Capitalism*). *315

The economy is currently transitioning from the old model of competition to a model known as the "social economy" (also known as the compassion economy). From a lifestyle of excessive materialism, we are now moving to a life of meaning and new values. When we are able to return to our true selves, able to return to our own hearts, we build up a kind of mental immunity to 'affluenza.' The economy will then no longer be oriented toward personal profit, but instead the mutual honor and glory of humans and the environment.

The clean economy provides an inner and outer power which allows us to transition to the social economy. It provides people of the future with a possible solution. Perhaps there might be a day when the planet will no longer be regulated by "currency," and instead a new type of lifestyle will emerge where all "people of the universe" will coexist in peace.

Clean Energy

"The trouble with most folks isn't their ignorance. It's knowin' so many things that ain't so." – 19th century humorist, Josh Billings

Energy controls the lifeblood of a nation. Whoever controlled energy throughout history was able to easily control the world. Yet as we continue to consume vast quantities of energy, we face the consequences of this consumption in the form of global warming and unpredictable natural disasters. The blowback from this energy crisis is gaining strength by the day.

In Taiwan, energy is a complex political issue that pertains to international strategy. Due to Taiwan's small land area, the density of its population, and the scarcity of natural resources, its reliance on imports reached 99.23 as early as 2008. This process of import still primarily involves the use of fossil fuels, such as coal, petroleum, natural gas, and uranium. Yet scientists have recently predicted that we will one day deplete all petroleum on the planet. If the supply of petroleum reaches (or exceeds) its peak in the next decade, many countries will soon be facing a threat to their energy security. Last year as well as in 2009, Russia suspended provision of oil to the Ukraine as a measure intended to admonish the latter. This measure alarmed many EU countries, such as France and Germany, who realized their vulnerability in relation to energy policy. *316

It is difficult to imagine how chaotic the human world would be if one day the supply of oil simply ceased. However, the issue of energy is deeply entangled and interconnected with a number of other issues, such as foodstuff issues, population issues, the environment, a lack of water resources, and international strategy.

We are faced with the problem of finite resources, yet we lack the awareness to stop wasting such resources; in this state of unconsciousness we have already squandered a large amount of energy. The endless greed of humans has caused excessive depletion of energy, which may well precipitate the greatest calamity in human history. Uncontrollable global warming has ushered in climate change and a host of natural disasters: typhoons, hurricanes, floods, and, most ironically, droughts. In the winter of 2014, we faced the most severe drought in history. A lack of water in all major reservoirs led to the imposition of water restrictions in each county and city, one after the other. This caused many people to reflect on the issue of climate change.

Our overreliance on fossil fuels seems to have severely blocked the path of human evolution. What is the solution for the Earth's energy use?

What I have written below some people might find hard to believe. I ask you to first calm your heart and keep an open mind as you read through these remarkable findings. A book I mentioned previously, *The Source Field Investigations: The Hidden Science and Lost Civilizations Behind the 2012 Prophecies*, written by David Wilcock, contains a wealth of valuable information. Let's have a look together:

At a symposium held at Zurich, Dr. Brian O'Leary, an astronaut at NASA, presented a large amount of information proving that humans had already created "free energy" (also called "clean energy") equipment, and that there was more than just one. Unfortunately, certain powerful vested interests had concealed all related information.

"Based on a report issued by the Institute for New Energy, David Wilcock notes that, as of 1997, "The US Patent Office has classified over 3,000 patent devices or applications under the secrecy order, Title 35, US Code (1952) Sections 181-188. The Federation of American Scientists revealed that by the end of the fiscal year 2010, this number had ballooned to 5,135 inventions, and included "review and possible restriction" on any solar cell with greater than twenty percent efficiency, or any power system that is more than seventy to eighty percent efficient at converting energy. According to Dr. O'Leary, some researchers are bought off and their discoveries put on a shelf. Others are threatened into submission, while others die under strange circumstances." *317

Wilcox cites comments made by Dr. O'Leary regarding Stefan Marinov, who was the "leader of the European free energy movement," and was the most optimistic, energetic person you could meet, and yet was found dead at the University of Graz after falling from the tenth floor. Dr. O'Leary also mentioned Dr. Eugene Mallove, who was considered a luminary in the field of alternative energy.

Wilcox mentions his friendship with Mallove, and how he once got so emotional that he broke down and cried in front of over 400 people. He recalls: "Dr. Mallove started out as the head science writer for Massachusetts Institute of Technology's own journal. Mallove claimed he was ordered to suppress research into cold fusion – during which they had gotten positive results suggesting free energy was being generated from the reaction. From there, he quit his job and went on to start Infinite Energy Magazine – and became arguably the top coordinator, publisher, and liaison for alternative energy inventors worldwide." *318

On May 15, 2004, Wilcox was originally scheduled to appear with Mallove in an episode of 'Coast to Coast', the largest night-time talk radio program in the United States, with Art Bell and Richard Hoagland.

"We were about to make a stunning announcement [during the program]: Hoagland and Mallove were going to visit Washington DC, the following week, and bring along a working, table-top free-energy device. This device apparently would begin spinning by simply being stared at and did not use any conventional power source...... Hoagland had lined up meetings with various senators and congressmen to demonstrate the device – and push for these breakthroughs to be released to the public for study and commercial application." Yet something shocking occurred: "Less than twenty-four hours before we were about to go live on the air, Dr. Mallove was bludgeoned to death outside his parents' home." *319

This happened right at the most exhilarating and critical moment, which was suspicious given that it happened right before Dr. Mallove was set to publicly reveal his secret device.

Furthermore, in the chapter *"Geometry Class Just Got Much More Interesting,"* Wilcox wrote: "In Lost Science, Gerry Vassilatos discovered that natural quasicrystal may actually exist within certain rocks......"

"Thomas Townsend Brown once obtained samples of these rocks, and discovered that they naturally emitted an alarmingly high voltage current. By simply placing an electrical cable on top of the rock, you can get several millivolts of power. When dissecting the rock into several pieces, you can get one volt of free energy......"

"According to Vassilatos, certain researchers at the Andes could extract as much as 1.8 volts of electricity from a single rock." *320

In the same book, Vassilatos also revealed the results of research conducted by Thomas Henry Moray, another scientist who has been suppressed. Moray discovered a type of rock that has the same properties but is even more powerful. He called it the Swedish Stone. Moray used this material to produce a free-energy device. A Swedish Stone the size of a mere wristwatch was enough to power a 100-watt light bulb and a 655-watt heater. Moray later developed the prototype for an energy device that could produce 50 kilowatts of electricity, enough to power a small factory for a whole day. It could have been used all day without worrying about electricity shortages, and it was all free. In 1931 Moray attempted to obtain a patent and was rejected.

He later discovered that the rocks contained other special functions. For example, using a standard wireless receiver, he could hear the everyday conversations and activites of people a great distance away without the use of a microphone. He also discovered that these rocks have a powerful healing effect.

In 1961 Moray found that the energy field his device produced could restore the soil used to mine gold, silver, and white gold, allowing it to once more produce microcrystals of these elements. Soil that originally only contained 0.18 ounces of gold began to produce as much as 100 ounces of gold and 225 ounces of silver. We now know that the chief element of these special stones is ultra-pure germanium. Yet moray was not the only one to discover remarkable stones. In the 1950s Arthur L. Adams, a retired electrical engineer from England, stumbled up a type of smooth, silver-gray material which could generate huge quantities of electricity. Its power could be further enhanced by slicing it into pieces to make special batteries and then soaking these in water.

You will not be surprised to learn that "British authorities seized all Adams's research papers and materials, claiming this was being done for 'future social distribution.'" *321

In this current period in which the planet is undergoing a serious crisis, we can see what would motivate someone to suppress and shut down sustainable free energy and clean energy. Clearly, there is an "invisible hand" behind all of this, as stakeholders attempt to control the world and avoid "losing their tight grip" on the planet's resources.

Clean energy is certainly not an empty dream. Richard A. Muller's final piece of advice for the president, offered in his book *Energy for Future*

Presidents: The Science Behind the Headlines, is as follows: "You should avoid using virtuous sounding names to describe energy, such as 'green energy,' 'renewable energy,' and 'clean energy' etc......"*322

I think that at this point, you get the picture. Throughout these years, I have often said that at one point in history humans will encounter a crisis, and that the answer to overcome the crisis already existed a long time ago within the vast, boundless super-consciousness. It is just a matter of whether we can purify our thoughts enough to coordinate and become one with this consciousness; connect with the big data in the vastdatabase of wisdom and spread the wisdom needed to solve this crisis so as to benefit all of humanity.

We hope to make use of this platform to connect with even more aspiring scientists and work together for the future of the planet! However, this requires your participation. Together, we can send out kind thoughts, raise the conscious of the planet, and integrate its oppositional side so that the collective consciousness of the planet no longer resides at the level of national interest, but instead at the higher dimension of sustainable life for all of humanity, thereby spurring the sharing of resources between countries, and the sharing of life's values and meaning between races.

In the current situation, where sustainability has encountered an unforeseeable crisis and the danger of total breakdown exists, we hope to combine the power of the people to transform this danger within the self, as well as in our lives, our lifestyles, societies, ecosystems, and countries; to transform the future of the planet and fill it with true hope.

Clean Life

Gandha Creation was established to implement our mission of leading a "Clean Life." It aims to care for the body, mind, and spirit of humans, as well as caring for the environment. Gandha Creations brings together companies from industries to do with culture, nature, and natural farming to cooperate and promote products beneficial to the overall health of the body, mind, and spirit.

Chinese incense ceremony can be traced to the Xia, Shang, and Zhou Dynasties and reached its zenith during the Tang and Song Dynasties. It is also one of the local cultural items that Gandha Creations is actively working to restore and nurture. The soul of Chinese incense ceremony is incense itself. Yet the primary focus is on passing down ancient methods of producing "traditional Chinese incense." The materials used are all of the finest quality, and every step of the production process is gruelling, processed using the most delicate ancient methods. The objective of all this is to make a superior stick of incense that contains true vitality, and to inject a sense of beauty and spirit into our busy modern lives, allowing people for a brief moment to gain spiritual nourishment and relief through the process of making incense.

In recent years, we have expanded the scope of our services. To help protect ourselves and the environment, we use entirely natural and pollution-free raw materials. Combining the elements of nature with high-quality "goods," we launched a line of healing oils and cleaning skin care products, as well as healthy high-energy food products, Tibetan tea, culture and creative products, and discounted products for annual festivals.

In a remarkable case of serendipity last year, we happened across a team of water resource experts who had been researching villages known for longevity around the world. They had been quietly going about their research for 14 years, having conducted in-depth analyses of the water quality in each area around Taiwan and created a "living water" dispenser custom-made for every region. Given that it is increasingly difficult to obtain water-based resources, the ability to give yourself and your family a cup of good quality water, one which truly contains energy elements from "the source of life," is a real blessing.

Protecting the body, mind, and spirit as well as the environment and ecosystem is Gandha Creation's inviolable spirit and mission. In order to promote sustainability in four major areas (production, lifestyle, our lives, and the ecosystem), we provide the following five categories of products that allow you to effortlessly feel the joy that comes from a clean life.

Clean body: Pure and natural daily lifestyle products that provide spiritual enjoyment.

Clean emotions: Create delight through a sense of joy, soothing, and relaxation; foster an atmosphere of cleanliness

Clean mind:	Notice the life force of beauty and learn how to establish a positive health self-dialog.
Clean soul:	Enhance your level of clarity and welcome all of life's possibilities with an attitude of openness.
Clean environment:	Purify the life space and care for the sustainability of the environment through pure, high-energy, non-toxic, pollution-free products.

2015 Gandha Creation Care Projects:

① Clean water and environmental protection: From the position of water experts, revealing the vital connection between water, illness, and the ecosystem. Meanwhile, as humans pursue the need for safe drinking water, how do we ensure that everyone drinks clean and good quality water and regains their health?

② Purification of the energy field: Purifying the energy field through traditional incense ceremonies, enabling everyone to become a master at purifying energy fields. From an internal balance of body and mind, to the reaping of good fortune in one's family environment and work situation, learn effective methods for bringing about ideal outcomes!

③ Lectures to promote better health: We invite the "godfather of health" who has been researching physical and mental health issues for over 20 years to deliver talks on maintaining one's health throughout the four seasons, having a simple diet, avoiding processed food, and the various illnesses caused by dietary misconceptions – cancer, etc.

④ Promotion of traditional incense culture: Embed breathing, meditation, and healing into one's life by making and playing with incense; creating a "nourishment room" in one's house, which will serve as an optimal center for soothing and relief in order to maintain the holistic health of the entire family.

⑤ Clean maintenance: Promote simple and natural cleansing and skin care methods and avoid the mutilating effects of all chemical-based cleansing products, skin care products, and make up; avoid using any kinds of additives, petrochemical materials, and metals, so as to bring about a bright future for all.

We welcome you to visit our website and to join us in creating a clean life! http://www.infinitassoul.com/en/gandha.html
Do not think any virtue trivial, and so neglect it; do not underestimate your own power. When it comes to changing the world, there will always be a role for you. We welcome everyone who wishes to support this large education platform for the sustainability of life; a platform which provides "ultimate care" to all people, to the environment, and the world.
Infinitas Educational Foundation

A New Heart and a New World – Ushering In a Golden Paradise across the Globe

"When you come to be sensibly touched, the scales will fall from your eyes; and by the penetrating eyes of love you will discern that which your other eyes will never see."
—Francois Fénelon

Enjoying tasty food; / Wearing beautiful clothes; / Feeling comfortable in their homes; / Delighting in their customs.
—Laozi Daodejing, Chapter 80

"And as to me, I know nothing else but miracles."
—Walt Whitman

The unbelievable power of love has brought us together once again on this heroic journey through life. Over these last 14 years, I do not even remember how many times I've said to people "Don't underestimate your own power!" Living on planet Earth with this "large human family," if we wish to have a brand new society, we need a new mind and a new set of eyes through which to look at the world and view its beauty, its value, and its meaning.

If our mind was awakened, the moment we opened our eyes and used direct intuition to see all things, the landscape of the world would take on a striking appearance. In every moment there is something striking happening, and it never "repeats." As early as 2,500 years ago, Greek philosopher Heraclitas said: "No man ever steps in the same river twice." A Zen master once said: "A pure heart is always vibrant and creative." Living in the moment in this state of wonder, every instant is vibrant and creative. Famous Catholic monk, Thomas Merton, once said "Love is our true destiny." We do not find the meaning of life by ourselves alone we find it with another.

Merton offers this description after opening the eyes of his soul: "Then it was as if I suddenly saw the secret beauty of their hearts, the depths of their hearts where neither sin nor desire nor self-knowledge can reach, the core of their reality, the person that each one is in God's eyes. If only they could all see themselves as they really are. If only we could see each other that way all the time. There would be no more war, no more hatred, no more cruelty, no more greed. . . . But this cannot be seen, only believed and 'understood' by a peculiar gift." *323

What a beautiful passage. This is the perfect portrayal of the "beginner's mind." Thai Zen master Ajahn Chah once said: "Man can return to the realm of innocence as long as he inhabits the beginner's mind." He told people that the beginner's mind exists in every moment, in the stillness between each thought, in the essence of the most fundamental awareness, clarity, and purity.

"The beginner's mind" is one of the best gifts the hero can give people after he returns to this world. That is, an omnipresent "intrinsic beginner's mind" – the true self, which already appears in every moment. Only in the state of being in a beginner's mind can we truly love ourselves; and only by truly loving ourselves can we truly love the world.

While meditating in seclusion after 15 years of practicing Zen, a psychologist once had an epiphany: "It is I who must love myself. No one else can make me feel whole. Only I can provide that love. Now I know that wholeness is always accessible to me and all beings everywhere. This knowing allows me to live with a new peacefulness and kindness to myself and others. In the simplest way, it has changed my whole life." *324

Eternal love that derives from the "beginner's mind" helps protect oneself, as well as all other people, and the world. The "beginner's mind" also symbolizes a mind like an empty cup; a broad and vast emptiness that can contain everything. Famous Japanese Zen master Shunryū Suzuki once said: "The practice of Zen mind is beginner's mind…The mind of the beginner is empty, free of the habits of the expert, ready to accept, to doubt, and open to all the possibilities. It is the kind of mind which can see things as they are, which step by step and in a flash can realize the original nature of everything."

It is due to love and the eternal upholding of the "beginner's mind" that this world takes on a new look. In his book *After the Ecstasy, the Laundry*, author Jack Kornfield cites the great Indian mystic Kabir, who shared the following with his disciples: "Dive into this life and experience the flow while you are still living…… Your so-called 'salvation' is your vocation for this life."

The "beginner's mind" of a hero does not mean being attached to this world, but actively participating in it. Christian mystic Symeon once stated that: "We awaken in Christ's body as Christ awakens our bodies." *326

If we want Christ to awaken our bodies, the best approach is to go out into the world. The realm of enlightenment is not separate to this world. By entering this world and shining our light it is actually more likely that we realize the "beginner's mind."

The beginner's mind enables Christ to "awaken" in our bodies, and allows us to become aware of the wonder of love and action; it allows Christ (Svabhava) to see through your eyes; allows Christ (Svabhava) to listen through your ears; allows Christ (Svabhava) to speak through your mouth; allows Christ (Svabhava) to act through your body.

In doing so, when faced with challenges either in your life or during great change, we can maintain our "beginner's mind" and remain open to the ensuing challenges or problems that arise, and thus welcome all possibilities. When we are once again visited by chaos, pain, fear, uncertainty, confusion, anxiety, or any other kind of mind-based demon, how do we know that we are on the right path? St. John put it this way: "If a man wishes to be sure of the road he treads on, he must close his eyes and walk in the dark." *327

Brave and openly facing these challenges is always the best method. A Catholic monk once wisely stated the following: "As soon as the spirit has matured, we become willing to open a dialog with our pain and our malevolence, and to incorporate them into our daily prayer. When a man experiences incredible suffering, he must consciously experience the impact of that suffering, and purify his mind until it becomes a vessel able to contain and process sorrow."

If we consciously experience something in its entirety, and fully embrace such experiences as the deepest and truest instructors for eternally cultivating the spirit, then one conscious action or prayer is helpful to the healing of the self and the world. Gandhi, full of compassion, taught us the following: "I believe in the essential unity of all people and for that matter of all lives. Therefore, I believe that if one person gains spiritually, the whole world gains, and if one person falls, the whole world falls to that extent." *328

Learn to love yourself, and pray and selflessly act to bring about the highest benefit to all beings on the planet. Only by doing so can you offer a supreme gift to the world.

Ram Dass asked his guru Nim Karoli Baba, "How do I become enlightened?" His guru responded: "Feed others and help others. Care for others and feed others, and serve God in a variety of ways." "God" refers to all people, events, and things in each moment. In a similar vein, Kabir the Indian mystic once said: "Only one thing in this world can satisfy my mind...... serving God in every single moment." *329

"Service" is the manifestation of an enlightened spirit, and is a specific quality of the "new human." The critical question is: as we serve others who are we really serving? In actual fact, we are really serving ourselves!

When this "beginner's mind," along with love, spreads across the world, the whole planet will be like a large family with no boundaries. Victor Hugo once prophesized the following: "In the Twentieth Century war will be dead, frontier boundaries will be dead, dogmas will be dead; man will live...... He will possess something higher than all these...... a great hope, the whole heaven." *330

When we no longer distinguish and discriminate between one another, and mutually combine our wisdom and power, we will live in abundance and everything will be possible. With a brand new mind, we will possess infinite power and a self that transcends the ego. We will get along harmoniously with others, and our new way of looking at the world will help heal our only homeland in the solar system – Earth.

The University of Southern California once held an international conference to discuss the future of the West. One thing all attending experts agreed on was that the name of the conference seemed to be something of a misnomer: without the East, they explained, the West would have no future.

Yet whether it be the East, the West, or any race or nation, we all must work together, keep one another company, as we jointly raise our consciousness.

Do not underestimate the power of any single deed. No matter how small it is, it emits a force large enough to shake the root of "avidyā" in the vast collective consciousness. Learn "transcendent" learning, and you will be able to bring about the fulfillment of your life during the splendid changes that occur in this century. Actively share with others the changes that occur in your mind and spirit. It is never too late.

Reassess your direction and once more get rid of the hunger and division that reside in your heart. While we work to eliminate the issue of famine in the world, work diligently to transform the hunger in your relationships, sense of meaning, finances, fulfillment, and consciousness.

By doing this we can "restore" the sacred order to our lives, and the world will naturally be "restored" to its sacred order and display its intrinsically perfect and tranquil side. And the history of the planet will at this moment change forever.

This vast path of awakening is never isolated, never lonely. "No man is an island." Decisions are the clearest indicator of the "beginner's mind" – the great power of the true self, Svabhava. It spurs us to choose a journey of change, a great journey of the self. This choice, this decision, is not made with knowledge that you will end up at a particular destination. The decision is made because this is the most meaningful journey in your life.

When caring for someone close to death, Tibetans always guide the person by whispering in his or her ear: "Remember the clear light, the pure clear white light from which everything in the universe comes, to which everything in the universe returns; the original nature of your own mind. It is your own true nature, it is home." *331

Regardless of which religion or tradition, we can all witness its trail. We see it in the singing of Jewish hymns for unity, in the love of the Holy

Spirit of Christianity, and in the eternal Brahma, the God of creation in Hinduism. This is the truth, the path, the essence.

If you don't realize the source,
you stumble in confusion and sorrow.
When you realize where you come from,
you naturally become tolerant, disinterested, amused,
kindhearted as a grandmother,
dignified as a king.
Immersed in the wonder of the Tao,
you can deal with whatever life brings you,
and when death comes, you are ready. *332

When you walk on the path of truth, life itself becomes a kind of blessing. No matter where you are located, what place, or what you are doing there, allow yourself to display the luminous smile that emanates from the sacred core; allow everyone who comes in contact with us to feel the freedom of our compassion, acceptance, deep understanding, support, and delight.

Finally, while you are walking on the path you have chosen to take you home, you should not let any person, event, or object influence your decision – including me.

Tolstoy offered this vivid description:

"Attack me, but attack me rather than the path I follow...... If I know the way home and am walking along it drunkenly, is it any less the right way......?"

"If I stagger and wander, come to my help......

You are also human beings and you are also going home." *333

At this moment, I do not think there are any words I could use to describe the greatness of your "beginner's mind" – your true self, Svabhava. I sincerely salute your self-realized mind, the part of you that has existed since the beginning of time. Awakening will call you, guide you, assign you tasks, for you are the seed of this power, and your Svabhava will blossom into the most radiant life flower.

This sacred promise, as well as all the power of Divinity and Buddha, will burst forth from you, the seed of Svabhava, into a dazzling, eye-catching light, for you have always been a conscious light. *334

I pray that love blesses you, and I offer my blessings to your whole family and to everything; to all life; and to all the nameless heroes who have lived from antiquity until today. Bless those soon-to-be-reborn conscious lights.

About The Clean Life Foundation

The Clean Life Foundation was established by Sat Dharma and a group of similarly spiritually enlightened people. Our group is dedicated to the lifting of consciousness and to spreading love throughout society. We conduct seminars, workshops, and volunteer projects, and also invite speakers from all around the world to spread spiritual philosophies and help Taiwanese to see deep inside themselves, and find their own strength and positive energy. The Clean Life Foundation hopes to preserve and perpetuate the spirit of Sat Dharma by publishing *Awakening Power*, and do our part to make the world a better place.

Notes

*Note 152: *The Wisdom of Imperfection: The Challenge of Individuation in Buddhist Life*, written by Rob Preece, translated by Liao Shide, published by Living Nature Culture Co. Ltd., p.43.

*Note 153: *The Wisdom of Imperfection: The Challenge of Individuation in Buddhist Life*, written by Rob Preece, translated by Liao Shide, published by Living Nature Culture Co. Ltd., p.120.

*Note 154: *Get Rich! With Peace of Mind*, written by Napoleon Hill, translated by Zhi-Zhong Dai, published by Leeds Publishing Co., Ltd.

*Note 155: *Get Rich! With Peace of Mind*, written by Napoleon Hill, translated by Zhi-Zhong Dai, published by Leeds Publishing Co., Ltd., p.7-p.8.

*Note 156: *The Synchronicity Key: The Hidden Intelligence Guiding the Universe and You*, written by David Wilcock, translated by Huang Haotian, published by Acorn International Publishing House, p. 206-p.207.

*Note 157: The painting, "The Ten Ox-herding Pictures", is based on the sutra, *The Buddha's Teachings of Ox Herding*. Here we refer to the last picture among these ten images created by the monk Guo An.

*Note 158: In "the Theory of Holes", holes refer to any part of you that has been lost, meaning any part of you that you have lost consciousness of. Ultimately, what we have lost awareness of is our essence or pure Being. When we are not aware of our essence, it stops manifesting. Then we feel a sense of deficiency. It could be the loss of "love", loss of "value", loss of "strength", etc. Therefore, you want to fill this hole inside you with values from the outside. To say we have lost parts of our essence doesn't mean that they are gone forever. You are simply cut off from the awareness of them.

*Note 159: In order to achieve your ends, for example, getting other people's attention, or hoping to win other people's love, you resort to some unusual ways or even to some drastic measures or extreme emotions, in the hope that you can get what you want. However, you end up fomenting discord among you and others. In *The Celestine Prophecy*, the author tells us that the battles for energy keep taking place among human beings. Because the energy we have is insufficient, we always try to grab more energy from others. We use different ways to perform our "dramas of manipulation". We act as if we are begging, interrogating, or intimidating others in order to obtain their energy. If we can't see clearly the roles others and we are unwittingly playing, we will never be able to escape from this battle.

*Note 160: To be connected with the energy of the earth, also known as the practice of touching the earth, refers to the act of expanding one's energy or consciousness in order to be connected with the earth (the planet Earth). Through breathing, your frequency and the frequency of the earth will be gradually merged. By reconnecting with the energy of the earth, you can get rid of your negative energy, replenish the supply of the dynamics of your life; so that while you can reduce the fatigue you are suffering from and restore your vitality, you will also experience the generosity and love of Mother Earth. Then, you will feel a sense of gratitude spontaneously.

*Note 161: The energy of Dharmadhatu permeates everything. The universe, the galaxy, the entire mankind, all the animals and plants, all the molecules and atoms are imbued with this energy. It keeps all the dimensions, time and spaces functioning normally. It is also the critical factor behind the balance between the order of one's life and the expansion of one's consciousness. Therefore, as far as the domain of the Dharmadhatu is concerned, it is present, and it is also absent. It exists in every aspect of everything. It is amorphous, but it can be turned into anything. You are the Dharmadhatu, and the Dharmadhatu is you. (The information in this note is extracted from the book, *The Light Awakening Cards*).

*Note 162: *Paths Beyond Ego: The Transpersonal Vision*, written by Roger Walsh and Frances Vaughan, translated by Yi Zhixin and Hu Yinmeng, published by PsyGarden Publishing Company, p. 211.

*Note 163: *A Hero with a Thousand Faces*, written by Joseph Campbell, translated by Zhu Kanru, published by New Century Publishing Co., Ltd. This book is the masterpiece of the great mythologist, Joseph Campbell. In this book, Campbell traces the similar stories about a hero's adventure and transformation that run through virtually all of the world's mythic traditions and discovers the archetypal hero that is present in all these stories.

*Note 164: *The Hero with a Thousand Faces*, written by Joseph Campbell, translated by Zhu Kanru, published by New Century Publishing Co., Ltd., p.61.

*Note 165: *The Hero with a Thousand Faces*, written by Joseph Campbell, translated by Zhu Kanru, published by New Century Publishing Co., Ltd., p.104.

*Note 166: For more information, please see *Power VS. Force: The Hidden Determinants of Human Behavior*, written by David Hawkins, translated by Cai Mengxuan, published by Booklife Publishing Co., Ltd.

*Note 167: *The Hero with a Thousand Faces*, written by Joseph Campbell, translated by Zhu Kanru, published by New Century Publishing Co., Ltd., p.121.

*Note 168: *The Hero with a Thousand Faces*, written by Joseph Campbell, translated by Zhu Kanru, published by New Century Publishing Co., Ltd., p. 121.

*Note 169: Experts in different fields.

*Note 170: The seven deadly sins are the categories of evil deeds committed by human beings. These evil conducts are derived from the eight evil temptations compiled by the Greek theological and philosophical thinker and one of the Desert Fathers, Evagrius Ponticus. They are: gluttony, lust, greed, sorrow, anger, sloth, vainglory and pride. In the second half of the 6th century, Pope Gregory I reduced the number of the evil doings from eight to seven. He combined vainglory with pride. He put together discouragement and sorrow; he called this combination the sin of sloth and added envy. He also ranked these sins in order according to the severity of their defiance against the spirit of love. As a result, they can be listed in the following order: pride, envy, wrath, sloth, greed, gluttony and lust.

*Note 171: These planktons are formed when the idea that we are unable to generate any active energy to help us move forward on our life's trajectory starts to drift about in our mind. It's similar to the feeling we have when we encounter something new, such as a new experience, a new belief system, a new piece of information, a new structure, and so on. We know that it is appropriate for us to change or adjust our attitudes or that it will help us live a better life if we do so, but we insist on preserving the status quo. We stay in the same place, unwilling to try to make any changes, and these planktons are what make us linger, refuse to change, and try to maintain the status quo.

Note 172: *The Hero with a Thousand Faces*, written by Joseph Campbell, translated by Zhu Kanru, published by New Century Publishing Co., Ltd., p121-p.123.

Note 173: Shankara (about 788 CE-820 CE) was an Indian philosopher and theologian from the Middle Ages, who consolidated the doctrine of Advaita Vedanta (also translated as the "not-two" theory). He believed the supreme Brahman (namely the only God—the Creator) was the origin of the world. Brahman is the absolute and eternal consciousness. It transcends anything subjective and anything objective. It transcends time, space, and the laws of cause and effect. All things were born out of Brahman, but Brahman doesn't depend on anything. Attainment of Nirvana means to witness the oneness of Brahman and oneself, that is, "Brahman and I are one and the same".

Note 174: *The Hero Within: Six Archetypes We Live By*, written by Carol Pearson, translated by Zhu Kanru, Xu Shenshu, and Gong Zhuojun, published by New Century Publishing Co., Ltd., p.8.

Note 175: *The Hero Within: Six Archetypes We Live By*, written by Carol Pearson, translated by Zhu Kanru, Xu Shenshu, and Gong Zhuojun, published by New Century Publishing Co., Ltd., p.9.

Note 176: For more information, please see the table of Six Hero Archetypes in *The Hero Within: Six Archetypes We Live By*, p.27. Source of reference: *The Hero Within: Six Archetypes We Live By*, written by Carol Pearson, translated by Zhu Kanru, Xu Shenshu, and Gong Zhuojun, published by New Century Publishing Co., Ltd., p.21.

Note 177: Reference: *The Hero Within: Six Archetypes We Live By*, written by Carol Pearson, translated by Zhu Kanru, Xu Shenshu, and Gong Zhuojun, published by New Century Publishing Co., Ltd., p.137.

Note 178: Reference: *The Hero Within: Six Archetypes We Live By*, written by Carol Pearson, translated by Zhu Kanru, Xu Shenshu, and Gong Zhuojun, published by New Century Publishing Co., Ltd., p.137.

Note 179: *Man and His Symbols*, written by Carl Jung, translated by Gong Zhuojun, published by New Century Publishing Co., Ltd., p.200-p.201.

Note 180: "Gebbeth" represents our shadow aspects, the aspects we don't want to see and accept.

Note 181: *The Hero with a Thousand Faces*, written by Joseph Campbell, translated by Zhu Kanru, published by New Century Publishing Co., Ltd., p.157.

Note 182: Leon Stein, "Hassidic Music", *The Chicago Jewish Forum*, Vol. II, No.1 (Fall, 1943), p. 158.

Note 183: These seven quadrants are: one's body, love life, interpersonal relationships, intelligence, family, career, and spirituality.

Note 184: *The Aquarian Conspiracy: Personal and Social Transformation in Our Time*, written by Marilyn Ferguson, translated by Liao Shide, published by BookLife Publishing Co., Ltd., p. 530.

Note 185: *The Aquarian Conspiracy: Personal and Social Transformation in Our Time*, written by Marilyn Ferguson, translated by Liao Shide, published by BookLife Publishing Co., Ltd., p.542.

Note 186: *World English Bible*, The Gospel of Luke, Chapter 6 Verses 28-38.

Note 187: *The Synchronicity Key: The Hidden Intelligence Guiding the Universe and You*, written by David Wilcock, translated by Huang Haotian, published by Acorn International Publishing Co. Ltd., p.389.

Note 188: *The Principle of Individuation: Toward the Development of Human Consciousness*, written by Murray Stein, translated by Huang Bihui, Wei Hongjin, et. al., published by PsyGarden Publishing Company, p. 57.

Note 189: *Why God Won't Go Away: Brain Science and the Biology of Belief*, written by Andrew Newberg, Eugene D'Aquili, and Vince Rause, translated by Zheng Qingrong, published by China Times Publishing Co., p.128.

Note 190: *Why God Won't Go Away: Brain Science and the Biology of Belief*, written by Andrew Newberg, Eugene D'Aquili, and Vince Rause, translated by Zheng Qingrong, published by China Times Publishing Co., p. 129.

Note 191: *Why God Won't Go Away: Brain Science and the Biology of Belief*, written by Andrew Newberg, Eugene D'Aquili, and Vince Rause, translated by Zheng Qingrong, published by China Times Publishing Co., p. 130.

Note 192: *Why God Won't Go Away: Brain Science and the Biology of Belief*, written by Andrew Newberg, Eugene D'Aquili, and Vince Rause, translated by Zheng Qingrong, published by China Times Publishing Co., p.130.

Note 193: *Why God Won't Go Away: Brain Science and the Biology of Belief*, written by Andrew Newberg, Eugene D'Aquili, and Vince Rause, translated by Zheng Qingrong, published by China Times Publishing Co., p.131.

Note 194: *Why God Won't Go Away: Brain Science and the Biology of Belief*, written by Andrew Newberg, Eugene D'Aquili, and Vince Rause, translated by Zheng Qingrong, published by China Times Publishing Co., p.132.

Note 195: *Why God Won't Go Away: Brain Science and the Biology of Belief*, written by Andrew Newberg, Eugene D'Aquili, and Vince Rause, translated by Zheng Qingrong, published by China Times Publishing Co., p.133.

Note 196: *A History of God: The 4,000-Year Quest of Judaism, Christianity and Islam*, written by Karen Armstrong, translated by Cai Changxiong, published by New Century Publishing Co., Ltd., p. 133.

Note 197: *A History of God: The 4,000-Year Quest of Judaism, Christianity and Islam*, written by Karen Armstrong, translated by Cai Changxiong, published by New Century Publishing Co., Ltd., p. 377.

Note 198: *Why God Won't Go Away: Brain Science and the Biology of Belief*, written by Andrew Newberg, Eugene D'Aquili, and Vince Rause, translated by Zheng Qingrong, published by China Times Publishing Co., p. 134.

Note 199: *The Varieties of Religious Experience: A Study in Human Nature*, written by William James, translated by Cai Yijia and Liu Hongxin, published by New Century Publishing Co., Ltd., p.473.

Note 200: *The Varieties of Religious Experience: A Study in Human Nature*, written by William James, translated by Cai Yijia and Liu Hongxin, published by New Century Publishing Co., Ltd., p. 496.

Note 201: *Why God Won't Go Away: Brain Science and the Biology of Belief*, written by Andrew Newberg, Eugene D'Aquili, and Vince Rause, translated by Zheng Qingrong, published by China Times Publishing Co., p.135.

Note 202: The two realms are the realm of desires and the realm of materials. According to the principles of general spiritual practices, these are the highest realms people who undertake these practices can attain.

Note 203: *The Hero with a Thousand Faces*, written by Joseph Campbell, translated by Zhu Kanru, published by New Century Publishing Co., Ltd., p.172-173.

Note 204: *The Hero with a Thousand Faces*, written by Joseph Campbell, translated by Zhu Kanru, published by New Century Publishing Co., Ltd., p. 230.

Note 205: *The Hero with a Thousand Faces*, written by Joseph Campbell, translated by Zhu Kanru, published by New Century Publishing Co., Ltd., p.206.

Note 206: *The Hero with a Thousand Faces*, written by Joseph Campbell, translated by Zhu Kanru, published by New Century Publishing Co., Ltd., p.220.

Note 207: *The Hero with a Thousand Faces*, written by Joseph Campbell, translated by Zhu Kanru, published by New Century Publishing Co., Ltd., p.220.

Note 208: *The Hero with a Thousand Faces*, written by Joseph Campbell, translated by Zhu Kanru, published by New Century Publishing Co., Ltd., p.175-p.176.

Note 209: *The Hero with a Thousand Faces*, written by Joseph Campbell, translated by Zhu Kanru, published by New Century Publishing Co., Ltd., p.200-p. 201.

Note 210: *The Varieties of Religious Experience: A Study in Human Nature*, written by William James, translated by Cai Yijia and Liu Hongxin, published by New Century Publishing Co., Ltd., p.492.

Note 211: *The Hero with a Thousand Faces*, written by Joseph Campbell, translated by Zhu Kanru, published by New Century Publishing Co., Ltd., p.241.

Note 212: *The Hero with a Thousand Faces*, written by Joseph Campbell, translated by Zhu Kanru, published by New Century Publishing Co., Ltd., p.232.

Note 213: *World English Bible*, Gospel of Matthew, Chapter 10, Verses 34~39.

Note 214: *The Hero with a Thousand Faces*, written by Joseph Campbell, translated by Zhu Kanru, published by New Century Publishing Co., Ltd., p.232.

Note 215: *The Hero with a Thousand Faces*, written by Joseph Campbell, translated by Zhu Kanru, published by New Century Publishing Co., Ltd., p.232.

Note 216: *The Hero with a Thousand Faces*, written by Joseph Campbell, translated by Zhu Kanru, published by New Century Publishing Co., Ltd., p.232.

Note 217: *The Hero with a Thousand Faces*, written by Joseph Campbell, translated by Zhu Kanru, published by New Century Publishing Co., Ltd., p.252.

Note 218: *The Hero with a Thousand Faces*, written by Joseph Campbell, translated by Zhu Kanru, published by New Century Publishing Co., Ltd., p.253.

Note 219: *The World's Religions: Our Great Wisdom Traditions*, written by Huston Smith, translated by Liu Anyun, published by New Century Publishing Co., Ltd., p.11.

Note 220: *The Hero with a Thousand Faces*, written by Joseph Campbell, translated by Zhu Kanru, published by New Century Publishing Co., Ltd., p.253.

Note 221: *The Hero with a Thousand Faces*, written by Joseph Campbell, translated by Zhu Kanru, published by New Century Publishing Co., Ltd., p. 279. Image no. 7.

Note 222: The *Zohar* (Zohar, "light, splendor") is a collection of writings of Jewish esoteric thought known as Kabbalah.

Note 223: *The Hero with a Thousand Faces*, written by Joseph Campbell, translated by Zhu Kanru, published by New Century Publishing Co., Ltd., p.285.

Note 224: *The Hero with a Thousand Faces*, written by Joseph Campbell, translated by Zhu Kanru, published by New Century Publishing Co., Ltd., p.285-p.287.

Note 225: *The Hero Within: Six Archetypes We Live By*, written by Carol Pearson, translated by Zhu Kanru, Xu Shenshu, and Gong Zhuojun, published by New Century Publishing Co., Ltd., p.4.

Note 226: *The Hero with a Thousand Faces*, written by Joseph Campbell, translated by Zhu Kanru, published by New Century Publishing Co., Ltd., p. 387.

Note 227: *The Hero Within: Six Archetypes We Live By*, written by Carol Pearson, translated by Zhu Kanru, Xu Shenshu, and Gong Zhuojun, published by New Century Publishing Co., Ltd., p. 5.

Note 228: *The Hero Within: Six Archetypes We Live By*, written by Carol Pearson, translated by Zhu Kanru, Xu Shenshu, and Gong Zhuojun, published by New Century Publishing Co., Ltd., p.14.

Note 229: *The Hero Within: Six Archetypes We Live By*, written by Carol Pearson, translated by Zhu Kanru, Xu Shenshu, and Gong Zhuojun, published by New Century Publishing Co., Ltd., p.218.

Note 230: *The Hero Within: Six Archetypes We Live By*, written by Carol Pearson, translated by Zhu Kanru, Xu Shenshu, and Gong Zhuojun, published by New Century Publishing Co., Ltd., p.220.

Note 231: *The Hero with a Thousand Faces*, written by Joseph Campbell, translated by Zhu Kanru, published by New Century Publishing Co., Ltd., p.386.

Note 232: This refers to an "Awakening Course" created by the writer of this book and founder of the Satdharma Institute – Guru Satdharma. It imparts the highest level of experience and wisdom to learners, provides instruction and guidance on various theories of super-consciousness, and conveys mystical theories for grasping universal wisdom in four phases, thereby gifting learners the four crucial keys for understanding the mysteries of wisdom and allowing them to experience the "mysterious power" that human beings innately possess. That is, the eternal and inextinguishable Higher Wisdom, the wellspring of happiness.

Note 233: *Power vs. Force: The Hidden Determinants of Human Behavior*, by Dr. David R. Hawkins, translated by Meng-Hsuan Tsai, Fine Press, p. 51.

Note 234: From the book *Rich Dad Poor Dad*, by Robert Kiyosaki, translated by Yang Jun and Yang Ming, Global Publishing Group.

Note 235: The "social enterprise" as a new model of enterprise originated from England. Such enterprises assist with public welfare, try to adjust social power through market mechanisms, and, by implementing certain business strategies, do their utmost to improve the conditions of human and environmental survival. They are not concerned with snaring maximum profits for a bunch of external stakeholders. Any surplus made is mainly reinvested into the social enterprise itself, so that the company may continue to solve social or environmental problems, and not simply optimize profits for the investors or owners. In this way, social enterprises combine the elements of social concern and profitability.

Note 236: The Five Aggregates consist of form, sensations, perceptions, mental activity or formations, and consciousness. The seven sufferings include the suffering of birth, old age, sickness, death, separation from loved ones, associating with those whom we dislike, and the suffering of unfulfilled wishes or desires. The flourishing of the Five Aggregates is the source of these even sufferings. In Sanskrit, the word for "suffering" is Dukkha. In Chinese, this has generally been translated using the word *Ku* (苦) or *Kudi* (苦諦). Semantically speaking, in Sanskrit "Dukkha" refers to a feeling of unease or disquiet, which, in modern times, corresponds to descriptions such as pain, sorrow, anxiety, dissatisfaction, or dejection (Wikipedia).

Note 237: The original text of the Vimalakirti Sutra is as follows: "When the Blessed Lord Śakyamuni was a Bodhisattva, his mind must have been impure, since today his Buddhakṣetra appears to be so impure. The Blessed One, knowing the Venerable Śāriputra's thoughts, said to him: What do you think of this, Śāriputra? Is it because the sun and the moon are impure that those who are born blind cannot see them?"

Note 238: Mapping the Mind, Rita Carter, Hong Lan (translator), Yuan-Liou Publishing.

Note 239: Source – Scientific American, Dec. 2014 edition, No. 154, P. 43

Note 240: Source – Scientific American, Dec. 2014 edition, No. 154, P. 43

Note 241: Source – Scientific American, Dec. 2014 edition, No. 154, P. 43

Note 242: *Taoism, Esoteric Buddhism, and Eastern Mysticism*, Nan Huai-Chin, Laoku Culture Foundation Inc.

Note 243: *The Source Field Investigations: The Hidden Science and Lost Civilizations Behind the 2012 Prophecies*, David Wilcock, Sonia Sui and Bai Le (translation), Acorn International Publishing Ltd, p. 68-69.

Note 244: *The Source Field Investigations: The Hidden Science and Lost Civilizations Behind the 2012 Prophecies*, David Wilcock, Sonia Sui and Bai Le (translation), Acorn International Publishing Ltd, p. 70.

Note 245: A more detailed description is provided in Chapter 3 of this book.

Note 246: *Nutrition and Physical Degeneration*, Winston A. Price, Chang Chia-Jui (Translator), Persimmon Books.

Note 247: *The Source Field Investigations: The Hidden Science and Lost Civilizations Behind the 2012 Prophecies*, David Wilcock, Sonia Sui and Bai Le (translation), Acorn International Publishing Ltd, P. 71-72.

Note 248: *The Science and Medicine of Meditation and a Journey of the Spirit: The Most Practical Guide to Transforming Your Body and Mind in the 21ˢᵗ Century*, Dingyi Yang and Yuanning Yang, CommonWealth Magazine, P. 216.

Note 249: *The Science and Medicine of Meditation and a Journey of the Spirit: The Most Practical Guide to Transforming Your Body and Mind in the 21ˢᵗ Century*, Dingyi Yang and Yuanning Yang, CommonWealth Magazine, P. 233.

Note 250: *The Science and Medicine of Meditation and a Journey of the Spirit: The Most Practical Guide to Transforming Your Body and Mind in the 21ˢᵗ Century*, Dingyi Yang and Yuanning Yang, CommonWealth Magazine, P. 225.

Note 251: The Varieties of Religious Experience, William James, Translated by Tsai Yi-jia and Liu Hung-Hsin, Li Xu Publishing, P. 473.

Note 252: *The Varieties of Religious Experience*, William James, translated by Tsai Yi-chia and Liu Hung-hsin, Li Hsu Publishing, P. 484.

Note 253: *The Varieties of Religious Experience*, William James, translated by Tsai Yi-chia and Liu Hung-hsin, Li Hsu Publishing, P. 486.

Note 254: *The Varieties of Religious Experience*, William James, translated by Tsai Yi-chia and Liu Hung-hsin, Li Hsu Publishing, P. 473.

Note 255: *The Varieties of Religious Experience*, William James, translated by Tsai Yi-chia and Liu Hung-hsin, Li Hsu Publishing, P. 475-476.

Note 256: Source: Taiwan Environmental Information Association; excerpted from a Washington DC report, ENS America, from Jan 16, 2015; translated by Chiang-wei and edited by Tsai Li-ling.

Note 257: *Paths Beyond Ego: the Transpersonal Vision* by Roger Walsh and Francis Vaughan; translated by Hu Yin-meng, Psygarden Publishing, p. 340.

Note 258: *Paths Beyond Ego: the Transpersonal Vision* by Roger Walsh and Francis Vaughan; translated by Hu Yin-meng, Psygarden Publishing, p. 341.

Note 259: *Paths Beyond Ego: the Transpersonal Vision* by Roger Walsh and Francis Vaughan; translated by Hu Yin-meng, Psygarden Publishing, p. 342.

Note 260: *Astrology / Karma & Transformation* by Stephen Arroyo, translated by Hu Yin-meng, Psygarden Publishing, P. 37.

Note 261: *Grow Rich with Peace of Mind* by Napoleon Hill, translated by Dai Chi-chung, Leeds Publishing, p. 239.

Note 262: *Paths Beyond Ego: the Transpersonal Vision* by Roger Walsh and Francis Vaughan; translated by Hu Yin-meng, Psygarden Publishing, p. 343.

Note 263: *Paths Beyond Ego: the Transpersonal Vision* by Roger Walsh and Francis Vaughan; translated by Hu Yin-meng, Psygarden Publishing, p. 345.

Note 264:

① Identifying with one of our roles: This refers to complete identification with the roles that we assume, such as police officer, professor, daughter, or subordinate, and thus forgetting that, in addition to these roles, there is also a "true self" inside us. Identifying this way may lead to a sense of inferiority or to arrogance. And as this role will be affected by the roles played by others, this individual might not know how to respect others. Only by clearly delineating between the "true self" and the role one plays can you maintain a distance with the role. Observe your own speech, conduct, and thoughts to retain a sense of freedom within.

② Identifying with first or second-order personality traits: Personality refers to traits or modes that have been acquired over time, such as interests, motives, attitudes, values, habits, ideals. These traits are not impervious to change. Second-order personality traits are lower-level structures in the personality that are semi-independent and stable. They also feature their own emotions, thoughts, and modes of behavior. Identifying with first or second-order personality traits results in the blurring of the true self and prevents the individual from being true to himself.

③ Identifying with self-concepts: Self-concepts refer to the concepts and judgments we hold about ourselves. The majority of these concepts and judgments come from the perspectives and feedback we receive from others. Self-concepts are the property of one's intelligence, and are not the actual true self.

④ Identifying with any of one's various states: After identifying with the roles we play, our first and second-order personality traits, and the self-concepts in our minds, by extension we also identify with the states that are generated by these, believing these states to be who we really are. An example is believing oneself to be an awful person or identifying with one's emotions and thus not being aware that our current state is not who we truly are.

The above text was reworded after being excerpted from *Transpersonal Psychology*, written by André Lefebvre and translated by Ruo-shui, Laureate Publishing, p. 222 - 228.

Note 265: Modified from *Transpersonal Psychology* by André Lefebvre, translated by Ruo-shui, Laureate Publishing.

Note 266: *Transpersonal Psychology* by André Lefebvre, translated by Ruo-shui, Laureate Publishing, p.246.

Note 267: *Transpersonal Psychology* by André Lefebvre, translated by Ruo-shui, Laureate Publishing, p.246.

Note 268: *Transpersonal Psychology* by André Lefebvre, translated by Ruo-shui, Laureate Publishing, p.248.

Note 269: *To Have or To Be?* by Erich Fromm, translated by Meng Hsiang-sen, Yuan-Liou Publishing; excerpted from *Transpersonal Psychology* by André Lefebvre, translated by Ruo-shuo, Laureate Publishing, p. 249.

Note 270: *Astrology, Psychology & the Four Elements: An Energy Approach to Astrology & Its Use in the Counseling Arts* by Stephen Arroyo, translated by Hu Yin-meng, Psygarden Publishing, p. 73-74.

Note 271: *Transpersonal Psychology* by André Lefebvre, translated by Ruo-shuo, Laureate Publishing, p. 250.

Note 272: *Transpersonal Psychology* by André Lefebvre, translated by Ruo-shuo, Laureate Publishing, p. 250.

Note 273: *Transpersonal Psychology* by André Lefebvre, translated by Ruo-shuo, Laureate Publishing, p. 252.

Note 274: One of Satdharma's courses: learning about negative energy states through steps such as perception and observation, and then using light to dissolve such states. This allows the self to return to a centered state and restore neutrality.

Note 275: *Transpersonal Psychology* by André Lefebvre, translated by Ruo-shuo, Laureate Publishing, p. 253.

Note 276: *Voluntary Simplicity*, Duane Elgin, translated by Chang Chi-chang, Li Hsu Publishing.

Note 277: *Paths Beyond Ego: the Transpersonal Vision*, Roger Walsh and Francis Vaughan, translated by Hu Yin-meng, Psygarden Publishing, p. 342.

Note 278: *Paths Beyond Ego: the Transpersonal Vision*, Roger Walsh and Francis Vaughan, translated by Hu Yin-meng, Psygarden Publishing, p. 367.

Note 279: *Paths Beyond Ego: the Transpersonal Vision*, Roger Walsh and Francis Vaughan, translated by Hu Yin-meng, Psygarden Publishing, p. 367.

Note 280: *Paths Beyond Ego: the Transpersonal Vision*, Roger Walsh and Francis Vaughan, translated by Hu Yin-meng, Psygarden Publishing, p. 365.

Note 281: Big data or megadata refers to data of a magnitude so large it cannot be captured, managed, processed, and sorted by humans into information readable by humans within a reasonable time frame. Under equivalent total data volume conditions, when this is contrasted with individually-analyzed, small-sized, independent data sets, each small-sized data set can then be merged and analysis conducted to obtain a wealth of additional data and relevant information. It can be used to examine business trends, judge the quality of research, avoid the spread of disease, fight crime, or determine real-time traffic conditions. These functions of big data are precisely why it has become so widespread. (Source: Wikipedia)

Note 282: Source of information: Liberty Times News Network

Note 283: *Chaos Point 2012 and Beyond: Appointment with Destiny*, Ervin Laszlo, translated by Chuang Sheng-hsiong and Chang Shu-tsai, Business Weekly Publications, p. 11.

Note 284: *Chaos Point 2012 and Beyond: Appointment with Destiny*, Ervin Laszlo, translated by Chuang Sheng-hsiong and Chang Shu-tsai, Business Weekly Publications, p. 20.

Note 285: *Chaos Point 2012 and Beyond: Appointment with Destiny*, Ervin Laszlo, translated by Chuang Sheng-hsiong and Chang Shu-tsai, Business Weekly Publications, p. 73-101.

Note 286: *Chaos Point 2012 and Beyond: Appointment with Destiny*, Ervin Laszlo, translated by Chuang Sheng-hsiong and Chang Shu-tsai, Business Weekly Publications, p. 116.

Note 287: *Chaos Point 2012 and Beyond: Appointment with Destiny*, Ervin Laszlo, translated by Chuang Sheng-hsiong and Chang Shu-tsai, Business Weekly Publications, p. 120.

Note 288: *Chaos Point 2012 and Beyond: Appointment with Destiny*, Ervin Laszlo, translated by Chuang Sheng-hsiong and Chang Shu-tsai, Business Weekly Publications, p. 125.

Note 289: *Chaos Point 2012 and Beyond: Appointment with Destiny*, Ervin Laszlo, translated by Chuang Sheng-hsiong and Chang Shu-tsai, Business Weekly Publications, p. 171.

Note 290: *Chaos Point 2012 and Beyond: Appointment with Destiny*, Ervin Laszlo, translated by Chuang Sheng-hsiong and Chang Shu-tsai, Business Weekly Publications, p. 179-180.

Note 291: *Transpersonal Psychology* by André Lefebvre, translated by Ruo-shui, Laureate Publishing, p.273.

Note 292: *Transpersonal Psychology* by André Lefebvre, translated by Ruo-shui, Laureate Publishing, p.272.

Note 293: *Transpersonal Psychology* by André Lefebvre, translated by Ruo-shui, Laureate Publishing, p.273.

Note 294: *Transpersonal Psychology* by André Lefebvre, translated by Ruo-shui, Laureate Publishing, p.274-275.

Note 295: *Chaos Point 2012 and Beyond: Appointment with Destiny*, Ervin Laszlo, translated by Chuang Sheng-hsiong and Chang Shu-tsai, Business Weekly Publications, p.180.

Note 296: An introduction to BIU: Since its inception, Spain's Bircham International University has chosen a unique and effective method of operation. For many years it has offered professional education for adults, and among a field packed with institutions offering online correspondence courses, it has stood apart from the crowd, partly thanks to its competitiveness. BIU is proud to announce that, thanks to the result of 15 years of combining quality, tuition, and instruction, it has consolidated its business model and reputation to become one of the top providers of correspondence courses. BIU is the only institution to provide over 200 courses and instruction in eight separate languages, and to be recognized in five continents. www.bircham.net/biu-references/world-references.html

Note 297: Hippocrates of Kos (c. 460 – c. 370 BC), also known as Hippocrates II, was a Greek physician of the Age of Pericles (Classical Greece), who is considered one of the most outstanding figures in the history of medicine. He is often referred to as the "Father of Medicine" in recognition of his lasting contributions to the field as the founder of the Hippocratic School of Medicine. This intellectual school revolutionized medicine in ancient Greece, establishing it as a discipline distinct from other fields with which it had traditionally been associated (theurgy and philosophy), thus establishing medicine as a profession (courtesy of Wikipedia).

Note 298: Hippocrates proposed the following view: "*Let food be thy medicine and medicine be thy food.*" This idea echoes the more holistic and balanced conception held by practitioners of ancient medicine. "*Knowing what type of people fall ill is more important than what type of illnesses they suffer.*" He pointed out that when a doctor enters a new city, he first has to pay attention to the direction of the city, its soil, climate, wind direction, source and quality of water, the dietary habits of its people, their lifestyle, and so on, as all of these affect the health of those living there. Moreover, as early as 400 BC, Hippocrates noted the significance of massage in medicine, asserting that "*Medicine is the art of massage.*" Massage is a vital form of therapy. Thus, he further added: *"Anyone wishing to study medicine must master the art of massage."*

Note 299: The Aquarian Conspiracy, Marilyn Ferguson, translated by Liao Shih-teh, Fine Press, p. 339.

Note 300: The Aquarian Conspiracy, Marilyn Ferguson, translated by Liao Shih-teh, Fine Press, p. 346.

Note 301: The Aquarian Conspiracy, Marilyn Ferguson, translated by Liao Shih-teh, Fine Press, p. 341.

Note 302: Back to Methuselah, Part 1.

Note 303: *Astrology, Psychology & the Four Elements: An Energy Approach to Astrology & Its Use in the Counseling Arts*, by Stephen Arroyo, translated by Hu Yin-meng, Psygarden Publishing, p. 33.

Note 304: *Astrology, Psychology & the Four Elements: An Energy Approach to Astrology & Its Use in the Counseling Arts*, by Stephen Arroyo, translated by Hu Yin-meng, Psygarden Publishing, p. 23.

Note 305: The Aquarian Conspiracy, Marilyn Ferguson, translated by Liao Shih-teh, Fine Press, p. 386.

Note 306: *The Aquarian Conspiracy*, Marilyn Ferguson, translated by Liao Shih-teh, Fine Press, p. 391.

Note 307: *Astrology, Psychology & the Four Elements: An Energy Approach to Astrology & Its Use in the Counseling Arts*, by Stephen Arroyo, translated by Hu Yin-meng, Psygarden Publishing, p. 22.

Note 308: *Astrology, Psychology & the Four Elements: An Energy Approach to Astrology & Its Use in the Counseling Arts*, by Stephen Arroyo, translated by Hu Yin-meng, Psygarden Publishing, p. 21.

Note 309: *The Aquarian Conspiracy*, Marilyn Ferguson, translated by Liao Shih-teh, Fine Press, p. 31.

Note 310: *Affluenza: How Overconsumption Is Killing Us – and How to Fight Back*, John de Graaf, David Wann, and Thomas H. Naylor, translated by Wu Shu-yu, Suncolor Publishing, p. 24.

Note 311: *Affluenza: How Overconsumption Is Killing Us – and How to Fight Back*, John de Graaf, David Wann, and Thomas H. Naylor, translated by Wu Shu-yu, Suncolor Publishing, p. 25.

Note 312: *Chaos Point 2012 and Beyond: Appointment with Destiny*, Ervin Laszlo, translated by Chuang Sheng-hsiong and Chang Shu-tsai, Business Weekly Publications, p. 130-131.

Note 313: *Chaos Point 2012 and Beyond: Appointment with Destiny*, Ervin Laszlo, translated by Chuang Sheng-hsiong and Chang Shu-tsai, Business Weekly Publications, p. 132.

Note 314: *Small Is Beautiful: Economics As If People Mattered*, translated by Li Hua-hsia, Li Xu Publishing.

Note 315: *The Zero Marginal Cost Society: The Internet of Things, the Collaborative Commons, and the Eclipse of Capitalism*, Jeremy Rifkin, translated by Chen Hsiu-ling, Business Weekly Publications.

Note 316: *Energy for Future Presidents: The Science Behind the Headlines*, Richard A. Muller, translated by Yen Cheng-ting, AzothBooks, p.11.

Note 317: *The Source Field Investigations: The Hidden Science and Lost Civilizations Behind the 2012 Prophecies*, David Wilcock, Sonia Sui and Bai Le (translation), Acorn International Publishing Ltd, p. 39.

Note 318: *The Source Field Investigations: The Hidden Science and Lost Civilizations Behind the 2012 Prophecies*, David Wilcock, Sonia Sui and Bai Le (translation), Acorn International Publishing Ltd, p. 393.

Note 319: *The Source Field Investigations: The Hidden Science and Lost Civilizations Behind the 2012 Prophecies*, David Wilcock, Sonia Sui and Bai Le (translation), Acorn International Publishing Ltd, p. 39-40.

Note 320: *The Source Field Investigations: The Hidden Science and Lost Civilizations Behind the 2012 Prophecies*, David Wilcock, Sonia Sui and Bai Le (translation), Acorn International Publishing Ltd, p. 39-284.

Note 321: *The Source Field Investigations: The Hidden Science and Lost Civilizations Behind the 2012 Prophecies*, David Wilcock, Sonia Sui and Bai Le (translation), Acorn International Publishing Ltd, p. 284-286.

Note 322: *Energy for Future Presidents: The Science Behind the Headlines*, Richard A. Muller, translated by Yen Cheng-ting, AzothBooks, p.315.

Note 323: *After the Ecstasy, the Laundry*, Jack Kornfield, translated by Chou He-chun, Oak Tree Publishing, p. 342.

Note 324: *After the Ecstasy, the Laundry*, Jack Kornfield, translated by Chou He-chun, Oak Tree Publishing, p. 132.

Note 325: *After the Ecstasy, the Laundry*, Jack Kornfield, translated by Chou He-chun, Oak Tree Publishing, p. 224.

Note 326: *After the Ecstasy, the Laundry*, Jack Kornfield, translated by Chou He-chun, Oak Tree Publishing, p. 224.

Note 327: *After the Ecstasy, the Laundry*, Jack Kornfield, translated by Chou He-chun, Oak Tree Publishing, p. 338.

Note 328: *After the Ecstasy, the Laundry*, Jack Kornfield, translated by Chou He-chun, Oak Tree Publishing, p. 320.

Note 329: *After the Ecstasy, the Laundry*, Jack Kornfield, translated by Chou He-chun, Oak Tree Publishing, p. 300.

Note 330: *The Aquarian Conspiracy*, Marilyn Ferguson, translated by Liao Shih-teh, Fine Press, p. 555.

Note 331: *After the Ecstasy, the Laundry*, Jack Kornfield, translated by Chou He-chun, Oak Tree Publishing, p. 346.

Note 332: *After the Ecstasy, the Laundry*, Jack Kornfield, translated by Chou He-chun, Oak Tree Publishing, p. 319.

Note 333: *The Aquarian Conspiracy*, Marilyn Ferguson, translated by Liao Shih-teh, Fine Press, p. 571.

Note 334: Please refer to the appendix of this book.

Printed in the United States
By Bookmasters